The Workplace *and* *Spirituality*

New Perspectives on Research and Practice

Edited by **Dr. Joan Marques,**
Dr. Satinder Dhiman, and **Dr. Richard King**

Walking Together, Finding the Way ®
SKYLIGHT PATHS®
PUBLISHING
Woodstock, Vermont

The Workplace and Spirituality:
New Perspectives on Research and Practice

2009 Hardcover Edition, First Printing
©2009 by Joan Marques, Satinder Dhiman, and Richard King

Grateful acknowledgment is given for permission from the following sources to print the material contained in this book:

"Letting the Heart Fall Open: Spirit, Vulnerability, and Relational, Intelligence in the Workplace" © 2009 by Birute Regine

"Liberating the Corporate Soul: Building a High-Performance, Values-Driven Organization" © 2009 by Richard Barrett

"Identifying and Managing the Shadow of Workplace Spirituality: Practical Guidelines" © 2009 by Marjo Lips-Wiersma

"Inspired Leadership: Leading with Spirit" © 2009 by Ellen Hayakawa

Library of Congress Cataloging-in-Publication Data

The workplace and spirituality : new perspectives on research and practice / edited by Joan Marques, Satinder Dhiman, and Richard King.
    p. cm.
Includes bibliographical references and index.
ISBN-13: 978-1-59473-260-7
ISBN-10: 1-59473-260-4
1. Work—Religious aspects. 2. Management—Religious aspects. I. Marques, Joan. II. Dhiman, Satinder. III. King, Richard, Dr.
BL65.W67W72 2009
201'.73—dc22

2009000436

10   9   8   7   6   5   4   3   2   1
Manufactured in the United States of America
♻Printed on recycled paper
Jacket design: Tim Holtz
Jacket art: © Ilja Mašík / Fotolia

SkyLight Paths Publishing is creating a place where people of different spiritual traditions come together for challenge and inspiration, a place where we can help each other understand the mystery that lies at the heart of our existence.

SkyLight Paths sees both believers and seekers as a community that increasingly transcends traditional boundaries of religion and denomination—people wanting to learn from each other, *walking together, finding the way.*

SkyLight Paths, "Walking Together, Finding the Way," and colophon are trademarks of LongHill Partners, Inc., registered in the U.S. Patent and Trademark Office.

Walking Together, Finding the Way®
Published by SkyLight Paths Publishing
A Division of Longhill Partners, Inc.
Sunset Farm Offices, Route 4, P.O. Box 237
Woodstock, VT 05091
Tel: (802) 457-4000   Fax: (802) 457-4004
www.skylightpaths.com

We dedicate this book to
current and future business leaders.

Contents

PART II *Work at the Organizational Level*

Acknowledgments

With gratitude to our families, friends, students, audiences, support groups, and all the sources we learned and unlearned from, on our way toward attaining the insights in producing this book.

With great appreciation to all the contributors, who generously donated their knowledge and insights to this book.

With enormous praise to management and staff of SkyLight Paths Publishing for their consistent and invaluable support, and with infinite respect to Marcia Broucek, for all her guidance and unremitting energy in making this project worthwhile!

Introduction

It becomes more apparent every day that events from even the far-thest corner of the world affect us swiftly and deeply. The entire world—and, therefore, the world of business as well—is experiencing a continuously unfolding stage of interconnectedness, nationally, regionally, and globally. This trend brings a large number of advantages—and disadvantages—at the personal, organizational, and societal level, creating opportunities for some to rise to heights never experienced before and, at the same time, thwarting long-established sources for others.

This is a time of shifting paradigms and puzzling paradoxes. On one hand, there are some disturbing trends to be dealt with, such as fundamentalism, terrorism, and inveterate corporate greed. These factors create a toxic antithesis to the changes some well-meaning leaders are trying to bring about. They thwart every effort toward celebrating diversity, acceptance, and mutual respect, and generate anger and hate among those that are taken advantage of.

On the other hand, there is an enhanced understanding of the need for change. Families, workforces, and entire societies are expressing their readiness to embrace change at an unprecedented rate. They are eager to partake in the caravan of human improvement, and they surprise friend and foe with their choices and level of holistic awareness. They increasingly unite forces in the realization that there are ways to grow jointly: not one group at the expense of another, but all groups growing together in a mutually supportive way.

Transformations are inevitable, and we always have choices about how to conduct them. While not always obvious, there are many ways to excel without harming others, to do well and to do good at the same time. As business leaders scan the world for resources, knowledge, creativity, and markets to meet today's challenges, they are coming to some important insights. They realize that, aside from the oftentimes fascinating and complicating differences among work populations, some universal values guide people of all cultures, countries, and continents: love, respect, honesty, and truth, to name a few.

We offer this book as a response to the growing challenges facing leaders in the twenty-first century. Its message of workplace spirituality transcends time and environment. We have assembled a team of like-minded individuals from various parts of the world, each with broad international experience in human interaction. Their message entails a united call for ongoing efforts in helping to make the workplace a more meaningful one. Each contributor is thoroughly aware of the importance of the human contribution. Each has written extensively about it, presented it on numerous forums, has lectured broadly about it, has earned international recognition and respect for it, and believes in it. While their styles are broadly divergent, their interests and convictions, and hence their message, are unified. This collaborative team of twenty-four highly respected authors, consultants, speakers, and pioneers in the area of workplace spirituality offers their perspectives in the spirit of sharing and continued growth for all.

This book is for current and future leaders of the workplace. It is a book for leaders who are centered and not self-centered, leaders who are willing to put service before self, and leaders who are keen to reinvent themselves through self-knowledge and self-reflection. The chapters are arranged in a sequence that first reviews personal, and then organizational, factors, but does not require any particular order of reading.

It is our goal to help leaders cope with challenges they might encounter; to suggest new alternatives for a spiritual approach to work; and to remind leaders of the simplest but most important component of work: *meaning* and *advancement for the human community as a whole.* We hope this book will provide strength in times of weakness, determination in times of doubt, inspiration in times of uncertainty, and continued support on a path from good to great.

PART I
Work at the Personal Level

Lance Secretan, PhD, is acknowledged as one of the most insightful and provocative leadership teachers of our time. He is a best-selling author who is revolutionizing the way men and women integrate inspiration and leadership. His teaching and writing on conscious leadership is radical and ingenious, and has been hailed as among the most original, authentic, and effective contributions to leadership thinking currently available. Individuals and entire organizations have experienced remarkable transformations through his unique wisdom and approach. Thirty of *Fortune's* "Most Admired Companies" and eleven of *Fortune's* "Best Companies to Work for in America" are his clients. *Leadership Excellence* has ranked him among the top "100 Most Influential Thinkers on Leadership in the World." For more information, see www.secretan.com.

Love and Truth

The Golden Rules of Leadership

LANCE SECRETAN, PHD

We are living in a society that has embraced fear as a weapon to coerce others to do their bidding. In marketing, leadership, coaching, politics, education, health care, parenting, and religion, fear is the base operating system. But while people can be motivated by fear, they are not inspired by it. This chapter presents a critical view on society's distorted perceptions of love and truth in business, and the wrongful act of repressing these behaviors out of fear for being seen as weak, or for the sake of short-term profits. The author argues that it takes courage, strength, and commitment to build and sustain relationships that are based on love and truth and, therefore, inspiration.

GOLDEN RULES OF LEADERSHIP

Nearly thirty years ago, I wrote my first book. At 496 pages, *Managerial Moxie*[1] weighed 1.4 pounds and was filled with complex diagrams, charts, matrices, models, formulae, theories, and other arcana chronicling the journey of my team in resurrecting a moribund business called Manpower Limited and turning it into a world-class organization that achieved international renown. My writing formula conformed to academic norms that required deep research, empirical validation of theories, double-blind studies, and peer-referenced material, which, after review and endorsement by cloistered committees, became part of a teaching curriculum. This accomplishment may have been the high-water mark of my intellectual arrogance and my personal need to meet the external needs of "a system." I had written an unnecessarily complicated book about a subject that is really not all that complicated.

Over the years, each book I have written on leadership has become smaller and simpler than the one before. As I have spent more time in the world, I have come to realize that living an inspiring life and making the world a better place is not a complex subject. It is actually very simple. I believe that Inspired Leadership boils down to following two golden rules: *the world would be a better place if we loved each other and told the truth*.

THE COURAGE TO LOVE

We are living in a society that has embraced fear as a weapon to coerce others to do their bidding. In marketing, leadership, coaching, politics, education, health care, parenting, and religion, fear is the base operating system. In so many different ways we have learned to rely on the stick and have forsaken the carrot. Yet we have choices in the ways we act and encourage others. We can act because we are afraid not to or because we love to. We have the choice between fear and love.

Individual experience tells us that fear is the psychological, emotional, and spiritual opposite of love. No one is inspired by fear. People are *motivated* by fear, but they are not *inspired* by it. Everything that inspires us comes from love—without exception. In fact, there is nothing in our lives from which we get inspiration that does not also give us love. If a sunset inspires you, it is because you love sunsets. If a person inspires you, it is because you love the person. Love is the place that gives rise to inspiration.

Yet how many people, including leaders, are afraid and embarrassed to include the word *love* in their vocabulary because they have grown up with an internal voice message that plays over and over, "If I express love, will people think I am weak, flaky, or lacking in resolve, purpose, or strength?" But this kind of thinking is based on the erroneous belief that courage and strength are found in aggression, and that gentleness reflects weakness. The bully, who believes that aggression is the best approach in any given situation, is by definition a coward. As the Iroquois have said, "The greatest strength is gentleness."

A leader who has the courage to be humble, forgiving, and loving—and therefore authentic—is a much more inspiring and effective leader. There is wisdom and power in having a big heart and using it to relate with others, heart-to-heart. I define love as *the place where my heart touches your heart and adds to who you are as a person.*

It takes courage, strength, and commitment to build and sustain relationships that are based on love and, therefore, inspiration. As Mahatma Gandhi once said, "Love is the prerogative of the brave." It takes courage to say to someone, "I love you," and to be a loving person. It takes courage to tell your colleagues how much you love their work, how much you love being part of a particular team or organization. Yet those are the things that inspire people. I am frequently shocked at how many people I meet in the leadership retreats that my company runs who tell me that one of their parents never told them they loved them. It should not surprise us that leaders coming from this experience will build and model their leadership theories and practices on the only life lessons they have known—fear, competition, aggression, motivation, ambition, and goal achievement.

THE ECONOMY OF TRUTH

Telling the truth could be the single greatest profit generator in corporate history. I estimate that some 20 percent of today's workforce is involved in checking up on the other 80 percent, making sure that company rules and regulations are followed, that the law is respected, that expenses are authentic, that budgets are met, and that there is honesty and integrity in the countless processes and procedures around which companies are structured.

This means that in an organization of ten thousand people, some two thousand are responsible for ensuring that their other eight thousand colleagues follow the rules, and they do this through audits, budget control, compliance, expense approval, and so on. If we assume that each of these people costs the company an average of fifty thousand dollars a year, including salaries, benefits, and overhead, the total cost is a staggering one hundred million dollars annually! But if we started a system-wide initiative on truthfulness and were even only 50 percent successful in doing so, then we could theoretically save one thousand jobs—half the people who are checking up on the other eight thousand.

We could then retrain those one thousand people to do more productive work, such as customer service, employee satisfaction and retention, product innovation and quality improvement, and—most important—inspiring others. These people are already on the payroll, and if their energy and enthusiasm could be redirected toward productive endeavors that *make* money rather than activities that *cost* money, they could make a more significant contribution toward organizational transformation, effectiveness, and profitability than any other single strategic initiative.

So, when we say that we cannot find enough quality people and that companies suffer from staff shortages, we need to think again! There are plenty of good people, but we have put them in the wrong jobs—jobs they are working in because we are not doing the right thing to start with: We are not telling the truth. Truth is a powerful economical tool.

When Mary Cusack was invited to start up a fifty million dollar packaging plant for Procter and Gamble's Light Duty Liquids (Dawn, Joy, and Ivory brands), she realized that the project was riddled with distrust and dishonesty. Working with human resources manager Don White, she initiated a truth-telling process inspired by Brad Blanton (author of *Radical Honesty*)[2] and Will Schutz (author of *The Human Element*).[3]

"We got people to look each other in the eye, share their appreciation, state their resentments, get over them, and move on," Mary reported. She was able to share all the information and opinions that she based her decisions on: "I became vulnerable in front of my people. As a woman in a manufacturing plant, I wasn't supposed to show emotions. But it worked to my advantage."[4]

The result was a dramatic improvement in decision-making speed and productivity. Although it usually takes eighteen to twenty-four months to build a plant, Mary did the job in six months, and developed new bottle designs in this time as well. "We saved twelve to eighteen months," she said. "That's ten million dollars."

Many years after speaking with Mary about her work with Procter and Gamble, I define leadership as "a serving relationship with others that inspires their growth and makes the world a better place." I write, teach, and consult to inspire others to see the sacredness in all relationships. The people you will meet in this book each follow their own unique calling to be leaders, and each of you who are now reading my thoughts on leadership will follow your own journey.

Imagine the impact in our world if we all infused our passion and purpose with the proof and power of loving one another and telling the truth—and then, one by one, moved it out of our offices and factories and boardrooms, and filled our homes, classrooms, hospitals, churches, and governments with it.

It would be—quite simply—inspiring and, therefore, revolutionary.

■ ■ ■

Birute Regine, EdD, is an executive coach, developmental psychologist, and coauthor of *Weaving Complexity and Business: Engaging the Soul at Work.* Her newest book, *Iron Butterflies: Women Leading in a New Era,* focuses on women leading in the new era by transforming the meaning of leadership, power, and success. While at Harvard receiving her master's and doctoral degrees, Dr. Regine collaborated with psychologist Carol Gilligan, author of *A Different Voice,* and was a teaching fellow for psychologist Erik Erikson. Dr. Regine was a visiting scholar at Wellesley's Center for Research on Women and an affiliate of the Stone Center. She has also trained in Gestalt therapy and family systems theory, and attended the College of Executive Coaching. As an international public speaker, group facilitator, and international consultant, Dr. Regine specializes in developing relational intelligence in high-potential people and using storytelling as a tool for organizational transformation.

Letting the Heart Fall Open

Spirit, Vulnerability, and Relational Intelligence in the Workplace

BIRUTE REGINE, EDD

Allowing vulnerability in ourselves and others in the workplace is a radical act in a culture where vulnerability is all but taboo. But when we allow, accept, and address human frailties and emotions, vulnerabilities can become strengths and can create conditions that invite the soul at work. This chapter presents ways to engage the soul at work by allowing vulnerabilities: creating mutual rather than hierarchical relationships; speaking to the highest self and expecting the best; embracing vulnerabilities as learning opportunities; and addressing stress by dealing with emotions and employing the power of appreciation.

VULNERABILITY IS KEY

Over the past several years, I interviewed more than sixty successful women from eight countries and three continents. They came from all walks of life and included doctors, artists, a federal judge, a novelist, businesswomen, a congresswoman, educators, a former nun, nurses, lawyers, a winemaker, a priest, CEOs, housewives, a Nobel

Peace Prize winner, and a governor. My goal was to uncover any common patterns of behavior that were central to these women's accomplishments, regardless of their chosen profession. To my surprise, I discovered that a key behavior that enabled all of them to transform themselves and their workplaces was how they handled vulnerability.

When I initially met these women, *vulnerability* would have been the last word I would have used to describe them because they all exuded an ease with themselves and a quiet self-confidence. This self-assurance was in part the fruit of their ability to manage and learn from vulnerable moments and times in their lives that led them to developing new strengths.

The *Merriam-Webster Dictionary* defines *vulnerability* as "being capable of being wounded physically or mentally; open to persuasion; easily influenced; open to attack; assailable."[1] Every aspect of this definition has negative connotations. In Western society, and particularly in the culture of male-dominated professions (which, essentially, means almost *all* professions), vulnerability is shunned and ridiculed as a weakness, something to be avoided at all costs—especially in its leaders. Yet the women in my study embraced vulnerability as a powerful element of their success *as leaders*.

If this sounds paradoxical, it is for good reason. These women independently developed a different kind of leadership, one that is the epitome of paradox: they are strong, as leaders are "supposed" to be, but they balance this with a degree of care and nurturing that is not on the traditional list of leadership skills. I use the term *Iron Butterflies* to describe women leaders of this ilk because they have the resilience of iron and the touch of a butterfly. The butterfly, of course, symbolizes transformation. It is an iconic phrase because I find that whenever I explain the concept, people often say they know an Iron Butterfly.

What do I mean by vulnerability? First, I call it "radical vulnerability" because to allow vulnerability in ourselves runs counter to deeply entrenched negative perceptions in our culture, where vulnerability is all but taboo. By vulnerability, I mean a profound openness. Think of the word as a coin. On one side is the openness that exposes you to the potential of being harmed. On the other side is the openness that allows you to be receptive to a depth of connection with others, and with all their thoughts and emotions, their humanity.

When we let ourselves experience vulnerability in this second way, we nurture the full range of our reactions and expressions to the world: all our yearnings, our needs, our shyness, our humility, our hopes. This does not mean we walk around with our beating hearts in our hands. Rather, it means that we are wise enough to embrace moments of openness in ourselves and in those around us because these moments offer opportunities to transform our lives. When we allow ourselves to be vulnerable, we replace harming with healing, weakness with strength, isolation with love, ignorance with wisdom. We invite what my colleague, Roger Lewin, and I described in *Weaving Complexity and Business* as "the soul at work."[2]

The capacity to handle vulnerability in this way requires a highly developed degree of what I call "relational intelligence." (The phrase was independently coined by management experts Joyce Fletcher and Judith Gordon, and psychiatrist Jean Baker Miller.)[3]

A highly developed degree of relational intelligence in leaders that allows, accepts, and addresses vulnerability in the workplace is the most essential step on the path to inviting the human spirit into the workplace and thus instigating a social transformation. Many studies have shown that people-oriented management leads to improved results in *all* traditional measures of business success: return on investment, shareholder value, employee retention, for example.[4] Moreover, people in these organizations say they feel happier and more fulfilled in their work than employees in more traditional management environments. Leaders who are adept with relational intelligence are therefore good for business, good for people, and good for the spirit. Everybody wins! It is the soul at work, individually and collectively.

The most effective way for me to describe relational intelligence at work in respect to radical vulnerability is to tell some of the stories I have heard while interviewing some of the Iron Butterflies.

CREATING MUTUAL, NOT HIERARCHICAL, RELATIONSHIPS

Linda Rusch is the vice president of nursing at Hunterdon Medical Center in New Jersey. Under Linda's leadership, Hunterdon Medical Center, a 176-bed facility, has consistently excelled, scoring in the high nineteenth percentile for patient satisfaction and quality outcome. In a world where most health-care institutions suffer a shortage of nurses and a high turnover, and when most nurses feel overworked, overwhelmed, and undervalued, Hunterdon boasts a retention rate of 97.5 percent.

One of the strongest leaders I have ever met, Linda exemplifies radical vulnerability. Among her many initiatives, Linda has addressed the hierarchy between nurses and doctors, what she calls the "not-knowing" nurse and the "all-knowing" doctor. Nurses often complain bitterly about the way doctors sometimes treat them, like handmaidens to omnipotent gods.

Linda dismantled that hierarchy, and not just because it hurt nurses' feelings. The old hierarchy actually threatens lives. For instance, a nurse, fearing a reprimand, intimidation—or worse, abuse—might refrain from calling a doctor at two in the morning to report an emergency with a patient. It was not easy to change that system because confronting abusive doctors is not something nurses learn in school. Linda got the word out that allowing abusive behavior was not part of a nurse's job. As Linda puts it, "What you permit, you promote."

In one particular case, a nurse, whom I will call "Jane," came to Linda with a typical tale of abuse. The doctor in question was generally well liked, though he did tend to lose his temper. He had yelled at Jane, derided her in front of patients over a small mistake she had made with one of his patient's charts. "I'll talk to him," Linda promised Jane. For the next week, the doctor appeared to avoid Linda, perhaps because he knew she would not let his misbehavior go unaddressed. Then one day, Linda found his attempt at leaving a humorous message on her answering machine: "Just want to report to you that one of your nurses intimidated me, and so I'm calling you as the hotline number." Was he trying indirectly to apologize for his behavior? Perhaps, but Linda did not feel comfortable letting the matter drop at that. So she sent him a handwritten note inviting him to have a cup of coffee with her.

The doctor scheduled an appointment and dropped by Linda's office with two steaming cups of coffee. Linda had decided beforehand that she was not going to talk to him about the incident with the nurse. She wanted to talk to him at a totally different level, not from anger or disapproval but, as she told me, from "a place of love."

Linda never uttered Jane's name during the conversation with the doctor. Instead, she started by saying, "I care about you. I don't like the way you are coming across. I know that's not who you are when you act this way." She could see a look of relief spread across his face. By coming from a place of care, Linda created the context for a very different conversation. As a result, the doctor opened up, confiding that he had grown up in poverty, that his mother had raised him and lifted him out of the ghetto, and had shepherded him through college and medical school. And here he was, a successful doctor. He admitted that growing up in the streets made him tough and angry and taught him to intimidate people. He was critical and tended to see a half-empty glass, an attitude that spilled over on the nurses.

Linda responded to him by saying, "I want you to be successful. I want people to love working with you because I know that's who you are." Any hierarchy that might have existed melted away as two colleagues chatted and formed a stronger relationship. They talked about how stress might be a factor in his edginess, and together they devised a plan for constructively dealing with it. "Speaking to the best in him," Linda recalls, "I could see the shift. Over time, I could see his behavior changing."

Note the dynamic here. By making herself vulnerable ("I care about you"), Linda set a nonthreatening context for their conversation, and the doctor felt safe enough to permit his own vulnerability to come out. Soon doctor and nurse were playing on a level field. Care had replaced intimidation, openness had replaced defensiveness, and trust had replaced fear. By working together on the problem, Linda modeled a different behavior, a cooperative one that the doctor could replicate with the nurses.

Linda proved that one person at a time, one relationship at a time, one opportunity at a time can create that profound opening between people that can change a workplace. Over time, it can transform an organization, an industry, and the world into a better place to work and live.

I love how Linda defines vulnerability: "Vulnerability is a power. It's letting yourself feel the love and be in the love." She describes it as an "incredible connectedness" with other human beings, in the moment, where you are heard and validated. "It's about being authentic and having this dance go on between you and the other person, when you can really understand what the other is feeling and thinking."

Opening ourselves as Linda did takes incredible courage and conviction, but the power it has to transform our lives and the lives of others—and the workplace—makes it well worth the risk. Radical vulnerability serves as a crucible in which a certain alchemy occurs, allowing for a deeper, more spiritual connection between people.

SPEAKING TO THE HIGHEST SELF AND EXPECTING THE BEST

While Linda's story is an example of dealing with an individual and speaking to his highest self, Cynthia Trudell shows how allowing vulnerability with a group can invite the highest self to work.

Cynthia, who is now a senior vice president with PepsiCo, was formerly with General Motors, head of the Saturn division, and then president of Sea Ray Group. She was the only woman at that time to attain that level of authority in manufacturing, which is a very male-dominated world. Her skill at allowing vulnerability in herself and in others enabled her to be a masterful leader.

"I'm the kind of person who will tell her people, 'I don't know where we're going, ladies and gentlemen, but I think we can go in that direction, over that hill. I am just as scared as you are, but, by golly, I want to go there badly. Will you come with me?' And they will follow me. If they never know that you have a vulnerable side to you, they can't deal with their own vulnerability. I've always believed that expressing your own vulnerability and getting people in touch with theirs goes a long way."

I was particularly struck by one story she told me from the time when she headed an auto plant in England that produced a product with serious quality problems. Television personalities were even making fun of the car. Cynthia felt compelled and determined to confront the executives and union people working on this car, but as a foreigner, she also recognized she needed to tread softly. "I cared about these people," she told me, "and I knew in their hearts that they wanted to win."

Cynthia went before the workers and said, "Together, let's go through this vehicle and see what we like and what we don't like about it."

The first reaction was, "Well, we think it's okay."

To that Cynthia responded, "Well, I don't, and I'm the customer."

The team went through a second evaluation and began to see things that they had overlooked on the first round. Cynthia seized the moment and engaged their soul at work by saying, "I want to tell you something. You are better than this, and you are going to prove it to me, but you are going to prove it to yourselves first. I can't believe that you don't want to be the best that you can be." They just stared at her, stunned, looking a little shocked and hurt. She then said to them, "You tell me what you want me to do. I will do whatever it is you want me to do, but I'm not going to be part of an organization that isn't passionate about quality and customers."

The next day, the team gathered and said, "We *are* better than this, and we *are* going to be better than this, but we're not sure how."

Together the team and Cynthia set down some rules of the game to guide them, and off they went to improve the car. "Eventually," Cynthia recalled, "they began to see, 'Oh, she believes in us and wants us to be better, and she isn't even beating us up. She can see something that we can't see.' For them, it was a relief that somebody believed in them. It was very gratifying to see them do something every day to improve the quality of that product, and they themselves felt a whole lot better. There was a sense of pride with the results."

By speaking directly to the workers' vulnerability, that they were, in fact, producing a poor product, Cynthia allowed an opportunity for new strengths to emerge. Instead of diminishing her people or telling them what they needed to do, she made herself vulnerable to their imperatives by telling them to *tell her* what they needed from her. Doing this, she engaged their highest selves by creating space, a crucible, where they could improve themselves, believe in themselves as she did, and maintain their integrity. Cynthia's leadership established mutuality, where her effectiveness and success as a leader depended on them, and vice versa. And they, in turn, like alchemists, turned base metal into gold.

Cynthia, like other Iron Butterflies, expects the best from people and is optimistic that the best will come. Some observers might think that Cynthia is naive for being optimistic and trusting, but might it not be better to err in trusting too much rather than not enough? The alternative to optimism is cynicism, which is a complete abdication of responsibility. And cynicism closes the door to the heart and soul.

Embracing Vulnerabilities as Learning Opportunities

Janie Burks, CFO of Volunteers of America, an organization that provides affordable housing and health care, helping people help themselves to overcome poverty and despair, told me how the people she worked with were willing to tell her what was really on their minds. I asked her how she created an environment where that was possible.

"Treating people well, listening to people well, being interested in them, attuned to them, are fundamentals of relationships," she responded. "And good relationships have a lot to do with productivity. I set a tone at work by being an example. You can't just ask people to be more open; you have to be willing to share something of yourself, too. I do that. I'll poke fun at myself, and it opens the group up. That might not be viewed as professional, but I think it's important. If someone brings a problem to me, I let him or her know that I can identify with that personally, and that fosters trust. It's just being very honest. If someone is in bad humor and creating negative energy, I confront them immediately. It takes time to sit down with people, but that adds richness to our experience of working together. Dealing with emotions has to be an all day and every day kind of thing. Over time, I have found that dealing with emotional realities is working in other ways. People come to me with information, such as telling me when someone is really stressed out, because they know I will address those kinds of things when they occur. They become part of the norm."

To illustrate her point, Janie told me about an incident involving a communication problem between her staff members and a member from another department. The problem related to a very smart and competent woman who worked hard but also operated within very narrow boundaries. She delegated any tasks or responsibilities outside those narrow lines to someone else. "There wasn't any reaching and stretching and flexibility, which I think is important in working with other people," Janie told me. "Her approach was, 'It stops here and then it's your job.'"

Janie decided to have a candid conversation with this person. "These are the kinds of conversations that it's all too tempting to put off for a very long time," Janie told me with a laugh. "When you start these conversations, you have to be willing to have them come back at you and listen to what the person thinks; that's not always easy. At the end of our conversation, the woman apologized for her behavior. Then I realized that I felt a need to apologize, too. I needed to recognize and be honest that maybe I could have done something differently here. I apologized because I was making an issue of her behavior and not recognizing her intent. It's a matter of knowing yourself and knowing you're not perfect and being true to your values. I got a smile from her. I felt we had settled some things and established a better understanding of how we could work together."

Janie sets an example for the rest to follow by admitting mistakes publicly, showing everyone that it is not the end of the world to err. After all, "To err is human." When someone makes a mistake, Janie makes it very clear that not only will they not be diminished, but they will be applauded for their courageous vulnerability. For example, she discovered that they had paid full annuity to an annuitant in advance. Generally, people get paid quarterly. There was not a lot of money involved, but these are donor relations, and as accountants they cannot be too careful. The staff accountant who made the mistake immediately admitted his error, saying that he had not been careful enough. He offered to call the donor and tell them he had made the mistake, which is what he did.

"I really appreciated that," Janie told me. "We very publicly let our staff know that this was a wonderful way to deal with this situation, taking away the threat associated with making mistakes. Instead, we celebrated his taking the responsibility by admitting it and going that extra mile and calling the donor."

Although Janie holds high expectations of others, she also makes allowances for their vulnerabilities. Under the wing of this Iron Butterfly, when people are vulnerable, such as when they make a mistake, they are never diminished for the error, but instead are recognized for their fortitude in owning up and taking responsibility. This openness to vulnerability not only allows them to learn from their mistakes and develop new strengths, but it also bonds people together in their shared humanity.

We all have frailties. Allowing for vulnerabilities in the workplace creates a culture of transparency and also helps prevent crisis. When people have to hide their mistakes or are afraid to ask questions, these errors can accumulate undetected until the house of cards tumbles and people find themselves dealing with a big problem—one that started as a small error and could have been avoided through honesty at the outset.

DEALING WITH EMOTIONS AND EMPLOYING THE POWER OF APPRECIATION

Justina Trott, director of the Santa Fe National Community Center of Excellence in Women's Health in New Mexico, describes herself as "a facilitator of processes to get people together and see how we, together, can make things work better." The following is an example of how she facilitates so the heart falls open and the spirit awakens.

Justina and her staff were meeting about a financial proposal and, as often happens with the topic of money, people began haggling over bits and pieces, getting testy with each other, grumbling. Justina could see the tension escalating, so in the middle of the discussion she pulled back her chair and said, "Wait a minute. Something else is going on here."

Justina recognized at that moment that her people were feeling overwhelmed, overworked, stressed, and unappreciated. "I said to them, 'In writing this proposal, I was trying to meet some of the needs people had. And I'm hearing from you, Jan, that it isn't working. I want you to know that I really appreciate what you have been doing.' Jan broke down and cried. And then I turned to another person and said, 'I know this is difficult for you.' And she broke down and cried. I addressed the CFO and said, 'You are probably feeling attacked right now because this is your financial proposal and they are making you out to be just money grubbing, so that can't feel very good to you.' I could see he was relieved to hear someone recognize that.

"So we switched from talking about the topic to processing how everybody was feeling. And, yes, they were feeling stressed, and they appreciated that someone took time to recognize it. I told them how much they meant to me because I couldn't be doing this work without them. This was a meeting where we had spent a good half hour on the topic and getting nowhere. We spent an hour dealing with the emotions in the room. Then in the last ten minutes of the meeting, we solved the problems. It was done. My guess is that if we had continued in the same negative vein and not addressed the underlying feelings, we would have solved nothing. People would have been angry, and the same topic would have been brought up in the next meeting. Although dealing with emotions is messy and takes time, in the end it is a more effective way of achieving our goals. This process works both ways. There have been times when I have gotten hot under the collar, and they have helped me deal with it."

Justina showed the power of reflection and action. By stepping back and reflecting aloud about what was really going on, she helped her people move forward genuinely as a team rather than being pushed forward for the sake of moving on. Dealing with relationships and emotions is time consuming, which Justina acknowledged, but it is ultimately more efficient. It is something like Chinese cooking: All the work is in the preparation, in chopping and marinating. Once the cooking starts, it goes very quickly.

Justina also demonstrated the power of appreciation and how this small action has a big effect in healing the tired soul and opening the heart. The fact that people's softness comes so quickly with appreciation speaks to just how little we take care of each other, and just how little it takes to feel cared for.

Companies spend a lot of money trying to motivate people. A study done on what motivated information technology workers had surprising results. The number one motivator was personal thanks; number two: written thanks; number three: public thanks. Money was number twelve. How simple it is to offer someone thanks, and it does not cost a dime! Appreciation is a small change that can have a huge effect on the quality of relationships at work. Psychologist William James once said that "the deepest principle of human nature is the craving to be appreciated." When we appreciate people and meet this craving, we invite the soul at work where the smallest gestures can make a big difference.

THE SOUL AT WORK

The kind of leadership and work environments exemplified by the above stories represent the future for enlightened organizations. It is, however, not a new concept, but rather one that has evolved from a participatory approach to management pioneered by Mary Parker Follett, a leader in the fields of human relations, democratic organization, and management, who focused on interpersonal relations for management and education. Her approach was not widely developed, however, and with her death in 1933, her contributions toward a people-centered approach to work were soon forgotten. A strictly mechanistic mode of management became the norm, based on Frederick Taylor's principles of scientific management and Henry Ford's and Alfred Sloan's practices of mass production. These principles and practices held sway until relatively recently.

Management experts Tom Peters and Robert Waterman, in writing their book *In Search of Excellence,* were given credit for promoting a people-centered style of leadership.[5] Scholars Pauline Graham, Margaret Karsten, and Joyce Fletcher, however, reminded management theorists that Mary Parker Follett was the founder of a humanistic approach to management, and so reclaimed her legacy.

Mary Parker Follett spoke to the heart of women's way of leading and a style that creates conditions for awakening the soul at work. As Joyce Fletcher described in *Disappearing Acts: Gender, Power, and Relational Practice at Work,* those conditions for organizational growth value connection, mutuality, interdependence, and collectivity—a definitive departure from separation, rigid boundaries, autonomy, individual achievement, and independence.[6] The Winds of Change Foundation and the Center for Research on Women at Wellesley College collaborated on a study of top female leaders, and author Sumru Erkut found that the descriptions of nearly every woman's leadership practice included elements of the democratic, people-oriented style.[7] The above stories reflect this people-oriented style in the women's demonstration of empathy, mutuality, authenticity, and empowerment. All of these female leaders are cultivating and inspiring others, eliciting their highest capabilities, and guiding people in transforming their vulnerabilities into strengths by engaging their soul at work.

Gallup polls show that most workers rate having a caring boss even higher than they value money or fringe benefits. In interviews with two million employees in seven hundred companies, Gallup found the relationship with a person's immediate boss determines how long employees stay at a company and how productive they are; people stay at a job because of relationships.[8]

Iron Butterflies create precisely these kinds of relational environments, where people enjoy working together as they develop their potential. And they are able to do this because of their relational intelligence and emotional strength. Howard Gardner, Elisabeth A. Hobbs Professor of Cognition and Education at the Harvard Graduate School of Education, and author of *Frames of Mind: The Theory of Multiple Intelligences,* called it "interpersonal intelligence."[9] He said that it is "getting more and more important all the time in business. It's not just about knowing yourself but having other people at work think a lot about themselves and about how they can use their abilities maximally ... and because historically that has been ruled as taboo—you don't want to talk about your inner feelings and thoughts and so on—I think there's a missed opportunity for people to mobilize themselves."[10]

It is indeed a missed opportunity. Given that people-oriented management practices enhance all bottom-line numbers in all business sectors, it seems reasonable that all business leaders would rush to embrace the approach. Instead, this way of running organizations is still a minority practice. The great majority of organizations still adhere to traditional mechanistic, *less efficient* management practices. The reason is not hard to imagine. The great majority of leaders are men, and leadership is typically defined in masculine terms: action oriented, aggressive, autonomous, and so on. The feminine attributes that are part of Iron Butterflies' leadership practice, such as nurturing and collaboration, are typically dismissed as being "soft," "unbusiness-like," and not leadership attributes.

As an aside, but illustrative of this attitude, is the history of my book *Weaving Complexity and Business.* When it was first published in hardcover by Simon and Schuster in 2000, it had a different title, *The Soul at Work.* When it was due to go into paperback, the new publisher told us, and I quote, "No one wants to hear the word *soul* in the business world." My coauthor and I hated the new, "more businesslike" title, but we were stuck with it.

Women's relational intelligence and collaborative ways of leading that allow for vulnerability are creating an alternative to the domination model of aggression and hubris in the business world, and are beginning to penetrate the business environment. Although the feminine attributes of nurturing and collaboration are often denigrated as being soft, they are, in fact, hard to put into practice. Selflessness, inclusion of others, dealing with vulnerability, and relational intelligence are simply not on the syllabus at business schools. When they are eventually included, and when the inculcation of the culture of aggression and myopic focus on financial bottom lines is set aside, the soul will indeed be at work in business environments, and the organizations themselves will be both more spiritual and more successful.

■ ■ ■

Linda Ferguson, PhD, is a human resources consultant specializing in organization development and personal transformation. Linda conducts workshops and retreats on emotional intelligence, Appreciative Inquiry (AI), empathic communication, leadership development, strategic planning, and working spiritually. She also provides coaching for people interested in making a positive change in their lives using a spiritual approach. Dr. Ferguson earned her PhD from Indiana University–Bloomington in organizational behavior, and also has a master's degree from Indiana University in social psychology. She has worked as an assistant professor of business administration at several universities, teaching organizational behavior, business ethics, Ethical Leadership, leadership and motivation, and entrepreneurship. Linda has traveled abroad extensively in Asia, Australia, Israel, and Europe, and currently lives in Virginia. She is the author of *The Path for Greatness: Spirituality at Work*. Linda is finishing her second book, *Staying Grounded in Shifting Sand*, where she introduces her process of Transformational Empowerment.™

Working Spiritually
Aligning Gifts, Purpose, and Passion
Linda Ferguson, PhD

We are all interconnected parts of a united whole, not just united in our tasks for the sake of the company or agency. We are interconnected emotionally, spiritually, and mentally as we do our work. So why are we afraid of spirituality at work? Why do we shy away from qualities that we know will help us be the best we can be at work and feel good being at work? Based on the conviction that each of us has activities, people, or places that feed us spiritually, this chapter presents a framework for working spiritually, supported by real-life examples and clarified with lessons from the field. The author concludes that there are unlimited ways to work spiritually, and that aligning our gifts, purpose, and passion in service to others will reveal our natural beauty.

WHAT IT MEANS TO WORK SPIRITUALLY

The Buddhist concept of a web of life exemplifies our interconnection. Imagine an endless web with diamonds at each cross-stitch, with each diamond bringing in the light around it and reflecting out the light of all the other lights shining on it. That is a picture of our life: we take in messages, imprints, and energy of others, and we reflect it all out through our unique self-expression.

So it is that we enter our workplace—as interconnected parts of a united whole. We are not just united in our tasks for the sake of the company or agency; we are all interconnected emotionally, spiritually, and mentally as we do our work. When we show up at work, we bring our emotions, thoughts, and beliefs to our workplace. Our attitudes and moods are felt by others, consciously or not. And our attitudes are contagious. A positive attitude helps raise people to new levels and sustains them through a crisis. Negative attitudes pull people down, suck out energy, and affect performance and mental health. Certainly, we have all felt the difference between a healthy, vibrant workplace and a toxic, stressful one.

I like to start my workshops by asking people to name all the descriptions they can for what it feels like to be spiritual. We usually generate a list of forty to fifty words, such as joyful, peaceful, content, energized, balanced, compassionate, caring, receptive, creative, aware, and mindful. You get the idea. Then I ask how many would want to work in such an environment. All hands go up. Then I ask if there is anyone in the group who thinks this type of workplace would feel better and have more energy. Not surprisingly, they all think it would.

So why are we afraid of spirituality at work? Why do we shy away from qualities that we know will help us be the best we can be at work and feel good being at work? Many people do not want to talk about spirituality at work because they confuse *religion* at work with *spirituality* at work. I draw a huge distinction between these two ideas. Religion is about creeds, rituals, and dogmas. Spirituality is more the state of being, the feeling we have when we are connected to something beyond ourselves. Even atheists in my groups describe what it is like to feel spiritual.

I like to use three key words to describe spirituality at work: *wholeness, meaning,* and *connection.* Most people agree that these concepts give us a basis for talking about spirituality at work. When we feel a greater sense of our own *wholeness*—our authentic self, our true nature, our center when all else falls away—we are able to best reflect our inner light, our highest qualities, our best expression of who we are. When we have *meaning* in our work and are doing things that are making a difference in the world in some way, we find greater energy to keep going under adversity and over the long haul. When we feel a *connection* with something greater than ourselves—such as a larger mission or richer connection to coworkers or clients—we find time goes more quickly, we enjoy what we do, and we receive as we give. When we find wholeness, meaning, and connection in what we do, we work spiritually.

In my workshops, once I get through with this exercise and discussion, people usually begin to see ways they can work spiritually. Then we start to identify how they can show up as spiritual beings at work. Every now and then, I find that some people feel they need "permission" from someone to tell them it is okay to work spiritually. They think of spirituality at work as some special new program the company is going to initiate. My response has been consistent: "Do you want permission to breathe?" Working spiritually is who you are, not what actions or initiatives your company does. Being spiritual at work isn't something that someone allows; it's a matter of how you are *being* as you do your work. When you are connected to your Source or Higher Power or whatever word you wish to use, you bring that energy and awareness to your work.

A FRAMEWORK FOR WORKING SPIRITUALLY

As I was developing ideas for my first book, *Path for Greatness: Spirituality at Work,* I wanted to capture visually what working spiritually looked like. I wanted the image to be a living representation, not an abstract diagram or model. As I pondered what image would best represent the vitality and beauty of who we are when we are being our best selves, fully alive and working as spiritual beings, the image of a flower came to mind (see figure 1). Let me describe each of the parts of this image and why it is a helpful way to consider working spiritually.

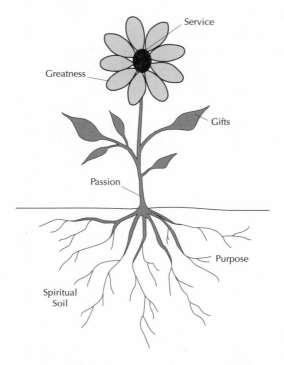

Figure 1: An image of working spirituality[1]

Spiritual Soil

Each of us has activities, people, or places that feed us spiritually. Some like to be outdoors, others in beautiful cathedrals. Some like to sing in a choir, while others prefer to sit alone in silent meditation. Regardless of how you reinvigorate and replenish your energy, you need that nourishment to sustain yourself in your busy life. Just like a flower needs fertile soil in which to grow, you need fertile soil for your life to flourish. Without ways and places to renew yourself, you could wither and die, just as a plant would die in soil that is too dry or without the right nutrients.

In my workshops, I ask people to consider what they do on a regular basis, either weekly or monthly, to renew themselves: How are you tending your spiritual soil? What does your life look like when your soil is fresh and fertile versus depleted and dry? I talk about how important it is to tend to your "soil," to do those activities that help revitalize and inspire you so you can meet your daily responsibilities.

Because life challenges can drain you and wash your spiritual soil out from underneath you, you have to be intentional to cultivate and replenish your soil continually.

Purpose

From fertile ground, your well-nurtured spiritual soil, your roots can grow deep and take hold. No matter the winds that blow, when your roots are deep and well grounded, you can withstand the external pressures and stressors. Your roots are your purpose. When you know clearly what you are supposed to do or have clear goals, you are much more effective in how you spend your time and your life energy. Meaningful work that helps you live your mission in life helps you stay focused on those things that are important, instead of spending time on busy work and running like a gerbil in an activity trap.

If you have ever met someone who was clear on his or her life purpose, you know what I mean. They are people with a mission. They have focus, determination, and dedication. I find it quite enjoyable and inspiring to be around these kinds of people because their energy exudes everywhere, and it is usually very contagious. They bounce back from setbacks, are highly motivated, and stay focused on what they need to be doing.

It is well worth your time to get clear on your life purpose and find your right livelihood. While your life purpose may change over time, the more clear your purpose is, the more you will be able to handle what life puts before you. This is especially true in work situations. Many people find that they are being stretched thin at work or asked to do more with less resources. Even in the most supportive work environment (and, sadly, too many of us work in toxic or unhealthy workplaces), the strain can be great. If you have a clear purpose on why you are doing what you are doing, and you can find meaning in what you do, you can persevere even under stressful conditions.

Passion

Once your purpose is clear, your energy will flourish. From your roots grows the stem of the plant, the center of your being, your passion. Just as a plant with a weak stem looks limp and sickly, so, too, when you do not have energy or passion for what you do, you may simply muddle through each day. With a clear purpose, you can bring forth your energy and passion to do your work and meet the challenges of each day.

Gifts

The leaves of the plant have cells that engage in photosynthesis, which feeds the plant and helps it thrive. A plant converts sunlight into energy through the leaves. So, too, do your gifts help you convert your purpose and passion into your daily life. It is through your gifts that you bring your purpose and passion to the world. Your gifts—which include your skills and abilities, personality traits, wisdom, and awareness—are unique. When your purpose is clear and your passion grows, you will best be able to use your gifts as your offering to the world.

Service

When you use your gifts in alignment with your passion and purpose, they become an offering done as spiritual service. Just as the center of the flower provides an offering of nectar for the bees to use and gives life to other plants, so can you make contributions to the well-being of others and the world at large through your service. When you work spiritually, your gifts become an offering, and you make the world a better place just by being in it.

Greatness

Just as the petals of a flower show the beauty of the plant, your beauty naturally bursts forth when you offer yourself in service to others. As the poet Rumi wrote, "Let the beauty of who you are be what you do." Working spiritually is about fulfilling your life purpose or larger mission with passion, using your gifts in service to others. When you do that, others will pick up on your beauty and gifts. Your beauty may even serve as inspiration to others, whether you know it or not. You will be working spiritually when you make your unique contributions, in your own corner of the world that enlivens and enriches others. When you make the world more beautiful by what you do, you will find greater wholeness and meaning for yourself and greater connection with others.

LESSONS FROM THE FIELD

I have had the opportunity to provide workshops on working spiritually to groups around the country, and I would like to share several stories from these workshops and conversations that exemplify ways people offer their work as spiritual service.

"This Is My Church"

A friend of mine, Julie, broke her ankle several years ago and had to take the bus to work for several weeks because she could not drive. Julie would hobble down to the street near her apartment to catch her bus. After the first couple of weeks, Julie found that if she timed her trip right, she would ride with one particular bus driver. This driver, whom I will call "Sue," was very outgoing and friendly and would talk to everyone as they got on the bus. Julie is *not* a morning person, so she would usually just nod as she entered the bus. She started to notice, however, that by the time she reached work, she felt more friendly and joyful.

As Julie paid attention to her morning rides to see what might be the explanation for her change of mood in the mornings, she realized that she really liked Sue. Sue took an interest in everyone who got on the bus and seemed to genuinely care about them. Julie found herself becoming more interested in the people who got on after her stop. Some would strike up long conversations with Sue, while others would merely nod or smile as they got on.

Julie assumed that those who chatted with Sue must be regular riders or friends. One day another rider asked Sue what church she went to. Julie was taken aback at the question but assumed that the rider must have known Sue personally. Sue then surprised Julie even more. Sue turned to the back of the bus and to the riders with a swoop of her arm she said, "This is my church." She went on to explain that she felt so connected to the people on her bus that it was her way of doing church. Sue evidently thought of her work as ministry. She knew it did not matter what kind of building or place she used to carry out her ministry of caring for others.

"I'm a Light"

In a completely different town, I heard a similar story. I usually start my workshops by asking people why they are interested in the topic of working spiritually and what kind of work they do. One woman said she was a bus driver as well as a Reiki master. When I asked her about that unusual combination, she said it was a perfect fit for her. She could drive around the town sending Reiki (healing energy) to people in her community and get paid to do it! This is another wonderful example of someone understanding her gifts and purpose and finding ways to offer her gifts to others in service.

People share their gifts and passion in service in many different ways. Some years ago, I met a woman who had worked as a waitress. She told me the story of one night that was really busy. The waitstaff was flying all over the floor trying to keep up; everyone was harassed and orders were arriving late. It was turning into a miserable night. She noticed how stressed out everyone was feeling and how chaotic it was getting and decided to do something about it. After taking a few deep breaths, she started saying to herself, "I'm a light, I'm a light, I'm a light." She said that several dozen times to help bring herself back to a place of balance and composure.

After she started feeling more grounded and peaceful, she then focused her energy on her coworkers and the customers. She again repeated to herself, "I'm a light," only this time she envisioned that she was sending that light out to everyone in the room. Her night went much smoother after that. At some point, still in the middle of the busy rush, one of her customers commented on how peaceful she looked, saying that she seemed to have a sort of glow around her. He asked what she was doing to achieve that calm and glow. They struck up a short conversation about related topics, and she realized the man understood what she was doing. After things died down, she went back to talk to him. He challenged her to use her gifts to do other kinds of healing work. From that conversation, she started thinking about how she could come to work every day and work from an inner place of peace and balance. She eventually sought training in energy healing and moved to the town next to mine to start her business.

Not Your Usual Chitchat

You never know what you will discover when you stay true to your gifts, purpose, and passion. When I stayed true to my gifts and passion, I felt called to write my first book, though talking about spirituality at work was not something I had always been comfortable doing. In 1995, when I first started writing my book, spirituality at work was not a popular topic. I was teaching at a small college, and it certainly was not seen as a topic appropriate for academia.

One day my department chair told me that I was scheduled to meet a certain dean of a prominent business school the following day. I had never heard of this dean and had no idea why he was coming to talk to our department, so when I met him, I was a little on guard. Doug was an older man, trained at Carnegie Mellon. He had been dean of two business schools, and he came with all the academic credentials. As we talked about our department's new business program, we went through the usual academic chitchat about where we had studied, and so forth.

Then he asked me, "What is your area of research interest?"

I gulped. Then I took a deep breath and said I was interested in spirituality at work and was starting to write a book about it.

To my absolute and complete surprise, Doug nodded and said, "You know, some years ago when I was a faculty member before becoming a dean, I wanted to write an article on the spiritually integrated manager. I never did write that article, but I've been interested in the topic ever since."

I nearly fell off my chair. Here was this traditionally trained, highly respected dean saying he had been wanting to address spirituality at work some twenty years earlier. I smiled, and we had an hour-long conversation about what the ramifications might be to businesses if managers were spiritually whole. I have cherished my friendship with Doug ever since. I would have never known about Doug's work and stayed connected with him on the topic of spirituality at work had I not claimed my gifts, purpose, and passion in that conversation.

"Calling in the Directions"

Shortly after writing my first book, I decided to take the chance to offer a spiritual activity in a strategic planning staff retreat I was facilitating. The retreat was held at a center designed and decorated with Cherokee themes, so I decided to open the retreat with a ritual of "calling in the directions"—a way of honoring the earth to focus our energy before starting our work. The director of the organization came to me later that day and said he felt the retreat had been so successful because we had started the day with that opening exercise. He thought it set the tone for a very different kind of experience and helped create energy that focused people to think in a broader way than they normally would have.

Put It Out There and See What Happens

I encourage you to offer your gifts and not shy from who you are as a spiritual being. You just never know who you will affect or how. I was in a staff training as a participant with some government workers. For the warm-up exercise, we each had to say what some of our hobbies were. Since my hobbies are almost all focused on spirituality, I figured there was no way out of talking about the subject. I said that I did drumming and Sufi dances. Not knowing if anyone there even knew what Sufi Dances of Universal Peace were, I just put it out there and waited to see what would happen.

During the break, a very large, middle-aged sheriff came up to meet me and say hello. Picture in your mind a heavyset man wearing his full sheriff gear—including a bulletproof vest. I had no idea what was going to happen as he approached me. But with the sweetest smile, he asked if I had been to the Coleman Barks program the year earlier in our town. Coleman Barks is the poet largely responsible for familiarizing the Sufi poet Rumi to Americans, and I admit I was surprised that this sheriff had attended the program. I found out that not only had he and his wife gone to the program, but he was very interested in many types of drumming. We talked for about twenty minutes about how marvelous the Rumi program had been and swapped titles of CDs we had of world drummers. I am glad that I took the risk to share my gifts and passion in that training session because that connection with the sheriff helped him claim his own gifts and passion more fully as well.

"Let the Beauty Inside Be Your Compass"

Over the years, I have used many different methods to help people connect to their spiritual core. I once worked with a pair of women who had had trouble working with each other for nearly ten years. We did several visualizations to help them find within themselves their highest best self, and I used Rumi's line, "Let the beauty inside be your compass," as the theme for our session. Two weeks later, they told me that they could see where they needed to shift, and that the work we had done together had helped them take steps to mend their relationship. One woman shared that our work had prompted her to get back to meditation, which she had given up some years earlier. She said she felt so much more peaceful having returned to her meditation practice.

There are unlimited ways to help people connect with their spiritual core. I have used Tibetan bowls to help a group get centered and focused before we start a meeting. I have often used visualizations and affirmations to set our intentions on what we hoped to accomplish as a group or individually. I have invited mediation by asking each person what the other person is there to show them about themselves and what they need to learn. I have invited people to honor their adversary as a teacher rather than an enemy. It is truly amazing what can happen when you can get people to shift their focus, intention, and energy to compassion, caring, or receptivity.

As writer Kahlil Gibran reminds us, "When you work you are a flute through whose heart the whispering of the hours turns to music."[2] When you align your gifts, purpose, and passion in service to others, your beauty will naturally come forth. You will find that the activities, tasks, or work you do from your spiritual center will flow more easily.

I wish for you clarity on what you are here to do in the world and courage to offer your unique gifts to the world in large or small ways.

■ ■ ■

Robert Rabbin is a renowned public speaker and an established author, executive coach, and self-awareness teacher. He has generated his insights and practical wisdom from more than thirty years of personal growth, spiritual self-inquiry, and meditative contemplation. He has traveled extensively, from the forests of Finland to the ashrams of India, from the boardrooms of corporate America to the lecture halls of Australia. Robert is the creator of RealTime Speaking, a daring style of public speaking that calls for integrity, vulnerability, and authentic connection. He works with a select clientele of business innovators, social transformers, and cultural thought leaders, assisting them to develop and deliver inventive messages that effectively engage their audiences. For more information and to contact Robert, please visit his website at www.robertrabbin.com.

YOU Are the Message!
The Power of Authentic Speaking
ROBERT RABBIN

This chapter makes a strong point for speaking in public with authenticity. In business, much of our speaking is really a hiding. We hide behind neutral masks, speaking neutered words. Yet we need to realize that if our audience does not immediately find us credible, they will not allow us to influence them. We need to speak with authenticity, predicated on vulnerability, honesty, empathy, transparency, and love. This chapter looks into the concept of vulnerability with others, entailing a willingness and capacity to see and be seen; to stand in front of others fully seeing them, and allowing them to see us, without putting up masks. Once we get used to telling the truth, living and speaking authentically, we also get used to discerning it. Authentic speaking is beneficial to our soul, the vitality and future of our organizations, and even the fate of our world.

ARE *YOU* FOR REAL?

I can think of nothing more essential, more urgent, more compelling for business executives and students of business and management than this: learn to speak in public with authenticity.

35

Why? What's at stake? Your soul. The vitality and future of your organization. The fate of the world. If you can speak authentically, you will bring untold blessings to yourself, your organization and its network of stakeholders, your family and friends, your community—the earth herself will be glad!

James Cagney, the actor famed for his tough-guy roles, pointed toward authentic public speaking when he offered a novice actor this essential teaching: "It's simple. You walk in the room, plant your feet, look me in the eye, and tell the truth."[1]

Can you do that? It is more difficult than you might think.

I define public speaking as speaking with anyone other than yourself, regardless of numbers, venue, or purpose. Do not confuse public speaking with lecturing or giving keynote addresses. Those are different types of public speaking. Everyone is a public speaker; *YOU are a public speaker!* Speaking itself is more than the words that come out of our mouths and more than the nonverbal signals of meaning and intent we transmit. Speaking is how we move in and through life. Our speaking tells the story of who we are and how we live. If we are to live a true life, a vibrant and vivid life, then our speaking will reveal, rather than conceal, our heart—the truth of who we are, what we are doing, and what we stand for.

At the end of one of her poems, Mary Oliver asks what it is we intend to do with our "wild and precious life."[2] If we take this question deep inside to the very depths, then our answer lies in our speaking. Our speaking represents the truth of how we live—or how we do not live—moment to moment in the here and now, without any spin or hype. Deep speaking reveals the self, unwrapped from rationalizations, justifications, and all the reasons why. Not the mundane self, not the blah blah blah self, but the primordial self, the pristine essence with a spine so strong that it stands as the axis of the world.

The question is, do you speak this way? Does anyone? Do you know what this sounds like?

As a public speaker, your first task is to tell your audience, the person or people with whom you are speaking, that you are for real. They want to know this one thing above all else, and they want to know it up front, immediately, before they are even willing to listen to what you have to say. They want to know if you are a real human being who is going to speak the truth, who is going to speak with transparency and integrity, with authenticity and vulnerability. Are you for real?

They may not agree with your message or point of view. They may not be persuaded to do what you want them to do, but they will not even get to these considerations if they do not think you are for real. We, as speakers, have got to be real, authentic, transparent. For their sake. For our sake. We must tell the truth. The deep truth.

HIDE AND SEEK

Being an authentic speaker is not a matter of content or technique or rote behaviors or scripted actions. As far as I know, there is no precise prescription, no how-to manual, no one-size-fits-all recipe for authenticity. In an interview with Larry King, master chef Julia Child suggested that real chefs do not need recipes, they just need to know the principles of cooking. If you need recipes, you will never be a chef. In the same way, you cannot become a credible, inspiring, compelling public speaker, which is to say a truth teller, by following a recipe or imitating someone else, or by raising your hand *just so* when you say *just this*.

Do not look for a model or precedent. It does not matter who else has done it, is doing it, or will do it. Maybe no one ever has. The principles of authenticity are universal: intimacy, vulnerability, and connection, as well as courage, truth, spirit, and passion. Authenticity means to meet people without a hiding mask, without a disguising role.

Authenticity is predicated on vulnerability, honesty, empathy, transparency, and love. A telling distinction must be made between those who speak *about* authenticity, and those who speak *from* authenticity. It may not be easy to speak from this place, but the willingness to do so is what will get you there. It means to speak from your depth, from the place where words are almost superfluous, where the truest speaking is the silent presentation of *you*.

Many of the business leaders I have coached find it difficult to embody my defining dictum of authenticity: *YOU are the message.* I ask them to speak, to lead, with themselves out front, but they would rather speak and lead with their title, their knowledge, their accomplishments, their plans, their forecasts and charts, their net worth, their positional power. In essence, they want to hide. Yet when the x-ray machine is scanning for their true heart, or their soul, what do we see?

I was once invited by the president of a company to listen to his keynote address to an international conference. The room was big and full, with eight to ten people per table, and maybe fifty tables in all. He stood to one side on the elevated stage that ran the width of the room. Two imposing screens, one on each end of the stage, were unfurled like white flags waiting to be emblazoned. And then they were—with slide after illegible slide. Even if I had been a speed-reader, I would not have gotten through the slides. There were charts and diagrams and bullet points and excerpts and quotes and flowing things and arrows going this way and back, and that way and—hey, now look here, this is important and you really need to get this, and while you're at it remember this because see these famous guys said it was so, and now we'll go on to the next slide and I do hope you're really getting all this and remembering it and integrating it into your consciousness and connecting it to your experience and frame of reference and—oops, I think I need to go back one or two, and now let's jump ahead to something you'll really like and be able to use—if you're still breathing and conscious.

When his talk was, mercifully, over, he invited me to have a drink with him in the lounge. We sat down at a small round table, and he asked, "So, what did you think?"

I was silent, weighing several options.

He said, "It's okay, I want you to tell me the truth. I want to know what you think."

I was waiting for that invitation. I said, "I really enjoyed that bit when you spoke about your values and why you do what you do, about the love you have for your family. I thought that was very revealing and refreshing. It lasted for about thirty seconds, and it came at the forty-two-minute mark. By my reckoning, you had thirty seconds of authenticity in a seventy-minute talk." I spoke a bit about the mind-numbing complexity of his slide show jumble and how no human being could possibly assimilate any of the information in a useful way.

Then I was silent.

So was he.

Finally, he said, "I don't like you. And I don't like what you just said. But I know that I need to hear you. I know that you are right."

I told him I thought he was hiding behind his slides and information. I asked him why he did not show up as a human being and say, "Here I am. Please see me. Please hear me. This is who I am and this is what I stand for."

In business, much of our speaking is really a hiding. We speak like newsreaders at their evening desks in TV world. *No one is home!* We hide ourselves behind neutral masks, speaking neutered words. This is not speaking. This is not communicating. This is not connecting. Giving out information, reading a script, pointing to slides— these are not speaking, not communicating, any more than random pressure on the inner ear is music. It is just hiding and pretense. It is a sham.

I do appreciate the value of information, especially information carefully gathered and clearly presented. It is important—in some cases, vital. But slides do not have eyes, and information does not have flesh, or feeling, or empathy. Information does not have love or a soul. People have these things.

Where are the people?

Why do we hide?

Why don't we speak authentically?

NOT GOOD ENOUGH

When we stand in front of others, we expose ourselves completely. This total vulnerability triggers every one of our insecurities and fears, especially the fear of not being good enough. I am not talking about being good enough to speak well; I mean good enough as a human being. We fear being the one that some celestial quality-control angel will point to and say, "Not good enough!"

We hide because we are afraid that if we are seen, we will not be good enough.

Almost everyone who comes to my RealTime Speaking workshops is afraid to stand in public and speak their truth. To speak our truth means showing ourselves, not our "knowing." It means showing the fingerprint of our soul, not all the red tape we have accumulated in the form of experiences, ideas, and beliefs. It means being willing to be seen by people without defense or pretense, without fear of their criticism and judgment, without hiding.

I ask people at my workshops to show themselves to others without masks and roles, without prepared texts or PowerPoint presentations. Until we can do this, our fear of being seen and judged as not good enough will rule us and run us from dawn to dusk and all night long. Until we can do this, we cannot really live authentic lives.

One of the most challenging exercises for participants in my workshops is the one in which I ask them to stand before the group without saying anything. I ask them only to see and be seen; to connect with each person in the audience, in turn, with their eyes and their hearts. I ask them to notice any tendency to hide, to retreat, to cover themselves. I ask them to notice any feeling of contraction or tension. I ask them to breathe, to open, to say nothing. To just be present with themselves and others. To see the audience and let the audience see them. To let people in.

Most want to run away. People want to laugh, to joke, to hold their hands tightly, to look away, to clench their jaws. One teacher kept turning around, wanting to write something on an imaginary blackboard. Another kept shifting from one foot to the other. Some say they want to sit down. It is difficult. People have a hard time connecting.

Most of the ills of our world are the result of a lack of real connection. We meet each other, yes, but we meet behind layers of protection. In other words, we hide, for safety's sake. Not only do we hide from each other, but also we hide from ourselves. Our communication, our public speaking, is a lie. It presents who we think we should be rather than who we really are.

I am not suggesting that we disclose the minutiae of our life indiscriminately. I am talking about revealing that *thing* in us that other people can trust.

Years ago, I did enough rock climbing to know that when it came time to pick a belay partner, the person to whom you were entrusting your life, I chose based on that *thing* in them that I could trust, their inner character that I knew would not betray the trust I was placing in them. I needed to see and feel something from their core that would match, "I've got you. Climb away." If I did not see it, if I did not feel it, well—no, thanks.

It is no different with public speaking, which should first and before all else reveal our inner character, motives, intentions, commitments. Our authentic speaking tells the truth of who we are with everything on the line. Another word for this is *credibility*. If our audience does not immediately find us credible, they will not allow us to influence them. The widespread notion that credibility comes from the content of our presentation is incorrect. Credibility in public speaking comes directly from the quality of our authentic connection, from the degree to which our speaking reveals, rather than conceals, our true self and character, motive and purpose, heart and soul. People want to know, and trust, *us*. That is why we get up to speak with people, to show who we are. If we are only going to be tour guides for a PowerPoint presentation, we should stay home. When people come to see us, to hear us, then we should show them *us*.

AUTHENTIC CONNECTION

Many business people confuse information with communication. Sydney J. Harris, an American journalist and author, sets us straight: "The two words 'information' and 'communication' are often used interchangeably, but they signify quite different things. Information is giving out; communication is getting through."[3] Getting through requires authentic connection.

Authentic connection means touching your audience by speaking from your heart to theirs, in a simple, direct manner. You look in their eyes and you tell the truth. Authentic connection has a precise formula: Authentic Connection = Intimacy with Self + Vulnerability with Others.

"Intimacy with Self" implies a willingness and capacity to know ourselves deeply, from the inside out, to excavate, through layers of repression, other people's ideas and beliefs, fears and inhibitions to a dynamic place of genuine enthusiasm for life. There is a depth within each of us that connects us, as individuals, to the whole—not just to others, but to all of nature, to the earth, to the cosmos. When we can open ourselves to this depth, we can receive what is already there, within us, waiting to be expressed. This is how we become most fully our unique self while being most fully connected to others and to life.

"Vulnerability with Others" implies a willingness and capacity to see and to be seen—to stand in front of others, fully seeing them and allowing them to see us, without putting up masks or barriers behind which to hide or distort our genuine presence. Vulnerability is risky business, at best. We scarcely open ourselves all the way with our spouse or partner, so how is it possible to do so in front of people we do not know, maybe hundreds of them? I know we can because I have seen it happen, many times.

It is this quality of establishing a connection with ourselves and our audience that creates the channels through which communication—distinct from information—is transmitted. It is a matter of embodying our message rather than presenting information.

Hardly a day passes that some scandal of corruption, fraud, or deception—by government officials, corporate executives, spiritual leaders, celebrities, sport figures—does not make the front page of a newspaper. Even the Catholic Church is not immune, paying out more than one billion dollars in penalties for not speaking authentically. I want to set things straight: We are not victims in this. The light is always on. What people do is always visible. Maybe someone is not telling the truth, but maybe we are not listening for the truth. Their lies reflect and mirror ours.

If we really want to, we can see with our light into the darkness that others may use to cloak and camouflage their speaking. As *we* begin to speak authentically and transparently, we begin to listen in the same way. This is how we begin to see who else speaks authentically, and who does not. But we have got to go first. We need to learn how to show who we are, from deep inside us. We need to tell the truth. Then we will be able to know who else is doing it. Once we get used to telling the truth, to living and speaking authentically, we get used to discerning the truth.

SPEAKING FROM THE HEART

In my workshops, I assign all kinds of topics for sample talks. Somewhere around the halfway mark of the session, I almost always say, "Give a three-minute talk beginning with the line, 'What I love most in the world is ...'" If people start too fast, or if I think they are too much in their heads, I stop them. "Saturate each word with the feeling of love. Don't describe, demonstrate. Feel it. Show it. If tears come, let them come. If your feelings overwhelm you, if you can't speak because of the emotion, then stand there without speaking, and just show us the emotion."

Sometimes I will share a story of times when I have sat on a stage in front of hundreds of people and cried. I am not telling them to do just this, or even saying that they should; I am saying that our true emotions are a part of our speaking. We do not have to bury these feelings, or be afraid of them, or manage them. We do not have to fear them. We can let them be a part of our speaking.

It never fails. When people begin to go deeper, their talks become dramatically different from their first attempts. Something happens to them when they share their connection to someone or something they love. Their faces are brighter, their rate of speech slows down, the quality of their connection is vastly stronger. They stop hiding. They become, in a word, real. They become present. They become beautiful and inspiring speakers.

I emphasize the importance of speaking from the heart. I want people to see for themselves that when they settle into themselves and talk about things that matter to them, when they open their hearts to the audience, when they are unafraid of deeply feeling and showing the emotion of what they love, it is transformative. I want them to see what happens when they speak from their hearts.

There is an intoxicating freedom and power in this realization that we do not have to fear our hearts. We can only speak from the heart if we know our heart. If we know our heart and speak our heart, we elevate and beautify our speaking beyond any technique or skill. In this elevation of our speaking, something magical, almost unbelievable, happens in us and in our audience. Please find out what that is. It is awesome. You will be amazed.

■ ■ ■

Julia Mossbridge, PhD, is the vice president of human potential research at Ergon Institute, LLC. She is currently researching methods of training psi-related perceptual skills, lecturing at corporations and not-for-profit organizations, and developing a book related to brain shaping. Dr. Mossbridge received her master's degree in neuroscience from the University of California at San Francisco and her PhD in communication sciences and disorders from Northwestern University. Dr. Mossbridge has published articles in the *Journal of Neuroscience, Learning and Memory,* and *Marine Mammalogy.* She was awarded the Oberlin Alumni Fellowship and the Laura Ann Wilber Scholarship in Audiology. She was the recipient of the Young Investigator Award by the Women in Acoustics Division of the Acoustical Society of America. She has written for *Shift, Conscious Choice,* and *Breeder: A New Generation of Mothers,* and was the body/mind health columnist for *Conscious Choice.* She also authored the book *Unfolding: The Perpetual Science of Your Soul's Work.* She has taught perceptual psychology at Northwestern University, mathematics at Shimer College, and biochemistry and biophysics at Pacific College of Oriental Medicine in Chicago.

Brain Shaping at Work

Wiring Our Brains for Integrity, Leadership, Creativity, and [Insert Your Favorite Trait or Skill Here]

JULIA MOSSBRIDGE, PHD

"Brain shaping" is a name for the neural rewiring that results from training or practice with feedback. This chapter focuses on three aspects of brain shaping. First, it is important to recognize that brain shaping is going on every day via practice, feedback, and attention. Second, it is possible to brain shape any skill or trait through practice, accurate and consistent feedback, and focused attention. And third, effective brain shaping in the workplace requires three things: repeated effort toward a common goal (practice); consistent and accurate responses from people who have the desired traits and skills (feedback); public, pervasive, and passionate focus on the traits and skills that are to be brain shaped (attention); and a deep trust and compassion for the learning process (brain-shaping awareness).

Brain Shaping Is Going on All the Time

A few weeks ago, my eight-year-old son practiced his usual delay tactics in getting out of the house, and I practiced something new. I did not freak out or get anxious or yell. I calmly told him there would be a consequence if he did not start to put on his shoes by the time I counted to three.

After a few days of using techniques like these to change my own behavior, as well as my son's, it worked. My son learned to get out of the house more effectively, and I learned how to reduce my not-very-effective angry behavior.

How did that happen? How did we both learn? Certainly, I first needed to change my perception of the situation. Instead of seeing his fixation on experimenting with magnets and lasers as a delay tactic, I needed to understand that he was actually more interested in his experimenting than in getting to school on time. Then I learned to change my language and my emotional tone, as well as my behavior. From my consistent feedback and my attention on his behavior, he learned how and when to take action.

The story of our mutual learning experience is certainly more complicated than this simple explanation and involves many intricate processes. We do not know all the steps involved in learning any skill or trait, but scientists have a few ideas. I have come to use the term *brain shaping* as shorthand for the way learning alters the connectivity and chemistry of the brain.

In a healthy person, every mode of repetitive human effort can result in brain shaping, whether at the workplace or at home. When we are told that our work is not good enough, we learn either to strive harder, change our tactics, or to ignore the feedback. Consequently, our brains are shaped according to what we choose to do in response to the feedback. When we are practicing a new skill, such as database administration, and get consistent feedback from the customer, the boss, and the functionality of the database itself, our brain is shaped to hone that specific ability and make our work both more efficient and more successful. Repeated practice, coherent feedback, and attention on the task or skill are in an intricate interplay that shapes our brains, leading toward changes that improve our day-to-day experiences and our chances to thrive.

A BRIEF HISTORY OF BRAIN SHAPING

We are learning beings throughout our whole lives, not just in child-hood. The idea that adults can learn, and that the brain is rewired as a result of this learning, has been a focus of much psychological and neuroscientific research in the past century. However, if we take for granted the idea that the brain is the source of our behaviors and per-ceptions, then the only explanation for being able to learn to under-stand the lyrics in rap music, speak a new language, or ride a bicycle is that the brain can rewire itself to master new skills. It is helpful to review some of the research of how brain shaping happens.

Early in the twentieth century, the school of behaviorism held that our sensory perceptions were fixed, that vision, hearing, smell, touch, and taste were just input channels, hardwired and inflexible. However, in the 1960s, developmental psychologist Eleanor J. Gibson established with her husband, James, that improvements in sensory perception could be achieved with practice.[1]

Michael M. Merzenich, a director of the Scientific Learning Corporation, built on this idea in the 1980s by investigating the neu-ral changes that occurred as a result of altered perceptual input to the brain. He used surgical techniques to change the information that reached the brains of adult monkeys and found that the brain's rep-resentations of the altered input were changed as a result.[2] This line of experimentation led from the realization that perceptual experi-ence can rewire the brains of adult animals to the eventual develop-ment of the cochlear implant, a device that uses brain rewiring to help deaf people hear again.

Later in the 1990s, Paula Tallal, a director of the Scientific Learning Corporation, working with Merzenich's team, showed that weeks of repeated practice and feedback on computerized speech-sound discrimination helped children improve their speech percep-tion. These children, who had been diagnosed with language perception problems, improved not only in understanding computerized speech sounds, but also in day-to-day speech and sound decoding.[3] This result showed that computer-assisted practice produces brain changes that generalize to everyday performance, and it led to the now-booming field of learning-software development.

At this point, science assumed that practice only resulted in learning when it was paired with accurate feedback. However, the importance of feedback was formally tested in the late 1990s, when Michael H. Herzog, head of the Laboratory of Psychophysics in Switzerland, and Manfred Fahle, coeditor of *Perceptual Learning,* presented an elegant series of perceptual learning experiments, in which they found that learning occurred significantly more quickly when feedback was accurately correlated with the performance of the task than when it was either incorrect or missing altogether.[4] Interestingly, feedback that followed a set of trials was just as useful as feedback that occurred immediately after a trial. That is, the participants were able to learn when general but accurate feedback was given at the end of a number of trials—such as, "You got 80 percent correct in that set of ten trials"—and the amount of learning was no different than when feedback was given after each trial. However, when participants received no feedback or when feedback was uncorrelated with correct performance, significant learning was rare. From these results, it became clear that feedback either allows or enhances learning, and that this feedback can be based on either each individual step in a process (one trial) or the end goal (percent correct over many trials).

Along with the criticality of practice and feedback, it was later shown that direct attention to the task at hand is critical for learning and the brain changes associated with it.[5] Daniel B. Polley, a student of Merzenich, decided to play sounds for two groups of rats and to train them to learn different distinctions in the sounds. Each sound could be distinguished based on either frequency or intensity, but one group of rats was trained to respond only to frequency differences, and the other, only to intensity differences. Each group developed changes in their brains associated only with the distinction they had practiced, but they had no brain changes associated with the distinction they had not paid attention to, even though they could have made that distinction with every sound. These results showed that attention to a given skill as we practice it encourages neural rewiring that supports the improvement of that skill. Although in some special cases learning can occur subconsciously, in most of these cases, subconscious reward structures or other shortcuts were likely being stimulated without accessing attention mechanisms.[6]

Into this scene came one of Merzenich's postdoctoral fellows, Beverly A. Wright, who studied the nature of perceptual learning and what that learning can tell us about the brain changes that are induced by training on simple perceptual tasks. Her experiments supported the idea that learning depends on many factors, including the particular task practiced during training, whether attention is paid during practice, and how that practice is distributed over time.[7] As a doctoral student in her lab, I followed Wright's learning-centered approach to gather insights about what kind of neural changes occurred during practice on perceptual tasks. We found that practice with feedback and attention can either produce broad effects that result in improved performance on related tasks, even when these other tasks are not trained, or result in narrow learning specific only to the practiced condition.[8] We are still trying to understand how to predict what kinds of tasks, when trained, will reveal generalization of learning to untrained tasks and which will not. One possibility is that practice on highly unusual or effortful tasks may result in broader learning.

On the high-tech side, another of Merzenich's students, Christopher deCharms, has founded a company called Omneuron that specializes in brain shaping using actual neural feedback. You may have seen him on www.ted.com, discussing the impressive results he gets when he uses real-time neural imaging as a biofeedback method. He has shown that, through feedback, practice, and attention, he can train people to control their own brain activity so they can reduce their experience of pain. His company is currently investigating other skills that can be trained using this remarkable approach.[9]

In summary, this research has demonstrated that neural changes accompanying learning are made as a result of repeated practice, accurate and consistent feedback, and attention to the task to be learned. These are some of the intellectual influences that have helped to shape my thinking, my brain. In the next section, I will draw on these ideas and others to speculate about how you can shape yours.

BRAIN SHAPING SKILLS AND TRAITS

I have no expertise in organizational learning, but I do know a lot about how practice, feedback, and attention can result in powerful rewiring of the brain. From this neuroscientific/psychological point of view, and with a sense of hope for the positive changes that can be created in any organization, I want to highlight some ideas about how well-run organizations can brain shape particular skills and traits.

BRAIN SHAPING INTEGRITY

Integrity is a trait that is both ill defined and, some people say, untrainable. Certainly, our early years are influential when it comes to learning to be truthful, to empathize with others, and to follow the golden rule—all elements of what people usually mean when they use the word *integrity*. However, Michael Shermer, science historian and author of *The Mind of the Market,* tells us that "fairness is part of who we are, but it only comes out and is rewarded when it helps us rather than hurts us."[10] In his book, he compares the classic cases of corporate evil and good, Enron versus Google.

When I asked Shermer to draw a connection between this idea and the learning process, he told me, "By nature we have the capacity to be either immoral or moral, both selfish and selfless. What gets expressed depends on the environment; that's the learning part." In *The Mind of the Market,* Shermer describes how people at Enron learned to cheat in order to survive in a culture that individually shamed and threatened its members. On the other hand, people at Google learned to play by the rules of fairness, honesty, and trust in order to thrive in its culture. Shermer says, "If you take an Enron person and put them into Google, I think they'd re-learn almost instantly, if they're not a sociopath."[11] The question is, why?

It seems to me that, in the new environment, the ex-Enron employees could practice integrity and receive appropriate feedback from those whose integrity is more highly developed. What's more, due to the high visibility of the principles of fairness, openness, and trust at Google, the environment would support focused attention on practicing these skills. Thus, practice, consistent feedback, and focused attention could brain shape integrity.

The conversation with Shermer reminded me of a similar one with Frans De Waal, an internationally acclaimed researcher in the field of primate behavior and author of *Our Inner Ape.* After a recent lecture about animal empathy, we talked about the evidence that empathy can be learned.[12] He mentioned that when two captive primate societies possessing different levels of empathic behavior are put in contact with one another, over time, the lower-empathy group starts practicing more empathic behaviors. Because the reverse does not occur—the higher-empathy group does not reduce their empathic responses—this suggests that primates have a tendency toward compassionate or empathic behavior.

Although it is clear that children learn empathy through imitation (a form of practice) as well as from clear and consistent feedback and attention to the person with whom they are empathizing,[13] the research on empathy learning in adults is just beginning. However, recently it was shown that practice with computer-simulated emotional expression software could successfully improve the capacities of adults who had difficulties in empathy and emotional understanding.[14]

What is going on with such learning? Hundreds of cognitive, cultural, and social learning theorists know better than I do about theoretical levels of learning and experiential learning styles that have crucial parts to play in these processes. But in a very simple sense, the question, how can you brain shape a seemingly nontrainable trait like integrity? can be answered this way: decide you want to learn it, put yourself in a group of people who already have it and will openly offer you feedback, and practice it repeatedly.

Brain Shaping Leadership

What is leadership? Whatever it is, we need leaders with skills that change with time, cultures, projects, and people. So how can anyone train leadership? We can try to imagine what behaviors are most desirable for a given situation and make an attempt to support those behaviors, but there is a problem with this approach. It is very hard to figure out correctly what those behaviors are. As management professor Richard A. Barker puts it in an article by the same name, "How can we train leaders if we do not know what leadership is?"[15] In this piece, Barker discusses outmoded definitions of leadership and how to introduce a more collaborative, collective approach to leadership.

In another attempt to address the same question, organizational psychology researcher David V. Day presents an impressive array of evidence on the success of leadership development methods, such as 360-degree peer review, mentorship, and action learning. He concludes that the ideas we have about how to improve leadership ability do not necessarily work. According to Day, what actually works seems to be less about the specific methods that are used and more about consistent use of those methods, in addition to the shared and openly professed pursuit of a truly common goal at all organizational levels.[16]

There may be many more complex effects of these factors, but it seems to me that using any method of leadership training consistently allows for practice and accurate feedback. Further, the shared pursuit of a well-publicized common goal results in an attentional focus on leadership itself, assuming the publicized goal is truly held by the entire community. So how can we brain shape leadership? The answer seems consistent: choose a leadership training method, choose a community goal, and make them both real and pervasive.

Brain Shaping Creativity

There are good arguments that creativity is partially, but not completely, genetic, and that certain early childhood experiences (such as parental conflict)[17] can nourish creative problem solving and expression in adulthood.[18] However, if creativity is like integrity and leadership, it, too, can be learned with practice, feedback, and attention.

Robert Epstein, researcher and psychology professor, worked with his colleagues to test and train creativity in one hundred and seventy-three government workers in Orange County, California. These workers were tasked with finding creative solutions to the city's problems. Epstein developed a test to assess what his research showed to be four elements of creativity, what he calls the "four creative competencies." Paraphrased, these are attending to and preserving new ideas for future use, challenging ourselves with difficult tasks, attempting to gain skills and knowledge beyond our current expertise, and surrounding ourselves with new input and/or new combinations of input. He used his test to evaluate each individual's level of creativity before and after an eight-month period, during which he offered one-and-a-half-day creativity training sessions, involving games in which participants practiced and attended to these competencies. Not only did the participants improve significantly on Epstein's test for creativity, but Orange County city officials were sold on the program due to an increase of six hundred thousand dollars in revenues and decrease in expenditures of $3.5 million, resulting from innovative solutions that were developed during the period the program was in effect.[19]

Science has shown that creativity can be trained, and the idea has entered into the popular media. A 2008 edition of *Scientific American Mind* featured a story titled, "How to Release Your Creativity."[20] Along with interviewing Epstein, the article's author also interviewed best-selling author Julia Cameron, who wrote the phenomenally successful book *The Artist's Way: A Spiritual Path to Higher Creativity.* Although the article does not really explore creativity training in depth, Cameron's twelve-week program does. Her process consists of repeated practice designed to foster an internal compassionate evaluation of yourself and your expression. This internal monitor becomes the central feedback provider for each creative attempt. Using quotes, stories, and insights about the creative process, Cameron focuses the reader's attention on the task at hand: learning to recover existing creativity and improve on current levels of creative expression.[21]

One of Cameron's contentions is that creativity is developed in environments that feel safe for the expression of unusual ideas and ways of being. Speaking to this point, Ken Robinson, author of *Out of Our Minds: Learning to Be Creative,* explains that emotional and intellectual ways of being have been falsely separated from one another.[22] We often assume that someone is either logical or emotional, but not both. The truth is that artists have to be pragmatic or else they cannot get their art materials or find space to work; scientists have to be emotionally driven or else they will not have the passion that is necessary to solve difficult problems. Some organizations are beginning to recognize the necessity of acknowledging the whole person in the pursuit of creative development, and Robinson discusses how these organizations can see the positive effects of making their communities safe for creative development.

What is the essential gift of an environment that acknowledges the intellectual, emotional, social, physical, and spiritual aspects of personhood? The gift is freedom to practice that which you have a passion to learn, to receive real feedback that matters to your whole being, and to attend to all aspects of your learning process.

Brain Shaping Anything

By now, I suspect the formula for brain shaping is clear: practice, get appropriate feedback, and focus your attention on what you are trying to learn. It seems simple, and it is certainly not revolutionary. In fact, at this point it may sound similar to the abandoned ideas of control theory, a management philosophy based on mechanistic principles describing humans as thermostats. This theory posits that we receive information about our performance relative to a set goal, correct errors internally, and calculate performance changes that are likely to get us closer to the set goal. But the problem with control theory is that people are not machines. Although we are affected by feedback, we have our own complex goals that change over time. Groups of people are even further from machines: we have group goals and individual goals, some of which can conflict with others.

For these reasons, creating a workplace that is *aware of* and *amenable to* brain shaping can be both difficult *and* revolutionary. A successful organization must be aware that it is and will always be a brain-shaping community. If it does not acknowledge this basic fact, then brain shaping will still occur, but not in a way that supports the goals of the organization.

Learning takes effort, and we have evolved to use valuable energy and resources only for effort that serves us. So the brain has to decide what to learn. It does this based on what repeatedly shows up in its attentional focus. However, our brains are smart: they use all the information at their disposal. Therefore, if a piece of paper tells you that your pharmaceutical company's mission is to cure disease, but your daily experience is that attention is really focused on cutting corners when testing medicines, your brain weighs the evidence accordingly. Your brain will be shaped, but not by words on a piece of paper. Hopefully, you will lose respect for the organization because of the mismatch between the stated and actual mission, and your brain will be shaped against the company itself.

At Enron, the motto "Respect, Integrity, Communication and Excellence" held little or no power over brain shaping. The power was in the feedback for and attention on the real goal, which was, as Shermer describes in *The Mind of the Market,* monetary gain at the expense of others. For a few whistleblowers, the disconnect between the company's goal and the external moral universe was, thankfully, too large. This disconnect thwarted Enron's brain shaping and led to the downfall of the company.

What if an organization is both aware of and supportive of the brain-shaping process? What happens then? First, brain shaping becomes a primary goal. When a new employee is hired or an old one moves on to a new project, she or he is asked, "How do you want your brain to be shaped when you're finished with this project? How can you help us shape other brains here?" As goals move fluidly throughout an organization and across time, an organizational commitment to brain shape any trait and skill essential to the goal allows the kind of adaptability necessary for survival and success in any living system.

In an organization with brain-shaping awareness, each member is both a learner and a teacher. All community members are engaged in *both* brain shaping in themselves the traits and skills they are committed to learning, and providing consistent and accurate feedback for others who are working on brain-shaping traits and skills that they themselves possess. Further, organizations with brain-shaping awareness know that brain shaping must be a conscious effort pursued with complete integrity. Thus, at every level of the organization, attention is focused on brain shaping the traits and skills each member wants to develop and feels are appropriate for the common goal. This means that openness about organizational priorities and goals is absolutely necessary. Without this kind of honesty, brains will get shaped in ways that do not match the actual goals of the community, and the organization will quickly collapse in on itself. Fortunately for the rest of the world, organizations that feel compelled to keep substantial secrets about goals and directions are, therefore, doomed to short life spans.

Finally, an organization with brain-shaping awareness holds a deep trust in the learning process. If an organization adopts the attitude that everyone is learning all the time, that mistakes are possible and even desirable, we might think that this would result in a dysfunctional organization that keeps making mistakes. But that is not how it works. What does result is a functional organization that keeps making mistakes—and keeps learning. The organization has ultimate integrity because it states publicly what is already true. The old idea that you have to know something perfectly before you do it is dead. Everyone is learning everything all the time, to greater and lesser degrees, depending on the experience of the person and the skill or trait to be learned.

BRAIN SHAPING THE WAY TO THE FUTURE

Dr. Stephanie Pace Marshall is the cofounder of the Illinois Math and Sciences Academy, a creative high school educating gifted students. She is also the author of, among other publications, the outstanding book *The Power to Transform: Leadership That Brings Learning and Schooling to Life*. She describes how schools shape the minds of their students, and, in fact, she calls schooling "mind shaping." In a larger context, she describes how mind shaping leads to changing the world, or "world shaping." Dr. Marshall has combined ideas from the neuroscience of learning with ideas from systems biology to propose a new, visionary structure for schools that are living, growing systems.[23]

I recently asked Dr. Marshall how the ideas in her book could apply to the workplace. She told me that because any human organization is a living system, she would treat the workplace as she does schools. "If we're talking about whole systems, how do we build common purpose, mission, language, vocabulary? What's the knowledge base? The knowledge base has to be available to the entire system, with fluid networks, communities of practice, sharing information across people, and no siloing of information. If our model is of a mechanistic universe, we will create social systems like mechanisms. But the universe isn't like that; it's about fields and potentials and relationships, so human systems must be built really differently."[24]

"Work" is another name for learning toward a mission. If we want to become *aware* of how brains are being shaped in our workplace, we have to acknowledge the learning process, consider all feedback, and observe where the real attention goes. If after that initial step of awareness we want to become *active* in shaping our brains toward skills and traits that will support a common goal, we need to give and receive clear and accurate feedback, attend to that common goal, and trust the learning process.

Luckily for us, this means we can take the basic concepts of learning—practice, feedback, and attention—and consciously create an environment in which they can work for us rather than against us. We do not have to understand all the intricacies of how every bit of feedback affects some kind of mechanistic system; in fact, that is a waste of time, since we are not mechanistic systems. We do not need to scrutinize every bonus structure and each meeting. If we did, we would be overwhelmed with the complexities and get off track. Instead, we need to do something that may be even more difficult, but significantly more effective: we need to be resolutely clear and gut-wrenchingly honest about what we actually want to accomplish as human beings working in communities, and then we need to let our brains shape the way there.

■ ■ ■

Margaret Benefiel, PhD, is CEO of ExecutiveSoul.com. She also teaches at Andover Newton Theological School in Boston, in the area of spirituality and organizational leadership, and at the Milltown Institute in Dublin, Ireland. Dr. Benefiel serves as chair of the Academy of Management's Management, Spirituality, and Religion group. She is the author of *The Soul of a Leader* and *Soul at Work*, and has also written for *The Leadership Quarterly, Management Communication Quarterly,* the *Journal of Organizational Change Management, Managerial Finance, Organization, Studies in Spirituality, Presence, America, The Way,* and other periodicals and books. She speaks widely, leads seminars and retreats, and offers consulting, coaching, and spiritual direction for leaders and organizations. Over five hundred executives and other leaders have participated in her courses and seminars.

Kerry Hamilton, CPCC, ACC, is a certified professional co-active coach and CEO of Kerry Hamilton, LLC, Executive, Personal Coaching, and Leadership Training practice. Kerry employs her leadership and life experience and enjoyment of people to foster a dynamic, personalized, and life-enhancing practice that helps people get unstuck and realize their personal and professional dreams. In her thirty-year career in leadership and management, Kerry has held senior positions in corporate and service company marketing, including vice president of marketing for the Marshalls division of the TJX Companies and senior vice president of marketing for BJ's Wholesale Club, as well as serving as a director of a corporate public board. Throughout her career, Kerry has focused on engaging people and teams in creating strategically sound and results-oriented work. Kerry is interested in the dynamics that lead to individual empowerment, team success, and professional growth, and accessing authentic leadership styles to create lasting influence and success.

Infinite Leadership

Authenticity and Spirit at Work

Margaret Benefiel, PhD, and Kerry Hamilton, CPCC, ACC

Infinite Leaders, having moved beyond the single bottom line, experience the power of personal authenticity, relationships with people and participatory decision making, and the transcendent. This chapter examines three Infinite Leaders and the values that keep them grounded: Gerald Macharia, a Kenyan business executive, who takes integrity as his guiding principle; Ted English, CEO of Bob's Discount Furniture, a chain of

*furniture stores in the northeastern United States, who focuses on rela-
tionship building and coaching; and Eileen Fisher, founder and CEO of
EILEEN FISHER Inc., a chain of clothing stores in the U. S., who holds
well-being for customers and employees as her highest value. The persons
highlighted in this chapter have consented to being named and quoted.
Their views do not necessarily represent the views of their organizations.*

LEADERS WHO MAKE A DIFFERENCE

What is making companies work today? In our view, a special kind
of leadership is making the difference, a leadership we call "Infinite
Leadership" because it is boundless and offers great possibility for
the future. Infinite Leaders have moved beyond the single focus of
bottom-line profit and have come to experience the power of three
distinct and related attributes that are manifested in their leadership.

First, Infinite Leaders understand that personal authenticity,
leading from deep personal values, is critically important to engage and
lead a workforce. Infinite Leaders choose to honor their personal values regardless of the impact that this decision will have on the short-
term bottom line. Indeed, these leaders understand that, ultimately,
the choice to honor their values leads to long-term sustainable profit.

Second, Infinite Leaders place high value on relationships with
people and on participatory decision making. These leaders understand that it is because of good relationships that the work gets accomplished in a meaningful and productive way. They also understand that
when people work together to articulate a mission and implement its
execution, a company achieves better results. Drawing on everyone's
wisdom and experience strengthens teams and enriches a company.
Good relationships are not just nice to have, they are an integral part
of the Infinite Leader's work.

Third, Infinite Leaders tap into their own hearts and souls,
and into the hearts and souls of the people who work for them.
Whether they call that spirit God, soul, well-being, or something
else, Infinite Leaders tap something deep that transcends their
particular organizations.

Infinite Leadership stands in stark contrast to Finite Leadership,
the norm in Western culture. While Finite Leadership focuses solely
on the bottom line and thus tends to neglect relationships, resulting in

slow death, Infinite Leadership opens up possibilities and leads to life. Infinite Leaders lead from their best selves and, in so doing, invite others to be their best selves. They liberate energy, joy, and creativity in their teams and organizations. By focusing on authentic relationships, Infinite Leaders get their egos out of the way and better serve their people and their organizations. They lead from the heart. They lead with values. They go beyond limits and achieve remarkable results.

Infinite Leadership is characterized by a clear mission and vision for the work of the organization. Infinite Leaders are transparent about what is working and what is not working. They admit to their own imperfections, and they accept mistakes in others. They have the courage to be in discovery every day about what it means to be a leader. They do not believe that they have all of the answers, or that they have solved all of the problems.

The Infinite Leaders highlighted in this chapter come from large companies and small. Some are at the top of their organizations, others, somewhere in the middle. These Infinite Leaders have a style of leadership unique to each of them. Each has a core value that she or he represents, a value that is true to her or his inner spirit, such as integrity, coaching, love of people, or well-being. In addition, these leaders value skill, intelligence, and results.

THE POWER OF INTEGRITY

Kenyan business executive Gerald Macharia is a genius at translating mission and vision into practice. How does he do it? He does it by living by his values. And first and foremost on his list of lived values is integrity.

Macharia lives by his Christian faith. In business, as in all other aspects of his life, he seeks God's guidance. Macharia turns to the Bible for direction in his work:

> I really admire Jesus and the way he approached things. He would probably be my best management guru and leadership guru. Basically, the gospels and the epistles are very, very rich in leadership principles.

Macharia, blessed with considerable gifts in helping companies grow and turning around troubled companies, understands his gifts as God-given. He believes that, in the creation story in Genesis, humans were directed to use their gifts:

> Our role was to maintain the good. So we can't sit back and admire creation; we have to work at it, to maintain the goodness. Wherever I go, I see opportunities, and I turn those opportunities into real benefit for the people, for whoever the stakeholders are. That is my role in the calling to shepherd creation.

Macharia has shepherded creation well. At age twenty-six, he turned around a division of a multinational company. A few years later, he served on a leadership team to develop products for the South market, the non-European, non-American market, for Colgate-Palmolive. At age thirty-two, he became CEO of Kenfin, a Kenyan financial services company, and he turned it around in seven months, bringing it back to profitability.

After his tenure at Kenfin, Macharia accepted an invitation to head up Faulu Kenya, a Christian microfinance institution. He was attracted by the opportunity to use his business skills to help Kenyans living in poverty build their own businesses. Macharia transformed Faulu Kenya from a nongovernmental organization (NGO) into a commercial microfinance institution, growing it by leaps and bounds, all the while maintaining its Christian orientation. He also spun off another company from Faulu Kenya, which, within a few years, had become a $2.5 million company.

Macharia holds integrity to his faith as his highest principle:

> If there's a temptation for me to make something good on my side that I know would not be right with the Lord, then I will not do it. Here I am in the international arena, and all sorts of people walk through my office, from pharmaceutical companies to government officials to all sorts of people, yet the questions I ask are always very simple: What is good for the people that we are serving? What is good for the government that we work with? But more importantly for me, what is God's position in this? And if it's not right, it's not right. I don't even bother to qualify. If it's not right, it is not right, period. Then it will not happen, and I will not do it. And I will voice that. I'll say, "I can't do that, unfortunately." And if it means my paying the price, I'm ready and willing.

Macharia's reputation for integrity has, indeed, forced him to pay the price. When encountering envy for his success or anger at his refusal to compromise his principles, he turns to biblical characters as role models. He remembers that God's people throughout history have often suffered for their adherence to their principles, and he turns to

God for strength and guidance. When he has faced social vilification and trumped-up charges in court, Macharia has trusted God to bring him through the trials.

In his work as the Clinton Foundation's representative in Kenya, where he heads up the Foundation's HIV AIDS initiatives, as well as in his position as chairman of his own consulting company, Macharia has a track record which demonstrates that living by biblical principles in business pays off. He has made an impact financially, turning businesses around and growing businesses dramatically. He has made an impact socially, strengthening microfinance and the lives it supports, and adding more years to the lives of HIV positive people through creating access to low-cost antiretroviral medicine. And he has made an impact for his faith, showing that living by Christ's principles can benefit everyone.

It's All about People

For Ted English, CEO of Bob's Discount Furniture, a privately owned regional chain of furniture stores in the northeastern United States, leadership is situational. Individual leaders need to tap deeply into who they are as unique persons to become the leaders they are intended to be in each situation. According to Ted, "There are many forms of leadership, and they all have a place: autocratic, democratic, personal, and impersonal leadership. In order to become good leaders, individuals need to adapt to who they are." Leadership, for Ted, is also about coaching people to be their best selves: "It is all about letting the people you are leading do their jobs. It is about understanding what they need to perform their jobs." Ted believes that an Infinite Leader never micromanages: "A leader's job is to set direction, have a clear mission and vision, step in to help with thorny or difficult situations, and be only marginally involved in the day-to-day business."

For Ted, this means not only trusting people but also needing to have the right people in the right jobs. As for knowing if you have the right person in the right job, Ted advises, "Usually performance will tell you, but not always. Sometimes, and often, it is fallout of the people around that individual."

When Ted says it is all about people, he means it: "I spend a lot of time with people. I get to know them. I ask questions. I look for consistency. I trust the people who are working for me to do their jobs, and at the same time I understand the complex nature of people. I pay attention to them and to what is going on around them."

Ted walks his talk: "It is very rare that I am in my office. I spend most of my time meeting with constituents. I made it my business when I came to Bob's to meet everyone in the organization (having left a company with 120,000 people). And I did it. Over my first eight weeks here, I met 1,600 people. I shook their hands, I looked them in the eye. I made that personal contact so they know that I think they, the people, are the heart and soul of the business."

Ted nurtures the heart and soul of the business: "The partners that started this business treat people with dignity and respect. Associates are expected to work hard, and have fun, and be an important part of this small business. The majority of associates here at Bob's feel that spirit."

In Ted's work at Bob's Discount Furniture, and his many years at the TJX Companies (owners of the T. J. Maxx and Marshalls off-price retail stores), his experience has taught him much about people— and results. It is not only a matter of innately caring about people, but also holding them to standards and expectations.

Sometimes, this leads to necessary decisions about changes in the organization that are not easy to make. What do Infinite Leaders do if they do not have the right person in the job? "One thing I needed to overcome," Ted reflects, "was being slow on the trigger about making people changes in the organization." After assessing capability and offering appropriate time for course-correction, it is important for the leader to make timely decisions about individuals. "I learned that being personally invested in someone can lead to being reticent to make a change that is needed. And this is deleterious to the whole organization. A leader needs to put personal feelings aside and make timely decisions for the good of the organization."

Caring for people, according to Ted, means upholding dignity and respect, while at the same time being in tough conversations about what is and is not working. He maintains that letting someone go can be done while honoring the person's heart and soul. In his definition of people skills, it is as important to be honest about what is not working, with empathy and trust, as it is to highlight what is working.

Great leaders are also good followers, according to Ted: "Great leaders are following all of the time. If you are willing to listen more than you speak, you'll follow more than you lead. If you have an organization that knows you have an open ear, the organization will give you the ideas. In a highly effective organization, most of the ideas come from the people. It is the people who are doing the work, who know what needs to be done, what needs to change. And it is staying in touch with the people, following their lead, that leads to great leadership."

Summing up his perspective on leadership, Ted identifies the three most important things a great leader needs to have: "a strong moral compass, a high level of intelligence, and great people skills. Without these three things, leaders will fail their people."

WELL-BEING FOR ALL

Eileen Fisher started her clothing business in 1984 with $350 and a few design sketches. Founded on the principles of well-being and simplicity, her business received $3,000 in orders at the first boutique show Fisher exhibited her wares at, and EILEEN FISHER Inc. was born. The company now boasts 42 company stores, 725 employees, and $254 million in annual revenues.

How can a business be founded on well-being? What does well-being look like in the workplace? Eileen Fisher's commitment to well-being begins at home and spreads in concentric circles outward to the company's individual employees, work teams, the organization as a whole, the communities that the stores serve, and the world.

Eileen Fisher practices what she preaches, in her own life and in her family. For example, Fisher practices yoga regularly and commits to being home by 3:00 p.m. every day to ensure that she makes time for family. Furthermore, she seeks to foster a sense of well-being among the company's individual employees and work teams. Each employee receives $1,000 every year to spend on "wellness and joyful activities," and another $1,000 per year for education. Some stores offer yoga and massages for employees as well.

Work teams learn to support one another, work by consensus, and foster a "joyful environment" in the stores. Lisa Ann Schraffa, a veteran employee at one of the Boston stores, states, "I think of my work as a spiritual practice."

Stores regularly clear out slightly damaged or extra inventory and donate the clothes to charities in their communities. Boston stores, for example, have donated to the Women's Lunch Place, a program serving homeless women, and New York stores have donated to "Dress for Success," a program providing clothes for job interviews for women recently released from prison. Each spring and fall, stores hold fundraisers for local charities. In addition, the company provides grants to women entrepreneurs and to organizations that elevate self-esteem in women and girls.

With its international suppliers, the company works with Social Accountability International to adhere to the SA8000 standards and to provide economic opportunity for women. In Peru, rural women gather to knit sweaters in their homes where they can tend to their families at the same time. In China, Eileen Fisher works to improve factory conditions and works only with factories that honor basic human rights, scrutinizing such areas as child labor, working hours, remuneration, health and safety, and management systems.

While it is not always easy to consistently view work as spiritual practice, and to translate the ideal into reality, Eileen Fisher employees don't stop trying. From day-to-day customer service, to seeking the best ways to offer economic opportunity to women in developing countries, daily challenges arise. "We're not perfect. But when we fail, we admit our mistakes and get back on track," says Lisa Ann Schraffa.

COMMON THREADS

Each of these Infinite Leaders approaches leadership in a different way. At the same time, common threads emerge. Each leader is true to values that are authentic for her or him, and measures the work she or he does as a leader against those values. Furthermore, each leader acknowledges that results are critically important.

Gerald Macharia honors his value of integrity and, most importantly to him, invites God as the final arbiter into his decision making. Throughout his career, and in his current work for the Clinton Foundation, this value serves to keep him grounded and to make him more effective as a leader. For Ted English, knowing his people and trusting them is foremost. Respecting and honoring people have made Ted's relationships strong and his leadership effective. And for

Eileen Fisher, delivering well-being to employees and customers forms the foundation for her company and ensures its success.

Gerald Macharia, Ted English, and Eileen Fisher are three examples, among many, of Infinite Leaders. Infinite Leaders are exhibiting the courage of authentic leadership that is transforming the way companies work today. Whether working in the United States or in other parts of the world, in large companies known for good works or smaller companies that are serving their customers' needs, Infinite Leaders know that putting people first results in decision making and leadership that serves the whole organization. Indeed, these leaders know that results that come at the expense of caring for people are short lived.

The creation of sustainable companies depends upon the daily and consistent actions that come through honoring one or more deeply held personal values, honoring people and relationships in the workplace, and bringing heart and soul to work. These Infinite Leaders ask to be measured by their ability to serve, and honor their personal values in the caring human interaction of their daily work.

■ ■ ■

Ellen Hayakawa is the author of *The Inspired Organization: Spirituality and Energy at Work* and coauthor of the best-selling and award-winning *Healing the Heart of the World: Harnessing the Power of Intention to Change Your Life and Your Planet*. An international keynote speaker, workshop facilitator, and corporate coach on spirituality in the workplace, Ms. Hayakawa has worked extensively with executives and employees in both the public and private sectors to explore the relationship between spirituality in the workplace and sustainability. Whether serving as a corporate coach and facilitator or as a keynote speaker at a corporate gathering or conference, Ms. Hayakawa facilitates the creation of community in an atmosphere of joy and fun. She has been interviewed on national radio and television, and was one of the ordinary creative geniuses featured in Teri Degler's *The Fiery Muse: Creativity and the Spiritual Quest*.

Inspired Leadership
Leading with Spirit

ELLEN HAYAKAWA

As awareness about spirituality in the workplace grows, we are seeing the next edge of the field emerging: a focus on Inspired Leadership based on spiritual principles. Inspired Leadership requires igniting an unstoppable passion; finding clarity in life's purpose, vision, and values; and making spiritually wise decisions. Spiritual wisdom is based on understanding that we are all one, that everything is a cycle, and that we need to combine head and heart wisdom. An Inspired Leader learns to develop the ability to use these intuitive abilities in decision-making processes to cocreate tomorrow's spiritual workplace.

THE EMERGENCE OF SPIRITUALITY AT WORK

In many ancient cultures and traditions, the spiritual life of an individual has been acknowledged as the source from which work is done, both as an expression of self and on behalf of community. In the modern world, however, we have only recently begun to acknowledge the central importance of spirituality in daily working life.

Consciousness about spirituality at work began accelerating in the early 1990s, as leaders who had been addressing aspects of spirituality in the workplace started to meet each other, to network, and to speak in organizations and conferences. Those early innovators, who included organizational consultants, professors, human resources directors, and business owners, were "coming out of the closet" and declaring their intention to advance the concept of spirituality at work.

Some had been speaking about or practicng spirituality at work for more than a decade; academic literature shows the concept being discussed as far back as the 1950s. We could argue that spirituality in workers has always been present, and always will be, yet it was not until the nineties that we finally began to recognize spirituality as the source from which individuality, creativity, wise decision making, excellence, genius, compassion, kindness, and heart arise.

In the 1990s, seeds were planted for the unfolding of the field of spirituality in the workplace. From a leadership perspective, the first issue was to dissolve the fear around speaking about spirituality in general, and about spirituality in the workplace specifically. Many feared imposing answers or religious or spiritual beliefs onto people. It was important to reassure those in business and organizations that acknowledging spirit and spirituality in the workplace could be approached from a universal perspective that acknowledged and honored all cultural, religious, faith, and spiritual backgrounds.

I discovered early on that, as a leader, I could facilitate the dialogue by asking questions and helping others find their own answers. It helped dissolve fears that I might be trying to impose my beliefs and values onto them. When there was some resistance, which I heard most often in the form of comments such as, "Do you *have* to use the word *spirituality*? Can't you use the word *values*?" my answer was simply, "Spirituality is much deeper than just values. Spirituality certainly embraces values, but it goes far beyond values."

When I first started speaking to students, business leaders, or organizations, I would ask the question, what is spirit and spirituality for you? What is spirituality at work for you? As you might well imagine, I heard many different definitions of *spirit:* Infinite, Mysterious Source of All, God, Goddess, One of a Thousand Names, Creator, Universe, Higher Source, That Which Remains Unnamable, Source of All Energy. After much listening and consideration, I have come to define "spirituality at work" as the process of connecting and aligning the energy of the individual, team, and organization while respecting our life-sustaining ecosystem, the earth.

Today, we have come a long way from the nineties, when those early innovative leaders would speak to small audiences in isolated spirituality-at-work conferences. In this century, those audiences have burgeoned to hundreds. Mainstream business schools are teaching courses on spirituality in the workplace. Both government and business are offering workshops and trainings on spirituality at work. Universities in both the United States and Canada have established spirituality-at-work centers. Numerous books on the subject, including my own *The Inspired Organization: Spirituality and Energy at Work,* are on reading lists at universities. All of this is evidence that spirituality at work has joined the mainstream.

Now we are seeing the next edge of the field emerging: a focus on Inspired Leadership based on spiritual principles. We are aware that we need leaders who can make better, spiritually wise decisions, leaders who can develop and apply their intuitive abilities from a heart-centered perspective. We need Inspired Leaders who base their leadership on these spiritual principles:

- Heart- and soul-based passion
- Sacred purpose, values, and vision
- Spiritual wisdom

HEART- AND SOUL-BASED PASSION

Statistics about the number of workers who are searching for jobs, even when they already have a job, reveal a disturbing fact: most people are not satisfied with their current job. More and more employees are suffering from burnouts, major depression, anxiety, or other mental health problems.

Spirituality at work suggests another way of working—by doing what we love. Inspired Leaders know that the only way to do work that is satisfying to heart, soul, and pocketbook is by knowing themselves. When we reject so-called opportunities, duties, and tasks that do not feed our souls and claim more and more parts of ourselves and our passion for what interests us, positive, expansive change will come.

When I was a wildlife biologist, I became depressed and bored with my job. Being depressed and bored is a painful experience. What I did not know at the time was that depression and boredom are signs and symptoms of a greater spiritual malaise that happens when we are no longer passionate, in love, and challenged by what we are doing. It happens when we are not using our gifts and talents to their full extent, when we are not discovering more about them. Boredom is a message to investigate new territory, both inwardly and outwardly.

Living spirituality in life and work means being committed to what we are passionate about. Inspired Leaders ask, "What do I love to do? What am I passionate about? What are my gifts and talents? How can my gifts and talents best serve my dreams and visions of sacred work, whether that be with one other individual, a team, or an organization?"

SACRED PURPOSE, VALUES, AND VISION

Inspired Leadership is anchored in knowing our life purpose, staying true to the values we hold sacred, and embracing our vision of work as the basis for cocreation in spirit. Inspired Leaders are aware that their purpose and sacred vision will be fulfilled only when they are aligned with their inner spiritual life.

Our sacred purpose is something that is unchanging over time, and every experience from birth through adulthood helps us fulfill that purpose. I like to think of life purpose as the theme of your life, and I often encourage leaders to encapsulate their sense of purpose in one short sentence, as a touchstone for their spirituality at work.

Another touchstone of Inspired Leadership is knowing the values with which we work. If we are to be spiritually based leaders, we need to name the values we hold dear, whether they include love, trust, respect, honesty, loyalty, or fun. Each of these values affects how we treat others. I encourage leaders to make a list of their values, to ask themselves, "How can I treat others as I wish to be treated?" and to align themselves with people and organizations who share the same values.

Inspired Leaders also embrace a sacred vision of work. This is not a static vision, but one that changes over time as we deepen in skills and wisdom. We may start out, for example, with a vision to complete a degree. Then it might become our vision to get a job that makes use of our training and abilities. After that, our vision might be to manage people or an organization. In each unfolding of the next vision, we learn about more gifts and skills, and it is in living out this vision of work and life that we continue to grow as Inspired Leaders.

In these times, it is rare that a vision can be accomplished alone. More frequently, the unfolding of a vision depends on finding others who hold pieces of the puzzle for our sacred learning and, therefore, our success. The more detailed we are about our vision of sacred work, the clearer it is. When I coach people on spirituality and the workplace, I give them a written assignment to help them connect with their vision. You might want to give this a try: Write down the details of your vision as you see it today. Continue to add to that document as you receive more pieces of your vision over time. Connect with other leaders who provide you with the pieces you need to manifest and accomplish your vision.

By recognizing your sacred purpose, values, and vision of work—and by articulating them—you will be on your way to living them.

BASIC SPIRITUAL LAWS

In many cultures, our material demands and consumption are excessive. Every ecosystem on the earth is in decline. Weather has become severe and unpredictable because of climate change. While there are people and cultures whose ecological footprint is far smaller than ours in Western society, we have to recognize that the decisions we make each and every day have an impact. In order for us to thrive together as humans and with all other beings on this planet, we must consider different ways of making decisions than we have used in the past. We must recognize the spiritual laws that govern this planet and the cosmos. We must employ spiritually wise decision making now and into the future.

To be Inspired Leaders, our decisions need to be based on three basic spiritual laws, each based on the values of truth, love, trust, respect for all beings and Mother Earth, integrity, and honesty. They are the basis for spiritually wise decision making.

First Spiritual Law: We Are All One

Perhaps the most important of all the spiritual laws is the first: we are all one. This means that everything and everyone is connected and interdependent. As Inspired Leaders, we need to consider the implications of our decisions not only in the way they affect us, but also in the way they affect others—both immediately and for the generations to come.

As an Inspired Leader, I invite you to ask yourself: What decisions am I making in my personal and work life that respect the law of balance, minimize the ecological footprint of both myself and my organization? What decisions am I making on behalf of the whole that are aligned with nature and her cycles, that will ensure a brighter and better future for all beings?

Second Spiritual Law: Everything Is a Cycle or Circle

Birth, growth, maturity, and death are a part of life. Everything in nature goes through these cycles, and all that is material is returned to the earth, while all energy or spirit returns to the Source. Currently, we consume material goods and then dump wastes that are synthetic and toxic—wastes that nature cannot metabolize—into the earth. We are killing our planet, ourselves, and other beings. As an Inspired Leader, ask yourself: what decisions can I make to work with and align myself and my organization with the cycles of nature?

Third Spiritual Law: Spiritual Wisdom Combines Heart and Head

Spiritually wise decision making combines heart (emotions such as love and compassion) and head (states of consciousness). We are continually learning how much the heart is deeply connected to the brain. The Institute of HeartMath, an international nonprofit research and education organization dedicated to helping people rely "on the intelligence of their hearts in concert with their minds," has found that the heart "possesses a far more developed communication system with the brain than do most of the body's major organs."[1] The heart not only pumps blood, but also transmits complex patterns of information to the brain and the entire body. In other words, the heart is a powerful entry point into the communication network that connects body and mind, emotions and spirit. With this knowledge as foundation, Inspired Leaders need to nurture the balance between their emotions and rationale in order to make decisions that are spiritually sound.

With the advance of scientific technology, we are also learning much about what happens in the brain during emotional responses, how our thoughts and emotions affect our brains and bodies. The more we can integrate and actively engage the right and left hemispheres of the brain, the more we can make spiritually based decisions in a holistic, balanced way. By understanding how our brains work, we have an opportunity to make decisions that come from the place of nonlinear holism rather than from linear fractions of rational information.

Each brain-wave range of frequencies holds a different gift. Too much or too little of any one set of frequencies results in perceptual challenges in working and living in the world. The brain is complex, and many of the states connect and overlap in ways that we are just beginning to understand, but it is helpful to understand the basics. Although I can only give a brief glimpse of what we understand about brain function, I hope this introduction will inspire you to learn more about your own brain and to learn how to naturally induce and maintain the various states of consciousness with your own free will.

- Beta (14–25 Hz) brain waves are the frequency of focus and concentration, and they are the brain waves used in survival mode. Beta is the state for which current mainstream education is designed.
- Gamma (27–100 Hz) brain waves are where whole-brain synchronization occurs, and they are connected to consciousness and perception. Meditating on love, kindness, and compassion, for example, puts brain waves into the range around 40 Hz.
- An alpha state (7–14 Hz) is a relaxed, pre-meditative state of enhanced learning and expanded awareness. It is an optimal state for learning new material, as well as gathering information for decision making.
- Theta (4–7 Hz) waves are present during meditation and deep relaxation. They are also present during accelerated learning. This is the state of the creative genius—those "Aha!" moments of creativity and solutions.

- The delta (.5–4 Hz) state, for most people, is achieved during deep sleep. It is the state of peace and healing.
- The theta (4–7 Hz) state and the delta state have been called the states of shamanic consciousness, when we experience being totally connected (spirit, soul, emotion, mind, and body) to spirit or the universe.

As Inspired Leaders, the more we cultivate the states of awareness, creativity, and peace within ourselves, the better we will be able to make spiritually wise decisions. Whether our tools are meditation, spending time in nature, drumming, dancing, or training our minds, when the whole person, including heart and the brain, is in a balanced state, we will be able to think, behave, and serve for the highest good of all. We will be fully present in the moment to make intuitive heart-based decisions for cocreating tomorrow's spiritual workplace.

THE COCREATIVE FUTURE

I have the privilege of coaching people of all ages to become Inspired Leaders. It is from coaching children and youth, however, that I have learned much about cultivating the intuitive senses and heart-centered abilities. Children and youth are among the best teachers and leaders in these areas. As much as we have gifts to offer them in mentorship, they have gifts to offer us. The more we are grateful for and appreciative of our intuitive gifts, and the more we use them in a state of love, compassion, and kindness, the more gifts of the spirit we will keep uncovering. Only then can we be the Inspired Leaders who will lead the workplace into a cocreative future.

May you continue to grow multidimensionally as an Inspired Leader, creating harmony and peace for this century in your families, communities, organizations, and the world.

■ ■ ■

Craig E. Johnson, PhD, is professor of leadership studies and director of the doctor of management program at George Fox University, in Newberg, Oregon. He teaches leadership, management, and ethics courses at the undergraduate and doctoral level. He also acts as faculty director of the university's interdisciplinary leadership studies minor. Dr. Johnson is author of *Ethics in the Workplace: Tools and Tactics for Organizational Transformation* and *Meeting the Ethical Challenges of Leadership: Casting Light or Shadow*, and coauthor, with Michael Z. Hackman, of *Leadership: A Communication Perspective*. His research interests include leadership ethics, organizational ethics, and leadership education.

Spirituality and Ethical Leadership
Moral Persons and Moral Managers
Craig E. Johnson, PhD

This chapter outlines strategies for promoting Ethical Leadership through individual and collective spiritual development. Spirituality equips leaders to act as both moral persons and as moral managers through providing a sense of mission and meaning; focusing attention on the needs of others; fostering humility, integrity, and justice; highlighting universal moral principles; and generating feelings of hope and joy. Leaders nurture their personal spiritual development by discovering their vocations at the same time they engage in self-reflective practices and serve others. Organizations encourage the development of spiritually sensitive, Ethical Leaders by creating a compelling vision, fostering intrinsic motivation, promoting shared spiritual values, and making space for the spirit.

> "Spiritual leaders are moral leaders."
> —*Gilbert Fairholm*

DUAL COMPONENTS OF ETHICAL LEADERSHIP

Providing Ethical Leadership is one of a leader's most important responsibilities. Those who fail to carry out this task put their organizations, as well as their careers, at risk. Corporate scandals at Quest, Hewlett Packard, WorldCom, AIG Insurance, Enron, Brocade

75

Communications, Sallie Mae, and Fannie Mae demonstrate the widespread damage done by Unethical Leaders. Conversely, leaders who fulfill their ethical duties prevent costly scandals and lay the foundation for long-term success. Members of ethical organizations are more collaborative and trusting, generating higher levels of satisfaction, commitment, and performance.[1] Corporations that act as responsible citizens build positive reputations and often increase market share.[2]

Researchers report that there are dual components of Ethical Leadership.[3] Ethical Leaders act as *moral persons,* behaving ethically as they carry out their leadership roles. They treat employees fairly and express care and concern for followers. They live up to the values they espouse and are perceived as open and honest. At the same time, Ethical Leaders act as *moral managers* who actively promote ethical conduct in followers. They serve as role models who focus the organization's attention on ethics. Ethical Leaders communicate frequently about the importance of ethics, outline clear standards, and use rewards and discipline to hold followers accountable for their moral conduct.

This chapter is based on the premise that spiritual development equips leaders to function as both moral persons and moral managers. The first section of the chapter describes the personal and shared nature of organizational spirituality and outlines how spiritual values and practices equip individuals to practice Ethical Leadership. The second section highlights strategies for promoting Ethical Leadership through individual and collective spiritual development.

ETHICAL LEADERSHIP AND SPIRITUALITY

Spirituality in the organizational setting operates simultaneously at two levels: individual and collective. Individual spirituality derives from the values, feelings, and practices of each person in the organization. Spiritually oriented individuals engage in behaviors designed to nurture their inner lives. They strive to get in touch with their deep desires and feelings, seek a sense of purpose, and want to establish deep connections with others and with a power greater than themselves.[4] Collective spirituality consists of organizational culture and climate that fosters shared meaning and connection. According to management experts Dennis Duchon and Donde Asmos Plowman, workplace spirituality is "a particular kind of psychological climate in which people view themselves as having an inner life that is nourished by meaningful work and takes place in the context of a community."[5] Spirit-friendly organizations nurture the entire person—emotions, self-worth, aspirations, and desire for purpose— while cultivating a sense of membership.

Individual and collective spirituality are interrelated. Spiritually oriented employees help create spiritual climates; spiritual climates reinforce the efforts of individuals to nurture their inner lives and to build relationships with others. Spirituality and religion, while they overlap, are not identical. Religious traditions and institutions encourage and structure spiritual experiences, but spiritual values and encounters often occur outside of religious channels.[6]

Both personal and workplace spirituality equip leaders for the task of Ethical Leadership by:

- Providing a sense of mission and meaning
- Focusing attention on the needs of others
- Fostering humility, integrity, and justice
- Highlighting universal moral principles
- Generating feelings of hope and joy

Mission and Meaning

Spiritual individuals and organizations are motivated by a sense of mission and meaning. Members believe that work is a calling, not just a job. The organization wants to serve worthy purposes, such as supplying needed products and services, meeting human needs, and improving the environment. This sense of calling and desire for meaningful work encourages leaders to make ethics a top personal and organizational priority. Ethical behavior is essential to the accomplishment of worthy objectives; unethical behavior devalues work and puts the mission of the organization at risk.

Other-Centeredness

Compassion, kindness, generosity, love, care, and concern all describe an orientation that puts others ahead of the self. Other-centeredness, or altruism, is encouraged by nearly every major spiritual tradition.

Love and compassion are two of the positive frames of mind in Buddhism, for instance, and charity is one of the Five Pillars of Islam.[7] Many humanitarian efforts, such as hospitals, colleges, soup kitchens, homeless shelters, and children's clubs, have their origins in religious and spiritual movements.

Spirituality can motivate leaders to put others above the self and to channel their energies into serving others. This other-centeredness, in turn, is key to Ethical Leadership. Ethical Leaders are marked by the care and concern they show to followers at the same time they foster altruistic behavior in others.[8] In contrast, Unethical Leaders put their own needs first and manipulate followers for their own ends. Spirituality also fosters altruistic behavior through its emphasis on connection and community. Connections cannot be developed or sustained unless members consider the well-being of others and treat fellow employees with compassion and respect.

Integrity, Humility, and Justice

Spirituality motivates individuals to behave in a consistently ethical manner, maintain humility, and treat others fairly. When these practices are repeated, they become the following positive character traits (or virtues).

Integrity refers to wholeness or completeness, to living up to espoused values and dealing honestly with others.[9] Such integration is a marker of spiritual progress, signaling that there is no distinction between the inner life and outward behavior. Integrity is also a sign of Ethical Leadership, contributing to the perception of the leader as both a moral person and a moral role model. Lack of integrity, on the other hand, quickly undermines a leader's moral authority. Followers watch the behavior of leaders closely, and one untrustworthy act can undo months and years of consistent behavior. Common "trust busters" include dishonesty, blaming others, secrecy, unfair rewards, and inconsistent rules.[10] For example, former American Airlines CEO Don Carty broke the trust of employees after word leaked out that he and other senior executives were receiving large bonuses at the same time they were asking workers to take significant pay and benefit cuts. Carty apologized and then resigned.[11]

Humility consists of three components.[12] The first is self-awareness or objective assessment of personal strengths and limitations. The second is openness, which is welcoming new ideas and knowledge based on an understanding of personal weaknesses. The third component is transcendence—acknowledgment of a power greater than the self. All three components are fostered by spiritual values and practices. Spiritual individuals engage in self-reflection that often reveals personal weaknesses. They recognize a power greater themselves.

The best-selling book *Good to Great* renewed interest in humility as an important leadership virtue.[13] Author Jim Collins and his team found that the leaders of the most successful companies in their sample were also the most humble. These "Level-5 leaders" downplayed their role in their company's success, gave the credit to others, were uncomfortable talking about personal achievements, and lived modestly. Humility has also been linked to Ethical Leadership.[14] Humility is a strong brake on immoral behavior. Humble leaders have a realistic view of their own contributions and demonstrate appreciation for others. They serve others, build supportive relationships, and are open to input from followers.

Justice involves both a sense of obligation to the common good and an obligation to treat others equally and fairly.[15] Like compassion, justice is promoted in most major religious traditions. Treating others fairly is also an element of Ethical Leadership. Just leaders feel a sense of duty and strive to do their part. They believe in providing the same rights to all of their followers, even when subordinates have differing abilities. Moral leaders recognize that equitable treatment communicates respect, compassion, and integrity. In contrast, unjust leaders ignore their responsibilities and the needs of the larger community. They deny the rights of followers and make biased decisions that favor some groups and individuals over others.

Universal Principles

Spiritually motivated individuals and organizations strive to live by universal principles such as love, truthfulness, and respect for human rights and dignity. Leaders who follow such principles are more likely to act as moral persons. They do not fall victim as often to greed and ego, destructive motivations that undermined the careers of former Enron CEO Jeffrey Skilling, former Tyco CEO Dennis Kozlowski, and former WorldCom CEO Bernie Ebbers. Instead, they seek to live up to spiritual ideals. Evidence of the motivational power of universal principles can be found in the lives of moral role models. Psychologists Ann Colby and William Damon studied the lives of twenty-three extraordinary moral leaders, including Virginia Foster Durr, who spent over thirty years fighting for civil rights in the South, and Susie Valadez, who fed, clothed, and provided medical care to poor Mexicans living near the Ciudad Juarez garbage dump.[16] Colby and Damon found that these ethical heroes lived by ideals or principles (honesty, equality, concern for others) that were often rooted in religious faith. These moral principles then became part of their core identities, tying together every aspect of their lives. The researchers concluded:

> Many of our exemplars drew on religious faith for such a unifying belief. In fact, this was the case for a far larger number of our exemplars than we originally expected. But even those who had no formal religion often looked to a transcendent ideal of a personal sort: a faith in the forces of good, a sustaining hope in a power greater than oneself, a larger meaning for one's life than personal achievement or gain.[17]

In addition to motivating ethical action, overarching principles also help leaders make better ethical choices. There is a positive correlation between spirituality and moral judgment.[18] Those who aspire to universal standards are more likely to recognize that ethical problems exist and engage in the most advanced form of moral judgment: principled reasoning.[19] Principled decision makers base their decisions on widely held ethical guidelines such as treating others with respect and seeking the common good. Less advanced thinkers focus on their own needs or look to others for guidance.

Hope and Joy

Positive emotions such as hope and joy are important products of personal and workplace spirituality.[20] It is easier to be optimistic about the future when engaged in a calling and meaningful labor. Setbacks such as low sales and stock downturns are less discouraging when they are part of a larger plan and purpose. Joy comes from living in harmony with personal values, serving others, and feelings of connection and transcendence. These positive emotions promote ethical behavior. Leaders and followers who are joyful and happy are more likely to follow through on their moral choices.[21]

PROMOTING ETHICAL LEADERSHIP THROUGH SPIRITUAL DEVELOPMENT

Because spiritual values and practices equip leaders for Ethical Leadership, encouraging the spiritual development of both individuals and organizations takes on added importance. In this section, we will examine strategies that leaders can use to foster their personal spiritual development. Then we will look at tactics that build spirit-friendly organizations that promote the spiritual development of leaders.

Enhancing Personal Spiritual Development

DISCOVERING VOCATION: Discovering vocation is key to developing a sense of mission and meaning that is at the heart of spirituality. In popular usage, the term *vocation* is generally limited to job or occupation. However, the original meaning of the term extended well beyond work. The English word has its origins in the Latin *vocare,* which means "to call" or "calling."[22] Discovering our calling encompasses every aspect of life—relationships, job, volunteer activities, leisure, and participation in spiritual communities. Leaders who have a clear sense of their individual purpose are more likely to join organizations that match their objectives and values. They are more satisfied and committed as members, focus on meaningful tasks that match their abilities, and are better equipped to serve others. Shell Oil, for example, is an organization that has incorporated a focus on discovering individual purpose into its leadership development programs.[23]

Discovering vocation is a three-step process.[24] First, leaders determine their unique gifts or skills by looking at past experiences and trying out a variety of jobs and volunteer experiences. Second, they identify their concern for others as well as their personal interests. Leaders' concern for others may take the form of solving educational problems, meeting environmental challenges, or providing technology to businesses. Interests, such as music, mathematics, or the outdoors, then motivate them to develop skills and knowledge that can later be used in service to others. Third, leaders find the right job fit, one that puts their gifts, concerns, and interests to the best use.

ENGAGING IN SELF-REFLECTIVE PRACTICES: Self-reflective practices put leaders in touch with their inner lives. These rituals involve self-examination and communication with God or a greater power. Such practices have practical as well as spiritual benefits for leaders, promoting mental and physical health, reducing stress and burnout, and helping them deal with crises.[25] Richard Foster, director of the Renovare spiritual renewal movement, suggests four inward disciplines that promote spiritual growth:[26]

- *The discipline of meditation.* Meditation is quiet contemplation, which can provide practical answers to problems, reenergize leaders, or point leaders in a new direction. Meditation can involve reflecting upon sacred texts, becoming still and embracing silence, thinking about creation, and reflecting upon the meaning of current events.
- *The discipline of prayer.* Prayer is not so much a means of getting something from a higher spiritual power, but rather the doorway to a new perspective. Through prayer, leaders may begin to see the larger meaning behind events, become more patient, and develop more compassion for enemies.
- *The discipline of fasting.* Fasting means going without food for spiritual purposes. Leaders may fast to focus their minds on spiritual issues, to reflect their commitment to God, or to draw closer to their spiritual center.
- *The discipline of study.* Study is an analytical discipline designed to change thinking. Effective study takes repeated effort over time, concentration, reflection on insights gained, and a learning attitude. A great many leaders and followers focus their study on the primary texts of the world's faiths and philosophies (the Qur'an, the Analects of Confucius, the Tao Te Ching, the Torah, the Bible) and spiritual classics. Leaders can also gain important insights from studying nature, relationships, themselves, institutions, and cultures.

SEEKING TO SERVE: Because other-centeredness is essential to spirituality, it is not surprising that the spiritual development of leaders depends in large part on their willingness to serve. Executive management consultant Krista Kurth notes that those who contribute to spiritually inspired service at work do so with no concern for personal gain.[27] Connection with a greater power sparks gratitude and love that encourages contribution to the good of the group. In serving a higher purpose, members set aside their personal agendas. Kurth suggests several practices that can build individual commitment to service, including:

- Practicing self-reflection and self-inquiry by stepping back, reflecting, listening to the inner voice, and paying close attention to what is going on
- Being attentive to underlying motivations and attitudes
- Maintaining a positive, accepting perspective on life
- Learning from life, particularly from challenging situations
- Keeping reminders of spiritual principles of service (pictures, quotes)

Enhancing Workplace Spirituality

An organization's level of spiritual development will have a significant impact on the spiritual development of its leaders. The greater the spiritual progress of the organization, the more likely it is to produce spiritually sensitive, Ethical Leaders. Steps for promoting collective spiritual development include creating a compelling vision, fostering intrinsic motivation, promoting spiritual values, and making space for the spirit.

CREATING A COMPELLING VISION: Spiritually friendly organizations craft inspirational visions that create a sense of mission and meaning and encourage members to live out their vocations.[28] Compelling visions speak to the emotions of individual members, sparking excitement and generating organizational commitment. These visions transcend the bottom line (few lower-level employees get excited about increasing stakeholder return on investment, for example) and reflect the core values of the group. Consider the mission/vision statements of these organizations that have been identified as spirit friendly:

"To honor God in all we do." —*Service Master*

"To contribute to human welfare by application of biomedical engineering in the research, design, manufacture, and

sale of instruments or appliances that alleviate pain, restore
health, and extend life."   *—Medtronic*

"We are committed to providing outstanding career opportunities by exceeding our customers' expectations through
continuous aggressive improvement."   *—TD Industries*

"Tom's of Maine will become the trusted partner in natural
care among consumers with whom we share common
values."   *—Tom's of Maine*

"The mission of Southwest Airlines is dedication to the
highest quality of customer service delivered with a sense of
warmth, friendliness, individual pride, and company spirit.
We are committed to provide our employees a stable work
environment with equal opportunity for learning and personal growth."
        —Southwest Airlines

FOSTERING INTRINSIC MOTIVATION: Traditional organizations try to
motivate through such extrinsic means as financial rewards, punishments, and regulations. Spiritual organizations, on the other hand,
tap into motivational forces within workers. Intrinsically motivated
employees put forth sustained effort because they find the organization's mission and their labor to be meaningful. Work becomes an
enjoyable activity that requires no external reward. Intrinsic motivation can be enhanced by emphasizing the group's shared goals, training workers so that they develop competence to master their tasks,
providing autonomy so individuals have control over their work, and
creating a warm, caring work environment.[29]

PROMOTING SHARED SPIRITUAL VALUES: Spiritually developed organizations operate under a framework of shared spiritual values.
Promoting these values can make organizations more productive,
and leaders who adhere to these standards are more sensitive to ethical issues. Carole Jurkiewicz and Robert Giacalone, professors,
researchers, and authors on workplace spirituality and organizational performance issues, offer a description of what one such values
framework might look like:[30]

Benevolence: kindness; promoting the happiness and prosperity of employees

Generativity: long-term focus; leaving something behind for those who follow

Humanism: asserting the dignity and worth of each employee; providing opportunities for personal growth

Integrity: adherence to a code of conduct; sincerity, honesty, candor

Justice: even-handed treatment of employees; impartiality in assigning rewards and punishments

Mutuality: recognizing interconnection and interdependence; contributing together

Receptivity: open-mindedness; flexible thinking; risk taking; creativity

Respect: regarding employees with esteem and value; expressing appreciation and consideration for others

Responsibility: following through independently to achieve goals; concern for doing what is right

Trust: confidence in the character and truth of the organization and its representatives

MAKING SPACE FOR THE SPIRIT: Spiritual organizations are intentional about nurturing the inner life of members. They may set aside space (chapels, meditation gardens) for reflection, meditation, and prayer, as well as time for such activities. For example, employees of DJ Jensen Construction in Portland, Oregon, are allowed to take paid time during the day to meditate.[31] Some spirit-friendly organizations incorporate moments of silence into meetings and other gatherings. Others invite spiritual speakers, study spiritual materials, sponsor spiritual discussion groups, send employees to workplace spirituality conferences and prayer breakfasts, and schedule collective service projects such as Habitat for Humanity work days, breast cancer relay teams, and neighborhood clean-up projects.

SPIRITUAL DIVIDENDS

The purpose of this chapter has been to demonstrate that spiritual leaders are moral leaders, and then to outline ways to promote Ethical

Leadership through individual and collective spiritual development. Spirituality equips leaders to function as moral persons and moral managers through mission and meaning; other-centeredness; integrity, humility and justice; and hope and joy. Leaders promote their personal spiritual development when they seek to determine their vocation; engage in self-reflective practices such as meditation, prayer, fasting, and study; and seek to serve others. Organizations can do their part to foster the spiritual development of leaders by creating a compelling vision, fostering intrinsic motivation, promoting shared spiritual values, and making space for the spirit.

Promoting Ethical Leadership through spiritual development pays significant dividends. Spiritual leaders are better equipped to avoid scandal, to create the conditions for long-term organizational success, and to provide meaningful, fulfilling environments for themselves and their followers.

■ ■ ■

Dennis S. Ross, MSW, is a rabbi at Temple Emanuel in Worcester, Massachusetts. He also directs Concerned Clergy for Choice for the Education Fund of Family Planning Advocates of New York State. Rabbi Ross has written for the *New York Times,* the *Boston Globe,* the *Jewish Daily Forward,* the *Journal of Reform Judaism,* and *MultiCultural Review.* He is author of *God in Our Relationships: The Spirituality between People from the Teachings of Martin Buber* (Jewish Lights Publishing) and "Abortion and Judaism," a contribution to the Jewish Lights *LifeLights* pastoral care pamphlet series. Through Family Planning Advocates of New York State, he is author of *Stem Cell Research: A Study and Advocacy Toolkit for Clergy* and lead author of *When a Woman Makes a Choice: A Curriculum on Reproductive Decisions for Clinical Pastoral Education.* He travels frequently to speak about spirituality, bioethics, and social justice.

I-Thou at the Workplace

An Interpersonal Spirituality from the Teachings of Martin Buber

RABBI DENNIS S. ROSS, MSW

The spirituality of the I-Thou relationship is fully compatible with the workplace. Associated with Jewish thinker Martin Buber, the I-Thou encounter speaks of a spirituality that passes between people. Unlike its counterpart, I-It, I-Thou respects every person—supervisor, employee, boss—for who they are. I-Thou opens spontaneously and unannounced, lasts for a moment or an hour, consumes full attention, is unique to the individuals and the occasion, but all too often passes by unrecognized and underappreciated. Calling attention to I-Thou and its signs can bring about greater awareness of this spiritual opportunity and enhance the tasks of the workplace and daily life.

TWO KINDS OF RELATIONSHIPS

It bubbles up in laughter shared with a colleague over a working lunch. It springs up in banter between boss and clerk while waiting for an elevator. It happens all by itself when receptionist and visitor strike up a conversation. I-Thou occurs spontaneously and frequently during the course of the day—at home, at work, and with friends. Opening modestly, without warning, and on its own accord, I-Thou often passes unnoticed, leaving behind a spiritual substance that goes unappreciated.

The term *I-Thou* became popular thanks to Jewish thinker Martin Buber (1878–1965). Buber, a religious intellectual, dedicated his life to study, teaching, and writing about Bible, theology, comparative religion, mysticism, and more. His fields of interest included psychotherapy, international languages, education, philosophy, anthropology, and sociology. Not content with just intellectual exercise, Buber put his beliefs into practice as a social activist.

Buber was born and educated in Vienna, where he rose to prominence as a philosopher and theologian. At age sixty-five, he fled the Nazis for Israel, settling with family in Jerusalem, where he taught, wrote, and engaged in social activism until his death in 1965. Buber's best-known work, *I and Thou,* released in 1923, outlines the interpersonal spirituality of I-Thou.

Buber taught that there are two kinds of relationships: I-Thou and I-It. As an example of the difference between the two, imagine heading to work on a daily route that includes a stop at one of the corporate coffee chain stores. You place the same order each morning, get the same stuff, throw down the money and pick up the change (grunt included, no extra charge). This automatic, mechanical, "It's early! I'm sleepy!" interaction with the person behind the counter is the kind of relationship Martin Buber would call I-It.

Then, one day, instead of a muffin, you order a whole wheat bagel with no-fat cream cheese. The barista smiles and comments, "On a diet?" and you are taken by surprise, to the point of embarrassment. Here you thought that the counter clerk did not even recognize you, let alone remember what you eat. The dull routine has broken; you discover that, unbeknownst to yourself, your presence makes a difference. Leaving the shop, instead of dragging with fatigue as usual, you realize your mood has lifted a little, thanks to the reaction you received. Martin Buber would say that this exchange was I-Thou, for the warmer, more personal words.

I-Thou is an individualized, unique interaction that consumes our full attention. I-Thou happens in the warm greeting of strangers or in a heart-to-heart conversation between old friends. The person is not a means to an end in I-Thou, but an end in herself or himself.

An I-It interaction, by contrast, is cold and impersonal, measured and calculated. I-It uses the person as an "it," as a means to an end, a tool toward a goal. I-It happens in analysis and diagnosis, in categories and competition. I-It happens between a barking boss and slacking employee, in the defiance one person shows another. However, I-It is not inherently harmful. In fact, it can be helpful, even essential, when providing food, shelter, or clothing, or social stability, economic security, and sound professional relations. Though necessary and important, I-It can become destructive when expanded to exploitation, bigotry, discrimination, or worse.

THE I-IT RELATIONSHIP

Before we can fully grasp the I-Thou, we need to recognize the significance of the I-It relationship, for there is no I-Thou without I-It.

I-It usually dominates interactions between boss and worker, employee and supervisor, salesclerk and customer. I-It rules the office, where people are more likely to use each other than to relate, where a person—a job performance, really—is evaluated rather than encountered fully as a human being. But it is possible to bring something of I-Thou into the I-It, and the incentive to bring I-Thou to work extends beyond growing a bottom line or any other improved corporate outcome. I-Thou may well bring those benefits, but that is not the point. Identifying I-Thou, being open to it, recognizing it, and encouraging it increases the spiritual at the office and makes for a more substantial and fulfilling work experience.

Consider the following scenario: You go to the bank, head to the teller's window, and hand over a deposit. The teller pecks at a keyboard while you look around and notice that car loans have gotten pricey. The teller shoves a receipt across the granite counter and mumbles, "Next in line please." You could have a warmer exchange with an ATM. This is an I-It relationship. It has five primary characteristics.

I-It Is Impersonal

I-It treats people indifferently and mechanically. It does the job, but nothing more. I-It identifies by an account number and it sorts, analyzes, and disposes. I-It mass-produces people as if people are interchangeable. I-It is the perspective of the movie ticket taker—one faceless person after another entering the theater. It is the view from the toll collector's booth—driver after driver passing through the plaza. I-It is in education when a standardized test determines student placement. In medicine, I-It is in the accurate but emotionless report on a medical procedure that reveals whether a symptom is life threatening or will go away on its own. I-It is in the bored, mechanical, and uncaring voice that asks, "Cash or credit?" And I-It is among familiar strangers, commuters who daily wait together for the train but never acknowledge one another. Yet I-It achieves a good when it brings mail to the door, food to the table, and electricity to the home. And were I needing immediate medical attention, I would not want chitchat or any I-Thou interactions. Make me comfortable and give me the help I need, right now! Treat me like an It, please!

I-It Uses People

I-It uses people as a means to a goal, as a tool for getting something or somewhere. The individual person does not matter—I-It is all about what "they" can do for "me." I-It is in the boss's pushing the mailroom to get the bills out before the end of the day or in the speech that tries to explain a bump or a dip in sales at a departmental meeting. It is in the "I need you to take that business trip, regardless of what is going on in your home life" command. In I-It, one person becomes a rung on someone else's ladder of advance.

I-It Is Competitive

I-It is vying for a promotion, going head to head with the competition to bring in a new account. I-It is in coffee break bragging and in the dog-eat-dog pressure from a person two cubicles away determined to be first in quarterly sales. I-It is in a competition where there is only one winner ... *and it better be me!*

I-It Is Calculated

I-It is measured by the hour, by the piece, by punching in and punching out. I-It dominates when there is too much to do and the schedule is tight, when deadline takes priority over person. I-It is the cashier trying to scan more items per hour than any other. It is when the claims adjuster tries to process even more forms in a day. I-It tries to get the most out of the people who work in a business or organization, ignoring the consequences on health or home life. I-It keeps an eye on the year-end bonus to the exclusion of the human factor.

I-It Is Reification to the Extreme

The German word for "reification" literally means "thing-ification." We reify people when we make things out of them rather than seeing their individuality. This is I-It, and it happens when the smallest part of a person swells up and defines them. The I-It of reification describes the promise of assistance in a restaurant when a kitchen apron identifies the waitstaff and evokes a question about the menu. Reification offers reassurance and relief when someone suddenly falls ill—there is a call to 911, and the white shirt, shoulder patch, and black bag of an emergency medical technician means help has arrived.

I-It relationships can be harmful when there is abuse of power and position, harassment or physical attack, racism or bigotry, or when the more privileged person takes advantage of weaker ones. Reification, for example, crosses the line from necessary and helpful to harmful when it becomes a bark at a hotel housekeeper over a lack of towels in the room or an ethnic, racial, or economic slur. I-It relationships become harmful when there is disrespect, exploitation, or abuse, when we treat the next person as less human than ourselves.

Yet I-It relationships are also essential at times. I-It is good when advancing collective well-being. Just imagine life without the health care that relies on I-It, or the transportation and other basics that I-It relations bring. What is more, I-It is the foundation for I-Thou when it conveys people from one place to the other, puts dinner on the table, or repairs the roof overhead. When I-It makes for comfort and security, the time is right to enter I-Thou.

THE I-THOU RELATIONSHIP

I-Thou defies description because it becomes I-It the moment there is analysis. Nevertheless, it is possible to communicate *something* about I-Thou, enough so we can identify it. Recognizing I-Thou is the important step toward bringing spirit to work. I-Thou is marked by these primary characteristics:

I-Thou Is Marked by an Absence of Concern for Time, Space, or Cause

Time: The duration of I-Thou, whether it goes on for an hour or lasts just two words, is irrelevant. The sense of time is abated in I-Thou; it is marked by a feeling of timelessness. When I-Thou ends, a person might look at the clock and remark, "My goodness! I didn't realize we went on *that* long!"

Space: Where an I-Thou conversation occurs, the location, the surroundings, who else is in the room, and whatever else is going on are beside the point. I-Thou occurs over a bite at the company cafeteria or at an upscale restaurant, where two people are so engaged with each other that they see no one else and nothing else. I-Thou happens in a noisy factory, where the attention turns from the action on the floor to a tight, instinctive focus on the conversation.

Cause: What brings people together in I-Thou, whether it is an appointment or a meeting by chance, and how they got there, whether by cab, bus, or by foot, are beside the point. I-Thou is consumed by what happens in the moment.

I-Thou Is Simple

Though I-Thou can be in the extended conversation between old friends, a long-standing relationship is not a requirement. It occurs in a smile or nod between strangers. It sparks in a word between a sales-clerk and customer, in a glance between a flight attendant and a passenger, or in a sigh at the office photocopier on the busiest day of the year. I-Thou lives in these simple exchanges.

I-Thou Is Mutual

Both parties have an equal investment in I-Thou. People, regardless of status, speak as peers with the same stake. I-Thou is a social equalizer.

I-Thou Changes Feelings, Yet It Is More than Emotions

Partners who feel one way when the conversation opens feel differently once it ends—anxiety turns to calm, anger turns to compassion, confusion turns to understanding. If you were looking for a fight and instead made a friend, or the other way around, I-Thou is present. A mood shift is the most reliable sign that I-Thou occurred. It is tempting to think of I-Thou as just feelings, but it is much more. Feelings change as a result of I-Thou, but the emotional shift is a by-product of the relationship, never the focus.

I-Thou Happens *between* People

I-Thou does not dwell within the person—not in the "I" or in the "Thou," but in the back-and-forth, in the exchange. I-Thou looks at the way people treat each other, not at how they feel when relating. To say, "I like you," and to act in a way that does not show it, to speak kind words but conduct oneself impersonally, fails the test of I-Thou.

I-Thou Is Time-Limited

Every I-Thou must end. Whether I-Thou is just a greeting or is part of an enduring relationship, I-Thou's end is built into the beginning. No matter how well people know each other, how long they work together, or how committed they are to one another, I-Thou comes to a close. Martin Buber used the term *holy insecurity* to point to the fragile and time-limited I-Thou, to the risk and tenuous balance of the relationship, as if the encounter teeters on the narrow edge of a knife blade.

I-Thou Involves "Imagining the Real"

Buber described the concept of "imagining the real" as standing in the place of the other and simultaneously being aware of yourself. It means seeing both sides simultaneously. Of course, one person never fully experiences what another undergoes, but it is possible to intuit. You can imagine the person's very real thoughts and feelings and hold your ground, all at the same time.

I-Thou Preserves Individual Integrity

Two people do not merge into one in I-Thou. I-Thou is not a capitulation of will since both parties retain their integrity. They keep their distinctiveness, standing at a distance and entering relation from where they stand. I-Thou can happen even in a disagreement: Something comes up between two people, but they clear the air. They may not settle everything, but their honesty illustrates I-Thou.

I-Thou Enters the Spiritual Dimension of Eternal Thou

When "I" meets "Thou," workplace communications attain a spiritual dimension. To describe the spiritual dimension of I-Thou is to say that each I-Thou enters what Buber called the "Eternal Thou." Of Buber's three terms, *I-It, I-Thou,* and *Eternal Thou,* Eternal Thou is the most difficult to explain. In brief, when people speak as "I" and "Thou," they meet God at the same time in Eternal Thou.

One way to think of Eternal Thou stems from Rabbi Abraham Isaac of Sadgora, an early Jewish teacher, whom Buber recalled as saying, "What we say here is heard there."

As surely as an early-morning watercooler conversation leaps from cubicle to cubicle in the office and fills the company cafeteria by lunchtime, what is said here on earth as I-Thou is heard there, abiding with God in the Eternal Thou.

I-THOU IN ACTION

I-It is inevitable, but not inescapable. There is great need to enrich I-It with I-Thou. We have the potential to strengthen the spirit in a workplace that can be impersonal, uncaring, and emotionless. We have the opportunity to expand I-Thou presence in offices and stores, classrooms and exam rooms so often noted for impersonal communication.

I-Thou and I-It wax and wane during the day, even during a conversation; they oscillate. An encounter flip-flops between the two, between work and relation, between the I-It business side and relating in I-Thou encounter. Herein lies the challenge and the opportunity: to recognize I-Thou in the workplace, to bring I-Thou into I-It, to invite a warmer exchange between clerk and client, salesperson and customer, waiter and diner, if only for a moment, softening the impersonal nature of the work relationship.

Contributing a measure of I-Thou to I-It enriches the routine with a measure of sanctity. Amid deadlines and meetings, with difficult clients and moody supervisors, when "I" finds "Thou," the workplace enters a spiritual dimension. With so many waking hours going into making a living—the education, the preparation, and the anxiety of bigger fish swallowing the smaller—the spirit cries out for a humanization and elevation.

Can I-Thou become a greater and stronger presence at work? Can an attorney and client review a legal document, all the while recognizing the personhood of each other? Will a supervisor walk over to a colleague's desk to speak face to face with candor and compassion instead of dashing off a trite e-mail? Can a receptionist offer a heartfelt greeting? Can a customer offer a cashier fully souled thanks, and will that measure of appreciation be reciprocated? Will a supervisor and worker be candid in disagreement, speaking respectfully, openly, and honestly? Can a doctor deliver bad news while making eye contact, placing a hand on a shoulder, allowing time for questions, and expressing compassion? Above all else, can I-Thou receive recognition in the workplace?

■ ■ ■

PART II

Work at the Organizational Level

Joan Marques, EdD, has been blessed with two exciting careers on two Western continents. She stands for more than twenty successful years in advertising, radio and television production, show hosting; and for dynamic entrepreneurship in Suriname, South America, where she founded and managed several businesses and a nonprofit organization focused on women's advancement. In Burbank, California, she is a founding member of the Business Renaissance Institute and ASPEX, director of communications of the Millennium Development Goals Global Watch, and chief editor of four globally available journals for scholars and practitioners. She holds a doctorate in organizational leadership from Pepperdine University, facilitates university courses, and regularly engages in workplace spirituality–related presentations and workshops. Dr. Marques has authored many articles and books pertaining to workplace contentment and emotional intelligence. Her current research interests include workplace spirituality, enhanced consciousness, and awakened leadership.

Satinder Dhiman, EdD, has guided business leaders for the last twenty-five years and served for ten years as a senior lecturer in commerce at DAV College in North India. He has coauthored various textbooks in the area of accounting and management, and currently serves as professor and chair of management, and associate dean of business in Woodbury University's graduate program. He is the recipient of ACBSP's prestigious International Teaching Excellence Award. Dr. Dhiman is a founding member of the Business Renaissance Institute and ASPEX, and serves on the boards of several scholarly journals. He regularly engages in workplace spirituality–related presentations and workshops. He holds a bachelor of science degree and a master's degree in commerce (with Gold Medal) from Panjab University, India; an MBA from West Coast University, Los Angeles; and a doctorate in organizational leadership from Pepperdine University. His current research interests include transformational leadership and spirituality in the workplace.

Dr. Richard King is a recognized authority on United States–Pacific Rim business relations, and he founded his company, King International Group, to carry out his personal commitment to strengthening these relations. He has held top management positions at major organizations and currently serves on the boards of various Pacific Rim–oriented organizations. He is a longtime member of the Noetic Institute and the World Business Academy. Dr. King is a frequent writer and speaker on Pacific Rim business issues, and is the initiator of the Business Renaissance consulting project, which focuses on "adding humanity to the bottom line." He is a founding member of the Business Renaissance Institute, and serves on the boards of numerous organizations. He regularly engages in workplace spirituality–related presentations and workshops. He holds a bachelor of science degree from Syracuse University, a master's degree from Occidental College, and an honorary doctorate of business administration from Woodbury University.

The *S*-Word Revisited

New Horizons in Workplace Spirituality

JOAN MARQUES, EDD, SATINDER DHIMAN, EDD, AND DR. RICHARD KING

*Conversations about workplace spirituality are becoming more fre-
quent, and with that, awareness about the topic continues to grow.
Some important factors, such as change, diversity, and the realization
that spirituality is not necessarily religion, have led to a more receptive approach toward this trend. This chapter reviews highlights from
dialogues conducted with business executives at various levels that
explored the questions and issues pertaining to workplace spirituality
and how to make it happen. Specific topics include the reason for the
growth of the workplace spirituality movement, our personal responsibility toward it, the place of spiritual intelligence at work, how a spiritual approach fits with a highly mechanistic work environment, and
how spirit at work enhances personal spiritual and mental growth.*

A wise woman who was traveling in the mountains found a
precious stone in a stream. The next day, she met another
traveler who was hungry, and the wise woman opened her
bag to share her food. The hungry traveler saw the precious
stone and asked the woman to give it to him. She did so without hesitation. The traveler left, rejoicing in his good fortune.
He knew the stone was worth enough to give him security for
a lifetime. But a few days later, he came back to return the
stone to the wise woman. "I've been thinking," he said. "I
know how valuable the stone is, but I give it back in the hope
that you can give me something even more precious. Give
me what you have within you that enabled you to give me
the stone."   —*Author Unknown*

EXPANDING HORIZONS

In the past century, some tremendous changes have occurred in our
human existence. We have become acquainted with levels of comfort
that our ancestors could not have imagined: the automobile, the

telephone, the airplane, the microwave, the fax, and the Internet are just a few of these horizon-expanding phenomena we accepted in our lives. And with this acceptance came a new way of perceiving our daily practices: we were exposed to other cities, counties, states, countries, cultures, and ways of thinking. We learned that our way of behaving was not the only way, and perhaps not even the best way! Thanks to our human curiosity and intelligence, we obtained a broader perspective than we had for centuries before.

With the expansion of our insights, along with the increased exposure to others from even the farthest corners of the world, came the understanding that change was here to stay. As change was happening in every area, and definitely in our work environments, we were increasingly confronted with greater insecurity, expansion beyond prior comprehension, faster-paced transformations, and diversity. New perspectives mingled with established ones. In particular, women and the broadest interpretation of minorities entered the workforce. And while this development may not have been accepted with great initial enthusiasm by all, it would not be reversed. Quite the contrary. So, thanks to our human flexibility, we members of the human cohort started to adapt. Diversity is now an established element of most workplaces, and with that diversity came the realization that other ways of thinking and behaving are not necessarily wrong. In fact, we realized that we could learn much from these other ways.

While past decades taught us the value of proper moderation and an open mind for alternatives, in today's workforce we are beginning to understand that there is interconnectedness in everything. While we still value the individual approach that has been part of the Western mentality for the longest time, we are now more likely to concede that human beings do not exist as separate entities, that we are interdependent on each other and many diverse factors to fulfill our daily tasks. The more we develop and learn from others, the more we realize the importance of treating our fellow workers—regardless of their positions—as equal human beings, and the better we understand the beauty of sharing. This acceptance of our differences, and the drive to enhance the quality of life for all who are involved in the process—our colleagues, customers, suppliers, community members, family, and ourselves—are keys to the discussion of spiritual behavior at work.

As facilitators of a Los Angeles–based movement toward improved workplace spirituality, the authors of this chapter regularly engage in dialogue sessions with local and regional business executives and members at all levels of the workforce. When we talk about the idea of workplace spirituality, the first thing we always stress is that spirituality is not religion, even though it may be derived from religiously nurtured perspectives. A spiritual worker does not have to adhere to any specific religion, or to any religion at all, to be seen as spiritual. In the past few years of dialogue sessions, five important issues have emerged. We offer these in hopes that they will illustrate some important causes and effects related to workplace spirituality.

Why are increasing numbers of people interested in spirituality at work?

There are several reasons why the topic of spirituality in the workplace is resonating so well with the general population (see figure 2). First and foremost, we all sense the growing discrepancy between workplaces and their focus on the value of individuals. Simultaneously, several other developments are occurring: the move toward large public companies and away from small family-owned companies; and a strong focus on profitability and goal achievement coupled with the loss of emphasis on the internal well-being of the company. This second development is in part due to the average life span of a CEO in a major company, which is now about three to four years. That is really a very short time to succeed, but enclosed in that short life span is the opportunity for a big payday if the CEO hits the target. Whereas in the past corporations were built to last, today corporations are built to sell, and the goal for CEOs is to achieve this objective while they are in charge. Again, that period of time is short; it is not a forecast of twenty-five years into the future. Rather, today's CEOs have an agreement with a set date that is likely only about three years down the road, and if they can attain the targets in stock price, revenue, or return on investment (ROI), they are looking at a phenomenal payday. However, if they do not achieve that goal, they will sink into oblivion. This may very well be the main concern among members of the workforce today, giving rise to the question: how can we change this focus?

The conscious or subconscious registration of the preceding realities, which also relates to a loss of personal connection in corporations starting at the highest levels, may be the crucial driver as to why so many people sense that something needs to be done. This, along with the augmented speed of development, increased exposure to insecurity and change, and expanded contact with other cultures, religions, and ways of performing, are just some of the reasons why spirituality in the workplace is becoming such an important topic.

Figure 2: Reasons for greater interest in spirituality in the workplace

How can we make our workplace better?

If you know the story of Johnny the bagger, you already know that position has nothing to do with a person's ability to help establish a more spiritual environment. In a nutshell, the story is a true one about a young man with Down syndrome who decided to bring a positive change to the grocery store where he worked. Each night he would find a thought for the next day and print out copies of it with help from his dad. Johnny would cut out copies of the thought for the day and sign his name on each slip of paper. The next day he would place one in each customer's grocery bag. With that one small gesture, he changed the environment of the entire store. People would wait longer just to be in his checkout line; others started coming to the store more often to get Johnny's thought for the day. When his colleagues saw how positively this simple act influenced the store's customers, they started to find creative ways that their departments could do the same. Customers were not only talking about the changes at the store, they were bringing their friends into the store, too.

The point of the story is that anyone can bring about a positive change. Spirit at work can be established without formal influence, in large and small ways (see figure 3). For instance, we might bring in a small token of appreciation to colleagues, demonstrating that we see them as more than just tools in the workplace, that we appreciate them for who they are, as fellow human beings with families, feelings, ups and downs. It might be as simple as offering a colleague lunch one day, showing some genuine interest in his or her whereabouts, or offering to cover for a colleague when he or she has some personal issues to take care of. These gestures create a lot of goodwill and go a long way toward establishing an atmosphere where people communicate more, support one another, and achieve better results overall—and the factor of mutual learning should not be overlooked.

Figure 3: Simple ways to enhance spirituality at work

How does spiritual intelligence fit in today's work relations?

When we posed this question, it raised a large number of refreshing perspectives, starting with another question: what is spiritual intelligence? We came to the conclusion that there could be just as many definitions of that term as there are human beings, but spiritual intelligence definitely has something to do with a sense of compassion for, and acceptance of, others just as they are. An interesting response came from one young participant, who asked how we should deal with evil. This young man explained that there are always people who will try to cheat, take advantage of others, or set others up to fail. His concern was that, when it came to spirituality in the workplace, we were focusing on a laudable, but perhaps unachievable target.

Fortunately, there were various mature members of the workforce present who responded from a broader perspective: We enter this life with certain qualities. Based on these, we may be seen as happy, sad, or even evil. Inherent in our being is a balance of two sides, which every tradition talks about: the positive and the negative. We all encounter people that are either more positive or more negative, and "evil" may very well be ingrained in all of us. It is not something out there in the ozone, it is what we bring in with our mental balance, and it is whether we allow the positive to reign over the negative, and allow ourselves to open up to others, or vice versa. When contracts get broken, people walk off the job, or employees need to be fired, our response is crucial. How do we choose to see these matters? As evil? Or as lessons toward future improvement?

Another participant underscored that, indeed, at some time in our career, we all encounter people who make our lives complicated. The art is to adjust our perception in dealing with these people. This participant then shared a story that was told to her when she thought, a number of years ago, she had encountered evil at her work:

> Once there was a Sufi master who had twenty students. Nineteen were very devoted to their study, very cooperative, punctual, and driven. Yet one of them was what we refer to as "evil": he was stealing from his fellow students, disrupting the lessons, and lacking the devotion of the others. One day the master had to leave for a few weeks, so the nineteen devoted students saw their opportunity to collaboratively get rid of

the evil fellow, and they did. When the master returned, he asked where the "evil" student was, and the nineteen devotees said, "He's gone, master. Now no one has to be miserable anymore!" Yet the next day the master got dressed and left again. He returned a few days later with the "evil" fellow. Upon the astonished looks of the nineteen devotees, he responded, "If he's not here, who is going to teach you patience, compassion, resilience, and understanding? Who is going to make you grow?"

In response to this story, other seasoned workers agreed that perception is everything. If we choose to see everybody as a teacher, even the most difficult persons and situations become bearable. And, ultimately, toxic situations seem to surface less and less, until they entirely disappear. To underscore the point, another participant cited a memorable statement by President Lincoln: "I don't like that person. Perhaps I have to get to know him better."

When we bring our spiritual intelligence to work, it helps us see things in a broader scope, take matters less personally, and accept others as they are and not as we would like them to be.

How does a spiritual approach fit into a highly mechanistic work environment?

The nature of workplaces differs enormously. Some workplaces are small and cozy, with a great level of interaction and a high sense of togetherness, and others are so large and so competitively driven that it is hard to maintain a sense of connectedness with anyone. Take the movie industry, for example, where things change nearly at light speed, oftentimes leaving employees confused and alienated because of the easy layoffs, the extreme protectiveness of positions, and the many overinflated personalities involved. An individual who wants to behave spiritually and engage in win-win outcomes may feel very unhappy in such a highly win-lose-oriented environment.

The approach to this problem may not be what most would like to hear, but in dialogue sessions, we tell people that, if you find yourself in an environment that has very little spirituality by nature, or in a workplace that engages in activities that, by nature, are destructive to existence or human health—such as the tobacco industry or the industry of warfare—you may need to recognize the fact that there might be a mismatch between your focus and the focus of this environment. The sooner you realize this, the sooner can you start to contemplate a new horizon. If the nature of the industry is not necessarily destructive to human existence, such as the entertainment industry, you may first consider shopping around for a different employer where the atmosphere may be less toxic and selfish. However, trends are usually industry-wide, and the chance of running into a more spiritually driven competitor is slim.

Another alternative, which may work for the entrepreneurial worker, may be to start a small service or production entity for this industry. Not everyone may consider him- or herself willing or able to do that. A third (but not final) option could be to consider an entire change in career, which might mean engaging in further education. While many people initially shy away from this option, it is important to know that it is now quite normal to have two or three different careers before retirement.

How does spirituality at work enhance personal spiritual and mental growth?

This question often leads to multiple interesting answers during our dialogue sessions (see figure 4). One important finding that has emerged from our sessions is that a spiritual worker connects with others and, therefore, learns from those others and their ways of performing. Yet the learning does not stop there. Because human connections usually extend beyond the workplace, mutual learning keeps happening in many areas, not only between workers but between workers and families, then between family members, and then between family and community. Those who choose spiritual connectivity keep on connecting.

Another interesting thing we have noted is that spiritual workers are individuals with a high internal locus of control. They are not reactive, but are proactive. They always start working from the inside out. They first try to discover, as Johnny the bagger did, how they can bring about a positive change. They ask themselves, "What capacities and skills do I have with which I can make a difference?" Then they execute their plan without immediately thinking of returns on their investment. They prefer to do good first, and they take steps to do well. They are convinced that by doing the right thing, right things will happen to them.

They focus on people who can serve as role models, not on those who will bring them down. This is not a matter of trying to copy a role model's entire behavior, but rather reviewing the positive traits and asking themselves what they can learn from these individuals. Spiritual workers adopt these positive qualities to improve themselves and the entire environment in which they perform.

One of the most interesting ways in which we have seen spiritual workers grow is through the realization of impermanence. When people realize that everything arises and passes, their tendency to engage in unnecessary stress diminishes. As an illustration, one of the participants in our dialogue session shared this story, which she heard in India:

> A father was living with his two grown sons on a large piece of land. Life was good, and both sons were living in their own house and working their piece of the land. One day the father passed away without leaving behind a will. The brothers conducted the necessary rites and rituals and started cleaning up their father's earthly belongings after the funeral. This is when they came across a small box, which the father had carefully kept in his closet. When they opened the box, they found it contained two rings: one was a beautiful, expensive diamond ring, and the other, a simple, solid, silver ring.
>
> The oldest brother, who was a bit on the greedy side, quickly thought of a reason to get the expensive ring. He told his younger brother, "I think that father would have wanted this ring to be a traditional family piece, so as the oldest son, I should keep it. Then I can give it to my oldest son later, and so on." The younger brother simply agreed and took with him the simple, solid, silver ring.
>
> Soon enough, both brothers continued their lives, and the older brother fell into his normal pattern of discontentment: winter was too cold and forced him to wear too many clothes; spring was too aggravating because birds were chirping early in the morning; summer was too hot, forcing him to take too many showers; and fall was too cumbersome with all the leaves falling from the trees. Life was never good enough.
>
> The younger brother had been sitting on his front porch one evening, intensely studying the ring he had inherited from his father, and wondering why the old man would have cherished such a simple ring. Then he saw that there was something engraved inside the ring. It read, "This too shall pass." The son smiled and cherished the ring even more from then on, as it helped him approach life from a much more balanced perspective. When he encountered great fortune, he would

not lose his head, but would realize that everything would pass, and he would remain down-to-earth. When he encountered hardship, he would not get too deeply depressed, but would realize that everything passes and become his normal equanimous self again soon.

We do not need to inherit a ring from our parents to realize that everything arises and passes; life teaches us that. Spiritual workers take this lesson of impermanence with them beyond the workplace as a means of internal growth, increased understanding, and better balance.

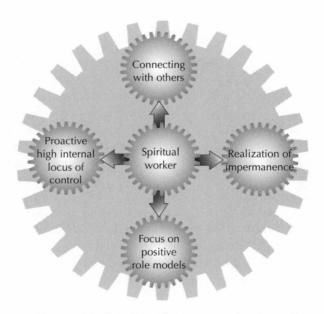

Figure 4: How a spiritual worker enhances spiritual and mental growth

New Horizons

Unfortunately, the general mentality in most contemporary workplaces is still highly individualistic and predominantly based on short-term advantages for the organization alone, instead of long-term benefits for all parties involved. Many leaders still perceive spirituality as incompatible with the bottom line.

Yet new horizons are emerging, and members of the current workforce are taking notice. Because of the dynamic and ever-changing nature of the workplace, many are recognizing that we need a spiritual approach now more than ever. What too often gets overlooked, however, is that we could *all* become spiritual workers if we decided to adopt a spiritual mindset at work.

Not only is a spiritual mindset positively related to the bottom line, but spiritual workers can also be a great advantage to the workplace, to the other stakeholders they interact with, and to themselves. Workplace spirituality can lead to tremendous advancement within the organization and among all those involved with it over a very long time.

■ ■ ■

Jerry Biberman, PhD, is professor of management at the University of Scranton. For twelve years he served as chair of the management/marketing department at the University of Scranton. He obtained his MS, MA, and PhD from Temple University. He writes, teaches, consults, speaks, and conducts workshops in the areas of work and spirituality, workplace diversity, and organization transformation. Dr. Biberman serves as editor of the *Journal of Management, Spirituality and Religion,* and has coedited several special editions on work and spirituality for the *Journal of Organizational Change Management.* Dr. Biberman was a founder and first chair of the Management, Spirituality, and Religion group of the Academy of Management. He is coeditor of *Spirituality in Business: Theory, Practice, and Future Directions* and *At Work: Spirituality Matters.*

What Makes an Organization Spiritual?

Applied Spirituality in Organizational Structure, Design, Processes, and Practices

JERRY BIBERMAN, PHD

If a person can be described as being spiritual, can a spiritual organization be described in a similar manner? Can an organization be described as if it were a person? Can the organization be described independently of describing its top leaders? In this chapter, the author argues that it is possible to do so, by describing the organization's structure and design, its processes and procedures. This chapter contends that spiritual organizations can be expected to have flatter organization structures and a greater openness to change. Their belief in abundant resources can lead to greater interconnectedness and cooperation between organization units and empowerment of workers at all levels of the organization.

THE NATURE OF SPIRITUAL ORGANIZATIONS

Most of what has been written about spirituality and work has tended to be focused on the individual or personal level. For example, several writers have described the behaviors of managers or executives who could be considered spiritual. In addition, a theory and several measurements of spiritual leadership have been developed.

Descriptions of spiritual leaders have been extrapolated from looking at behavioral descriptions of "enlightened" people, and of people who have committed themselves to spiritual values and who have engaged in spiritual practices for a number of years. Leaders operating from a spiritual paradigm perspective have been described as being open to change, having a sense of purpose and meaning in their life, appreciating how they are connected with a greater whole, and having individual understanding and expression of their own spirituality. In contrast to a scarcity belief, they possess what has been referred to as an abundance mentality—a belief that there are abundant resources available to all, so that there is no need to compete for them. They are also more likely to trust others, share information, and work in concert with teams and coworkers to accomplish mutual objectives, and to empower their coworkers and people below them in the organization hierarchy. They are more likely to use intuition and emotions in reaching decisions. They are also more likely to use win-win collaborative strategies in conflict situations.

If a person can be described as being spiritual, can a spiritual organization be described in a similar manner? Can an organization be described as if it were a person? Can the organization be described independently of describing its top leaders?

The answer is yes, by describing the organization's structure and design, its processes and procedures, and its stages of spiritual growth or change.

Structure and Design

Spiritual organizations tend to have flatter, organic (as opposed to mechanistic) organization structures. Their design is more likely to be decentralized and informal, most resembling matrices, networks, boundaryless organizations, or some similar loose integrated design. Their design allows for maximum communication with constituents both inside and outside the organization.

Processes and Procedures

Spiritual organizations are likely to have a greater openness to change. Their belief in abundant resources leads to greater interconnectedness and cooperation between organization units, and empowerment of workers at all levels of the organization. Rather than believing in the preservation of the self at all costs, these organizations can be more concerned with existing in harmony with their environment and, therefore, may be more supportive of ecology and the environment, and more concerned with meeting the needs of internal and external customers. Spiritual organizations encourage creative thinking and the cooperation of organization units to establish and accomplish mutually agreed-upon mission statements and objectives for the organization.

Stages of Spiritual Growth or Change

Individuals on a spiritual journey are often characterized as going through several stages, which are variously described in different spiritual traditions but have several things in common. In the Christian tradition, the process of spiritual transformation is known as the three ways: the purgative way, the illuminative way, and the unitive way.[1] Along the way, spiritual transformation includes "dark night" experiences.

Similarly, organization and group theorists have described organizations and groups as going through stages. Many organizations go through changes that could make them less spiritual as they grow from a small entrepreneurial company to a large successful company. While the owners of a small startup company may have begun with spiritual values or intentions, as the company grows and becomes more successful, they are more likely to follow traditional management policies and organization design policies, resulting in large companies run by traditional command and control policies.

There are companies, however, that choose to remain faithful to the spiritual values with which they were started as the company grows. In these cases, organizations can go through stages that mirror the spiritual growth stages of an individual. For example, in *The Soul of a Leader,* Dr. Margaret Benefiel, CEO of ExecutiveSoul.com (coauthor of "Infinite Leadership: Authenticity and Spirit at Work"), tells the story of Tom's of Maine. As the company became more successful, it almost lost sight of its spiritual values, and Dr. Benefiel outlines the steps that the company took to get back on track and remain true to its spiritual values:[2]

- Purgative: During the company's first decade, Tom and Kate Chappell chose a spiritual path and started and grew a company in alignment with their spiritual values.
- Illuminative: When Tom was ready to leave the company for the ministry, he decided instead to stay with the company and pursue his ministry education at the same time. It was through this process that Tom and Kate discovered (through wisdom Tom gained in divinity school) that they needed to reclaim their original values. Holding a leadership team retreat, followed by a gathering of the entire company, the company developed and implemented a new statement of beliefs and a new mission statement.
- Dark night of soul: When there seemed to be no way forward for the company to continue to grow and still remain true to its values, Tom and Kate called a family meeting, at which they decided to try to sell the company, but only if the new owners would commit to keeping the company in Maine and continue to adhere to the company's values. When they could not find a buyer who could take the company to the next level, Tom and Kate refused to sell to an inappropriate buyer, and they committed themselves to taking the company to the next level, with the help of a yet-to-be-hired COO.
- Unitive: Tom and Kate returned to the company committed to product development. They created three-person development groups to develop new products, and they partnered with Tom O'Brien as COO.

EXAMPLES OF SPIRITUAL ORGANIZATIONS

Spiritual organizations can be either for profit or nonprofit, and can exist in a variety of settings. Since 2002, the International Center for Spirit at Work (ICSW) has awarded an annual International Spirit at Work Award to organizations that have implemented specific policies, programs, or practices that explicitly nurture spirituality inside their organizations. To date, forty-two organizations in thirty-seven countries have received the award, including consumer product stores such as the Body Shop and Eileen Fisher, Inc., health-care hospitals and services, software services such as Ternary Software, and food processors such as Tyson Foods.

It is instructive to note what ICSW considers to be the qualities of a spiritual organization:[3]

- An organization deeply committed to nurturing the human spirit
- An organization where people can incorporate their spirituality into the workplace
- An organization where employees can find nourishment for "vertical spirituality" (between themselves and God, or the Divine, or Higher Power), which might include meditation rooms, time for shared reflection, silence before meetings, ecumenical prayer, and support for employees to take time off for spiritual development
- An organization where employees can nurture "horizontal spirituality" (service to others), which might include caring among coworkers, service commitments to customers, a social responsibility orientation, environmental sensitivity, and well-aligned vision/mission and values
- An organization that explicitly nurtures spirituality, where the topic of spirituality is openly discussed, not just assumed or implied

A number of writers have cited companies as being spiritual. In *Soul at Work,* Dr. Benefiel describes several spiritual organizations such as Southwest Airlines, Reell Precision Manufacturing, Mercy Medical, Our Lady's Hospice, and Greyston Bakery.[4] More recently, in *The Soul of a Leader,* Dr. Benefiel describes Landry's Bicycle and several nonprofit agencies.[5] Several of the contributors to the author and management professor Len Tischler's *Spirituality in Business* describe a variety of spiritual organizations,[6] and in 2008, Joan Marques, founding member of the Business Renaissance Institute and coeditor of this book, cited Starbucks as a spiritual organization.[7]

It should be noted that organizations change, just as people do, and their levels of spirituality may go up or down because of various factors, such as mergers, acquisitions, leadership or directional changes, and the like. Over time, organizations cited as being spiritual may lose some of their spiritual characteristics. Tom's of Maine, for example, is now a part of Colgate, but still claims to have the same company values and products. It will take some time to see if it can remain spiritual within the larger organizational context.

Making Your Organization More Spiritual

Influences or drives to make an organization become more spiritual can come from any level of the organization. In most cases, the influence comes from the top, from the founder or CEO of the company. But the influence can also come from the bottom, or from any level of the organization—especially if there are mechanisms in place to elicit employee input and feedback. For example, in some cases, employees have requested prayer and meditation groups and opportunities.

In addition to understanding that companies go through stages of spiritual development just as individuals do, it is helpful to consider several questions when thinking about how to make your organization more spiritual:

- Does the leader have to go through the changes first, and then influence the rest of the organization to change, or can the change occur at any level? Does it need to be an individual change first, or can a group or organizational unit begin the change process?
- While change is most often initiated by leadership at the top, it could also be initiated at other levels of the organization. In every case, however, spiritual change begins first in a specific individual or group who is then motivated to change the organization in a similar direction.
- Just as a person encounters opportunities to grow spiritually or to begin on a more spiritual path, does an organization encounter the same type of opportunities? If so, what would they be?
- An organization encounters opportunities to begin on a spiritual path just as individuals do. In much the same way a crisis or other opportunity for self-examination and reflection can lead to a personal spiritual transformation, so, too, can a similar opportunity occur in an organization, either through a

financial or other crisis in the organization, a change in leadership, or a company takeover.

- Just as an individual encounters challenges along the spiritual path, does an organization encounter the same type of challenges? If so, what would they be? Organizations obviously encounter challenges along the spiritual path. A common example is when an entrepreneur starts a small company with spiritual values, with the members of the company all in agreement about those values. As the company grows and becomes more successful, it experiences an influx of new managers or employees who no longer are familiar with or "buy into" the original values of the founding entrepreneur. Dr. Benefiel's case example of Tom's of Maine is a good example of this. Sometimes a company either restructures or gets bought out by a larger company that is not familiar with or does not "buy into" the original values of the founding entrepreneur, and the challenge becomes how to retain the original spiritual values.

- Is there an organizational equivalent of the dark night of the soul? How would an organization deal with it and transcend it?

- An organizational crisis can be the equivalent of the dark night of the soul, especially when the members of the organization begin to lose sight of or begin to question the spiritual values they once held. For example, members of the organization may question whether their practices are in keeping with the values expressed in their mission statement. When such a crisis occurs, the organization needs to provide mechanisms, such as executive and employee retreats and speak-out sessions, to help members revisit the organization's values.

STAYING ON THE SPIRITUAL PATH

Even the most spiritual organization faces challenges to remain on the spiritual path. These are most likely to occur as the organization becomes bigger and more formalized, or as the organization faces greater competition or economic challenges. The question for any business leader committed to spirituality in the workplace is how the organization can remain true to its spiritual values and practices.

First, the organization needs to remain open to challenges and criticisms from all of its internal and external constituencies. Second, it needs to be flexible in its ability to respond to these criticisms and challenges. Third, the organization needs to provide frequent and ongoing opportunities to revisit and celebrate its mission and values, and to critically examine ways in which it can respond to challenges while remaining true to its spiritual values. These opportunities could include company retreats and celebrations.

The organization could also appoint people or units to provide ongoing feedback on its processes, as well as people or units to look for ways to promote an abundance (as opposed to scarcity) interpretation of, and response to, ongoing challenges from within and without the organization. Finally, since the impetus for change can come from any level of the organization, not just from top leadership, leaders of organizations need to create mechanisms or positions throughout the organization to monitor and be ready to respond to the impetus for change.

What can you do as a member of an organization to help make the organization more spiritual? Whether you are in the top echelons of management or working your way up the organizational ladder as an individual organization member, regardless of your title or position in the organization, your personal spiritual life matters. As you work on your own spiritual development and deepen your own spiritual practices by engaging in daily prayer, meditation, and spiritual study, look for ways in which the insights you gain from your spiritual practice can be applied to your organization and work situation—particularly in the areas of decision making and interpersonal communication. The more you engage in your own spiritual growth, the more the organization will benefit from your spiritual growth. If you are a manager or a senior officer in your organization, look for ways in which insights you gain from your spiritual practice can lead to better ways of motivating and leading other organization members, and to better ways of designing the organization and improving organizational processes and practices.

■ ■ ■

Frederick T. Evers, PhD, is a professor of sociology and director of teaching support services at the University of Guelph in Guelph, Ontario, Canada. Dr. Evers received his MS and PhD from Iowa State University and his BA from Cornell University. He received the prestigious 3M Teaching Fellowship. Dr. Evers has worked on numerous projects related to the scholarship of teaching and learning. With Drs. James Rush and Iris Berdrow, he published *The Bases of Competence: Skills for Lifelong Learning and Employability*. With Rev. Lucy Reid, he published *Working with Spirit: Engaging Spirituality to Meet the Challenges of the Workplace*. Rev. Reid and Dr. Evers have conducted many workshops and presentations related to *Working with Spirit: Engaging Spirituality to Meet the Challenges of the Workplace*. Dr. Evers has worked as a volunteer with youth groups in the Anglican Diocese of Niagara. He is married and has two adult daughters and a granddaughter.

Rev. Lucy Reid is an Anglican priest currently working in a parish in Victoria, British Columbia, Canada. She has served in parishes in England, Montreal, and northern Ontario, as well as in university chaplaincy in Guelph, Ontario. As a chaplain, she convened a Spirituality in the Workplace group for faculty and staff for more than twelve years. From experience with this group came much of the material for *Working with Spirit: Engaging Spirituality to Meet the Challenges of the Workplace,* coauthored with Dr. Frederick T. Evers. Rev. Reid is also the author of *She Changes Everything: Seeking the Divine on a Feminist Path*. She is married and has three young adult children.

Addressing Wellness Problems in the Workplace through Spirituality

Six Risks and Six Spiritual Solutions

FREDERICK T. EVERS, PhD, AND REV. LUCY REID

This chapter looks at wellness problems of the workplace and how spirituality can address them. To start, the authors consider why we work and conclude that it is not just to earn a living but to be self-actualized persons and all that this entails. Yet as essential as work is, there are potential negatives. The authors address six risks—being defined by work, workaholism, burnout, downsizing and underutilization, impersonality, and fear—and show how spirituality offers solutions to these critical problems. By bringing balance to our work, and reminding us that our lives are more than our work, spirituality in the workplace can

*help us and our coworkers, our families, and our friends live balanced
lives with integrity and authenticity.*

THE MEANING OF WORK

Why do we work?

"A silly question," someone might say. "I need to work to earn a
living, buy food, and have a roof over my head." Most people must
"work to live"; most of us need to earn an income to live in our society. Work is an essential part of our lives.

Work also gives meaning to our lives. We try to choose work that
we find interesting, work that fits who we are. Some of us feel that we
are called to our work. Many of us are lucky enough to have jobs that
are satisfying, challenging, and fulfilling. Of course, the lifetime job
guarantee is no longer a reality, and many of us change jobs and professions during our lives. Yet even this is not necessarily a bad thing;
changing jobs can be revitalizing for the individual and the work
organization.

Work meets human needs on many levels. In psychologist
Abraham Maslow's famous hierarchy of needs, all five levels of need
have a relationship to work, starting with physiological and biological
needs, moving to safety, belongingness and love, esteem, and self-
actualization.[1] While not everyone's work will meet all five of these
needs (especially self-actualization, which is essentially being "all
that you can be"), many people find personal growth and fulfillment
in their work.

Yet there are many jobs that do not provide self-actualization
and, hence, spiritual meaning. For many people, work is routine,
repetitive, and even hazardous. This kind of work may meet physiological, safety, and belongingness needs, but does not contribute to
spirituality. Certainly there are other ways that people in routine jobs
can achieve self-esteem and self-actualization, such as through family, volunteer work, music, and many other outlets. But if work and
other activities do not promote spirituality, or even negate spirituality, then we have potential alienation and normlessness, a life devoid
of meaning, a life that becomes a struggle just to get along day-to-day.

The key is not to "live to work," not to let work become a
destructive force by invading our lives. We are all more than our

work. We are sons and daughters, spouses, parents, grandparents, friends. We are volunteers. We care for other people. We have hobbies. We are tourists. We sing in the choir. When people survive a life-threatening disease or disaster, they typically conclude that they will enjoy life more now that they know what is important to life—and the answer is not more work.

Yet this does not mean that work cannot contribute to our spirituality. If spirituality is a search for meaning in our lives, then work can help provide answers to the search. If work is relevant to self-transcendence and spirituality, then we can conclude that work has its place at all levels on Maslow's hierarchy. Some authors have posited that spirituality, or self-transcendence, should be a need one level higher than self-actualization,[2] which implies that a spiritual sense of being is the ultimate need of humans. It takes us beyond our ego needs to a concern for universal needs.

There is a great deal of interest in spirituality among organizational leaders, and a growing body of literature on this topic. Joan Marques, Satinder Dhiman, and Richard King, researchers and authors on workplace spirituality and organizational performance issues, and editors of this book, make a strong point for why spirituality in the workplace matters. [3] William Guillory, another researcher and author on these topics, argues that "spirituality is the life force that permeates and drives a Living Organization in the pursuit of its business objectives."[4] And the authors of this chapter have addressed the topic of "engaging spirituality to meet the challenges of the workplace" in our book *Working with Spirit: Engaging Spirituality to Meet the Challenges of the Workplace.*[5]

The question for business leaders is how organizations can create a climate of spirituality. Is it possible to do our work and find serenity, to give work its proper role in our lives without being consumed by it? How can spirituality address work-related problems?

There are many potential problem areas of work that we could investigate, but we believe spirituality can offer a countering life force that can offset the problems created by work in six particular areas: the risk of being defined by work, the impersonality of the work world, workaholism, burnout, downsizing and underutilization, and fear in the workplace.

The Risk of Being Defined by Work

Why do we tend to introduce ourselves to others in terms of the work that we do ("I'm Fred Evers, director of teaching support services at the University of Guelph," or, "I'm Lucy Reid, Anglican priest in Victoria, British Columbia") rather than by the relationships that are key to our lives ("I'm Fred Evers, husband of Susan, father of Jerry and Courtney, and grandfather of Halle," or, "I'm Lucy Reid, married to David, mother of Tom, Kate, and Ben")? As with most people, we would both say that our families are more important to us than our jobs, yet it is common to define ourselves by our work. In most cases, this is not a serious problem. It becomes a problem, however, if we define ourselves *exclusively* by our work. If we are what we do at work, then what happens when we retire or are laid off or are unable to find a job? Are we then no one? Are we no longer a person?

Allowing ourselves to be defined by our work can potentially lead to psychological problems—even suicide, in extreme cases where people lose their jobs or feel as if they have failed completely at their jobs. No matter what the status of our work, we need to know that we are more than our work. We need to recognize that we, and the people we work with, have feelings and abilities. We each have a unique place in a larger social network.

Spirituality can be a powerful force for self-definition and fulfillment. Because spirituality concerns issues beyond the material and quantifiable, it takes us past the usual job-related norms of success and failure and reminds us that, ultimately, our "doing" is less important than our "being." Spirituality can be a key component in helping us understand who we are and honoring what is important to us.

People need to be proud of their work and feel that it relates to their spirituality. The problem emerges when work becomes 100 percent of who we are. We need to feel that we are a whole person with work, family, volunteer activities, hobbies, and so forth all contributing to who we are. Employers need to be aware of the whole person: Do employees have families? What do employees do outside of work? Are there ways that employees' outside pursuits can be assisted by the organization? Workplace teams, for example, can provide an opportunity for employees to know each other better. Team members will form stronger relationships with each other than they may have otherwise, and employers can check with team leaders to ensure that employees are not feeling consumed by their work.

THE IMPERSONALITY OF THE WORK WORLD

"It's just business." A statement like this is often used to justify poor behavior or hurtful comments. The workplace can force us to define who we are as less than who we really are. It can promote a personification that is stripped of anything that is judged as nonessential in terms of the jobs we do. Asking a colleague how his or her family is doing is a small break in the norm. Some organizations connect with their employees more effectively than others, realizing that a holistic view of employees is important. But the norm is impersonality, a climate where what someone can do for the organization is the most important factor.

It is interesting to look at people's desks. Most of them include pictures of the family and little tokens that relate to the other side of who they are. An archaeologist researching organizations in a few hundred years might make a lot out of these artifacts on our desks. Are they an attempt to make the job relate to the whole being of who we are?

Spirituality is the opposite of impersonality. Spirituality promotes integrity of individuals, all aspects of their being. It celebrates the unique aspects of individuals and affirms their humanity in all circumstances. No one is a mere cog in a machine.

A workplace that values the spirituality of its employees promotes all aspects of their being. Large organizations might provide daycare facilities, exercise rooms, or meditation rooms to take a break. Company parties might include partners and families. "Check-ins" at meetings could invite personal stories of activities outside of work. In-house Web pages could include information about the employees' families, hobbies, and volunteer activities.

It should be noted that this openness might feel odd to some employees at first. "Why are they doing this?" they might wonder. "Is there some ulterior motive?" Once it becomes clear, however, that this climate of personalization is the norm within the organization, most employees will embrace it.

Workaholism

Workaholism is a matter of letting work take over our lives. Just as an alcoholic is consumed and controlled by alcohol, a workaholic is consumed and controlled by work. Work always comes before family, leisure, and other activities. A workaholic typically puts off vacations for a long time, and when he or she finally goes on vacation, takes work along on what should be a total break. Workaholics display an addiction to work and what it symbolizes, as well as a fearfulness about the consequences of not working. They can also use work as an anesthetic to numb underlying pain and difficulties.

Many of today's technologies contribute to being immersed in work. Personal digital assistants allow people to check e-mail no matter where they are. Is e-mail really that important? Would it really hurt to be unharnessed from 24/7 electronic work? A spiritual culture within a company can go a long way toward defusing workaholism. What if slowing down at appropriate intervals and enjoying all aspects of life were encouraged? What if Sabbath time, simplicity, and balance were values as important as productivity and profit? It could be a lifeline to a saner relationship with work.

Burnout

In their review of research on job burnout, authors and reseachers Cynthia Cordes and Thomas Dougherty describe burnout as "a unique type of stress syndrome, characterized by emotional exhaustion, depersonalization, and diminished personal accomplishment."[6] Burnout is a situation where the individual can no longer cope with the demands of work for a short or long period. All of us feel burnout to a certain extent, regardless of our jobs. It can be caused by stress over layoffs in various industries, or it can occur when people are in a job or career position they do not like.[7] Sometimes employees may feel they are not getting the rewards or the gratitude they deserve. This may cause them to work longer hours and become more frustrated by the situation. Burnout can then result from the extra hours they feel are important to obtaining positive feedback.

Dealing with burnout might result in the decision to change jobs. It might involve reassessing the fit between our jobs and our personalities and abilities. Less extreme solutions than quitting include leaving on time each day, taking vacation time, and prioritizing tasks.[8]

Spirituality can help level out the stresses of work by reminding us that there is much more to life than work. It can also put work into its appropriate context as an important, but not all-important, part of our lives. Spirituality can also help us with self-evaluations that can aid us in determining the best job fit for us. "Know thyself" is a core spiritual goal, and along with self-appraisal comes self-acceptance, so that we can pace ourselves, be realistic about ourselves, and settle into our work with more peace.

A spiritual workplace has many opportunities to reduce burnout. Job evaluations might help people consider their "fit" in a position, as much as what they can produce. Perhaps another job in the company would more closely fit their personality, or work with their family schedule better, or help them use their potential more. A spiritual workplace might put a high priority on giving thanks for a job well done, or expressing appreciation for that extra stretch of long hours to meet a deadline. A spiritual workplace would appreciate the whole person, not just for work-related abilities, but for personality, unique abilities, and contribution to the spirit of the work environment.

DOWNSIZING AND UNDERUTILIZATION

Organizations change over time. They expand and contract in order to meet market fluctuations. Universities, for example, are going through a downsizing due to the retirement of baby boom generation professors. While not necessarily downsizing intentionally, some institutions may take advantage of the high number of retirees to meet shrinking budgets. The auto industry is also going through intentional downsizing due to lagging sales and increasing gas prices. The impact is great not only on automakers but also on all of the industries that relate to automakers. In Ontario, Canada, for example, for each job lost in the auto industry, it is estimated that seven people in the wider community are affected.[9]

In a study on the effect organizational downsizing has on the health of employees, researchers and authors Mika Kivimäki, Jussi Vahtera, Jaana Pentti, and Jane E. Ferrie found that "downsizing results in changes in work, social relationships, and health related behaviours."[10] They noted that sickness absence was attributable to adverse changes in work characteristics, the most important of which were increases in physical demands, job insecurity, and reductions in job control.

Downsizing not only affects the people laid off but also those who remain in the organization. Using the National Longitudinal Survey of Youth for the years 1992–1994, researchers and authors C. David Dooley, JoAnn Prause, and Kathleen A. Ham-Rowbottom found a relationship between inadequate employment (part-time or low wage) and depression (controlling for previous depression). They also found that the relationship existed despite mediator variables such as income, job satisfaction, and marital status. Marital status did buffer the relationship, while education and job dissatisfaction amplified the relationship.[11]

How can spirituality address this situation? For starters, a spiritual company can approach the issue of downsizing and layoffs with compassion and support. While layoffs might be inevitable, the way they are handled can be empathetic and caring. Recognition should be given for the employees' service, sadness expressed for the hard realities, and every effort made to treat people with kindness and realistic help to survive the changes ahead—both for those losing their jobs and for those remaining. Counselors could be brought in, job-search firms contacted, reasonable lead times offered, and follow-up support put into effect.

While spirituality cannot remove the worry of losing a job or the frustration of underemployment, it can put these things into the context of a person's whole life. The Serenity Prayer, attributed to Reinhold Niebuhr and used by Alchoholics Anonymous and other recovery groups, is perhaps the best example of a spiritual prayer to help people cope with difficult situations:

> *God grant me the serenity*
> *to accept the things I cannot change;*
> *courage to change the things I can;*
> *and wisdom to know the difference.*

This prayer acknowledges a higher being, a force that can help us with life's most difficult situations. It speaks to the truth of needing to find the inner equilibrium to deal with adversity. It does not promote acquiescence to difficulties, but asks for courage to make changes to life's circumstances. This kind of spirituality is not a soft cushion to escape into, but a source of resilience, stability, and purpose. In an uncertain work world, fostering this kind of personal spirituality will go a long way toward helping people find the inner serenity and wisdom to withstand the chaos of downsizing.

FEAR IN THE WORKPLACE

Unfortunately, fear at work is a silent problem that we do not address very often. Some may feel intimidated by others. Others may fear using different equipment at work. Some workers may fear being open with their colleagues. In their book *Driving Fear Out of the Workplace,* consultants Kathleen Ryan and Daniel Oestreich identify four key themes about the fear of speaking up at work: the relationship with the boss is of key importance; a little bit of fear goes a long way; when threatened, people react with strong emotions; and in spite of fear, the organizations they studied seemed to operate satisfactorily.[12]

The relationship between employee and boss is about climate: is there an open climate created by the way the boss interacts with workers? Ryan and Oestreich point out that 70 percent of the 260 people they interviewed said that they hesitate to speak up because they fear repercussions. They also found that people are not objective about their jobs; they take their jobs personally, so they are strongly affected by the climate. Overall, Ryan and Oestreich found fear to be an undercurrent even in the organizations that are generally successful. They argue that reducing fear changes the underlying characteristics of the organization, and they conclude that "reducing fear is an essential component of organizational transformation."[13]

Spirituality in the workplace can help reduce fear by promoting and fostering mutual respect, honesty, and courage. In cases where an employee has blown the whistle on the employer or organization for unethical practices, for example, there has to be a high level of courage and honesty for the individual to face the fear of speaking out. A supportive community of those who share values and ethics can be invaluable, and because spirituality is closely linked with community, this is another way in which the work environment can be enhanced and made healthier through spirituality.

The Path to Serenity

These, then, are some of the core problems that can impact wellness within organizations. Understanding the role of spirituality in the workplace environment can address and alleviate these problems. Whether by creating a mutually supportive sense of community; or by refocusing priorities; or by promoting balance, self-knowledge, and integrity, fostering the spirituality of employees and employers can foster wellness at work. The means might be lunch-hour discussion groups, meditation times, workshops, prayer groups, or individual practices. But whatever form it takes, spirituality looks beyond the surface and calls forth a deeper response to life's challenges, based on authenticity, wisdom, and courage.

The ancient Chinese Sage Lao-tzu, in the classic text we know as the Tao Te Ching, advises that if we "chase after money," our hearts "will never unclench"; if we seek "other people's approval," we will be "their prisoner." In the end, doing our work and then stepping back is "the only path to serenity."[14]

Perhaps these words from 2,500 years ago hold the key to addressing wellness problems in the workplace through spirituality. We can do our work and find serenity. We can give work its proper role in our lives without being consumed by it. We can enjoy our work and our lives.

■ ■ ■

Tanis Helliwell, MEd, is the founder of the International Institute for Transformation (IIT), which offers programs to assist individuals in becoming conscious creators to work with the spiritual laws that govern our world. IIT programs are offered in Canada, the United States, Germany, Ireland, Italy, and Holland. She is the author of *Take Your Soul to Work, Summer with the Leprechauns, Decoding Destiny: Keys to Mankind's Spiritual Evolution,* and *Embraced by Love.* Tanis is also a sought-after keynote speaker and has worked for almost thirty years as a consultant to businesses, universities, and government, both to create healthy organizations and to help people develop their personal and professional potential. Her clients include the McKinsey Corporation, IBM, the World Business Academy, the David Suzuki Foundation, the Banff Centre–Leadership Programs, the Alberta Medical Association, and the World Future Society. She lives on the seacoast north of Vancouver, Canada, and for over twenty years has led people on tours and pilgrimages to sacred sites. Both in her corporate and spiritual work, she is committed to helping people develop right relationships with themselves, others, and the earth. For information on her upcoming retreats and books visit www.iitransform.com.

Overcoming Fear and Building Trust
Creating Healthy Organizations

TANIS HELLIWELL, MED

Helping others to develop their potential not only translates into sound economic sense, it also builds long-term loyalty, high productivity, and enthusiasm. Like a magnet, it attracts people. To create healthy organizations, it is essential to have trust among the executives, managers, and staff. Individual fears undermine trust and manifest in the forms of territorialism, aggression, depression, and escapism. This chapter offers a questionnaire to help you identify the major areas that you and your organization need to examine in order to build trust, commitment, and morale, as well as offering concrete and simple, but effective, ways to motivate others, and better still, to motivate yourself to rise to your potential.

"Life is either a daring adventure or it is nothing."
—*Helen Keller*

FEAR IN ORGANIZATIONS

A great many of the decisions made in organizations in North America are driven by fear. Fear is the flipside of motivation. Motivation in the workplace gets lots of attention, from incentive programs to performance rewards to inspirational posters. Understanding motivation is important because it helps us examine what people strive for in their lives and why there are differences among us. Studies on how people are motivated range from psychologists Frederick Herzberg and Abraham Maslow's research on the reasons why people work, through management consultants Peter Drucker and Peter Block's studies in management, to business founders Daniel Yankelovich's writings on ways to motivate different age groups and Patrick Lencioni's work on teams.[1]

However, these studies on motivation provide only half of the picture—the half that is concerned with what pushes and drives people to get what they want. Let's call this the positive (+) force. If we are to fully understand what keeps people—and their organizations—from becoming all that they could be, why they do not actively seek what they want, both in their organizational and in their personal lives, we also need to look at the negative (-) force. This comes from the fears that hold people back. While motivation increases the chances of attaining our goals, fear decreases them (see figure 5).

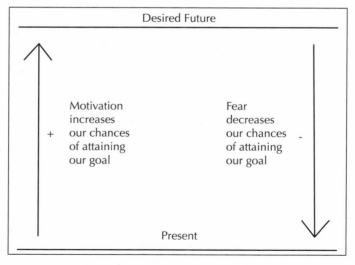

Figure 5: Motivation vs. fear

Human energy naturally moves outward to strive, create, change, learn, and develop. Unlike animals, people have goals, hopes, and dreams that pull them out of bed each morning, and, most important, people measure the success of their lives based on whether they have achieved these goals. These goals are highly individualistic and depend on each person's set of values. For example, some people say their high point in life was having children, others say it was becoming a vice president, and still others say that life began at fifty, when they packed in their one-hundred-and-fifty-thousand-dollar-a-year job to write a book.

What is important to people is not so much *which* goals they set for themselves, but that they *achieve* their goals. These are the intrinsic motivators of which Frederick Herzberg speaks in *Work and the Nature of Man.*[2] People work at their full potential when they are physically, emotionally, mentally, and spiritually engaged in striving for the goals that they desire. However, this does not happen very often in our organizations, and one of the major causes is fear, both on the part of the individual and of the organization.

Negative Effects of Fear

One of the insidious characteristics of fear is that even irrational fears appear rational. When people are fearful, they are in an unbalanced emotional state. They lose their perspective. They take examples of what is not going right and extend them into visions of doom. Fear has a clinging quality that covers everything in a murky gray. When people are fearful, they see the glass as half empty instead of half full and look for supporting evidence for why they cannot get what they want.

Although fear is an emotion, there is an erroneous thought that lies behind it: the scarcity mentality that there is not enough love, success, money, and happiness for everyone. This thought inevitably leads naturally to the next, that there are winners and losers. Having made that connection, people then put themselves into one of these two categories, based on their self-esteem and life experience.

How people react to fears depends on their temperament. Aggression, depression, escapism, and territorialism are four of the most common reactions.

Aggression

Some people become angry with others and see others as the reason for their own lack of movement toward their goal. They see others as tyrants and seek revenge in the coffee room by defaming the character of their opponents. These people have a great desire to be number one, the one above the crowd, the winner. When they do not achieve this because someone else gets a job that they want, they resort to aggression.

The life view of these aggressors contains only two kinds of people: winners and losers. If they are not the winner, they must be the loser, and this thought causes them great distress. This reaction is often seen in organizations when individuals become jealous of another's success and use their energy negatively to sabotage the other person, rather than constructively to clean up their own act and change their behaviors or skills in order to become promotable.

Depression

When passive individuals are fearful, they have a tendency to sink even further into themselves and become self-pitying and depressed. They are all too willing to accept the label of victim and wallow in thoughts of loss and deprivation in their lives. In this mental state, these people may resort to addictions to cigarettes, alcohol, pills, or food to anaesthetize the pain of a life not lived. They lack energy and are lethargic because they are holding their energy back from taking action to achieve their goal. These individuals are easily recognizable by their "poor me" and "nothing good ever happens to me" approach to life.

Escapism

Other individuals refuse to confront their fears by engaging in escapist activities. They are not prepared to commit to taking charge of their life and so engage in fantasies to stay in a childlike state with little or no responsibility. This may be your "Peter Pan" man or woman who does the minimal amount of work to keep his or her job. He or she drifts through the office, socializing, wasting other people's time, living from weekend to weekend and holiday to holiday.

Territorialism

There are also those individuals who respond to fear by channeling their energy into protecting their territory. These people are suspicious and guard information. They are narrow-minded, opinionated, and rigid. They do not want anyone to know how to do their jobs because they want to be irreplaceable. They do, in fact, often achieve that goal, because they are not promotable. No one knows how to do their jobs, and so they get to hang on to them for years. The best managers hire the best subordinates and train them to master their jobs so they are able to move on, but a mediocre boss wants to have even more mediocre employees because he or she is afraid of being eclipsed.

■

These negative effects of fear manifest when people hold themselves back from doing something they really want to do. Whether it is a fear that someone will not like them, that they will be fired, or that they will fail, the end result is that fearful people end up denying themselves the potential of what they are able to become. The same thing happens with organizations.

HOW ORGANIZATIONS CREATE FEAR

It is important to separate fears that organizations cause from fears that individuals have regardless of what the organization does. This is not an easy task, as the two are often interconnected and feed each other. A good place to start is by examining some prevalent fears that executives, managers, and employees have when they work in organizations that have been adversely affected by external forces, such as an economy in recession.

Executive Fears

- There are shrinking markets for our products.
- Our employees can't think as well as our company's biggest competitor.
- We don't have the right technology or people or answers to solve our problems.

Manager Fears

- I'll be a victim of downsizing and the current trend to level the organizational structure.

- I'll be caught in the middle between what my bosses, my employees, and my customers want.
- I'll lose control and seniority after years of working my way up in this organization.

Employee Fears

- I'm the lowest on the totem pole and have the least power, so I'll be the first to go.
- I can't say what I want because I'll be fired.
- I can't trust anyone to look after my needs.

The negative effects of these fears in organizations are self-evident. Fearful people do not do their best work. If you are spending your time and energy watching your back, covering yourself, playing it safe, and falling in step with someone else's idea of what is important, then you are not fulfilling your potential. Not only are you miserable as an individual, but the organization is getting only a fraction of what you could give if you were not controlled by fear.

Fear contaminates. Executives may be fearful because their organization has a decreased market share and reduced profits hurt organizations. The decisions they make to turn the company back to prosperity may have long-term ramifications for the employees.

Take the case of someone I will call "John." John has worked for Company X for twenty years. He is a loyal employee, a hard worker who is willing to put in extra hours to get the job done. He prides himself on his dependability, and one of the major reasons he has worked for Company X is that they reward their employees with security and a feeling of being part of a family.

Within the last few years, however, John feels as if the rug has been pulled out from under him. Because of a downturn in Company X's profits, many people have been let go. Friends and colleagues with just a few years more seniority than he has were strongly encouraged to retire and are now gone. Worse still, many of them have been unable to find work.

Still reeling from the withdrawal of his support system, John has to implement new management practices. He is no longer a manager but a team leader. John sees this as a demotion and no longer knows what is expected of him. Furthermore, his company is not recovering in the marketplace, and there will likely be more staff cutbacks. John is afraid that if he does not catch on quickly and prove his worth, he will be the next to be terminated.

It is easy to see how John, with his fears of failure, rejection, the unknown, and losing control, is not going to do his best job. When people are fearful, they contract. They become less than they were. When people are secure in their jobs and the roles they play, they expand. They become greater than they were.

If we look at the same situation from Company X's viewpoint, we might conclude that Company X acted to survive. They were over-staffed and had to let people go. Their old organizational practices were not working, so they implemented self-managed work teams. Company X does not guarantee lifetime employment and believes that those people who wish to stay employed must be willing to change.

Company X may have taken the best solution available to them, but the point is that they generated a great deal of fear in John and other employees by these events. Organizations can offer courses in project management, strategic planning, and team building, but changing the outer form of the organization without dealing with the inner concerns of the people is a recipe for disaster. If the spoken or unspoken fears of employees like John are not defused, it will take the organization longer to create the new working structure that it wants. That is the best-case scenario. In the worst case, the organization will not survive because the underlying needs of the employees are never met.

TAKING INVENTORY OF THE FEAR IN YOUR ORGANIZATION

While understanding fear—what it is, what causes it, and what its effects are—is important, we need more than just intellectual knowledge if we will make any changes in the workplace. The place to start is where you are. The following questionnaire has been designed to help identify the major areas that need to be examined if your organization wishes to rebuild trust, commitment, and morale among its employees.

FEAR INVENTORY

Answer the following questions by circling the numbers that best represent your opinions.

Never	Sometimes	Often	Most of the time		
1	2	3	4	5	1. I am afraid to tell people in my organization what I really think.
1	2	3	4	5	2. People say one thing and do another in my organization.
1	2	3	4	5	3. The rules in my organization change too often for me to figure out what I'm supposed to be doing.
1	2	3	4	5	4. My ideas and opinions are not encouraged.
1	2	3	4	5	5. My loyalty and hard work are not being rewarded.
1	2	3	4	5	6. It seems as if we are always attempting to fix symptoms but are not dealing with the underlying causes of the problems.
1	2	3	4	5	7. People who play it safe and uphold the status quo are rewarded; people who question it are not.
1	2	3	4	5	8. I do not trust the ethics of people with whom I work.
1	2	3	4	5	9. I do not respect the abilities and skills of my coworkers.
1	2	3	4	5	10. I am not involved in decisions that directly affect me.
1	2	3	4	5	11. People are unwilling to take responsibility for their mistakes and try to pass the buck.
1	2	3	4	5	12. I do not get support and credit for my ideas.

Scoring

Write the number you chose for each of the questions in the table below. Add each column down, placing the total in the bottom box. Finally, add the bottom row across to get a total.

Self-Expression	Ethics	Leadership	Total
1	2	3	
4	5	6	
7	8	9	
10	11	12	

Interpreting Your Scores

- The greater your total score, the greater you perceive the fear to be in your organization.

  12 to 25: indicates a reasonably healthy organizational climate

  26 to 36: indicates areas where your organization needs improvement

  Above 36: indicates a high level of fear in your organization

- In which area—self-expression, ethics, or leadership—is the fear greatest?

- To check your perceptions, you may wish to give this questionnaire to others (e.g., coworkers, subordinates) for their opinion.

Reducing Fear in Organizations

Psychologist Frederick Herzberg said that there are two reasons why people work: intrinsic motivators and extrinsic hygiene factors.[3] Intrinsic motivators are things that make us grow, feel productive, and learn. Extrinsic hygiene factors make our life comfortable and safe. Herzberg discovered that no number of extrinsic factors would give us happiness or purpose in our life and work. Only intrinsic motivators can do that. However, without extrinsic factors, we may, in their absence, experience severe discomfort.

Intrinsic Motivators	Extrinsic Factors
• Challenging work	• Job security
• Learning	• Comfortable routine
• Personal growth	• Society approves of us
• We work at something we value	• Money is our reason for working
• We push our boundaries	• We know our job inside out

In today's working world, fear is running rampant because people have lost their former extrinsic factors, and their intrinsic motivators are not being met in their jobs. People will move more quickly to embrace new ideas if both intrinsic and extrinsic rewards are present. That is the ideal solution, but it is difficult to achieve in these economic times.

I believe that there is a tendency in evolution for people to move toward intrinsic motivators. It is increasingly difficult for organizations to promise extrinsic factors, such as job security, money, and unchanging jobs. Therefore, it is in the best interest of organizations to build intrinsic motivators into their companies to attract good workers. If organizations give people the opportunity to do challenging work that they personally value, they will have an incredibly dedicated and creative work force. This is just the opposite of fear.

How can organizations reward the intrinsic needs of employees? Although there is a lot of talk about Total Quality Management (TQM) and learning organizations, there is often a gap between the theory and the practice within organizations. This gap creates and feeds people's fear. If we are seriously interested in transforming organizations to a new productive structure, we need to find ways to close this gap.

FOUR STEPS TO A HEALTHY ORGANIZATION

1. Display competence, vision, and ethics.

Warren Schmidt conducted a survey of 1,500 managers for the American Management Association and asked, "What is the most important quality a leader needs?" The top answer, given by 88 percent of respondents, was "honesty," which was followed closely by "competence" and "vision."[4]

2. Encourage trust and dispel fear.

If employees believe that their leaders are ethical as well as competent, trust will greatly increase within the organization. When trust increases, fear decreases. People will have a feeling of pulling together; one for all and all for one.

3. Develop a sense of support and belonging.

When employees feel that they are an essential part of the team, they become more tolerant of interpersonal differences, more understanding, and more helpful, while at the same time becoming more direct and honest. They have a greater willingness to take risks in their relationships because they understand that both parties are striving toward the same goal.

4. Encourage creativity.

Taking the first three steps leads to synergistic problem solving. Synergy is based on the principle that one plus one equals three, and that two heads are better than one. Both individuals and teams become more creative, and this starts a spiral of expanded growth for both the organization and its members.

■

Taking these four steps will help fear-filled organizations transform into organizations where people feel that their intrinsic physical, emotional, mental, and spiritual needs are met. Stephen Covey, author and internationally respected leadership authority, said in his best-selling *The Seven Habits of Highly Effective People* that it is difficult to find organizations that reward the spiritual needs of employees.[5]

By "spiritual," Covey means that people feel that they are doing something that they intrinsically value.

Decades ago, psychologist Abraham Maslow called this quality "self-actualization" and said that only 10 percent of people are leading self-actualized lives.[6] That leaves 90 percent of people unhappy in their work and/or personal life. Why does this happen?

I think it comes back to fear. As a consultant, I sometimes start my work with an organization by asking its executives, managers, and employees, "What are your physical, emotional, mental, and spiritual needs and to what extent are they being met by the organization?" I have discovered repeatedly that people can easily identify what these needs are; they know what they want. It is seldom, however, that the organization is meeting these needs.

People are not asking for a million dollars, to be head of the company, or to be a vice president at age twenty-one. Their goals are, on the whole, reasonable and in keeping with their innate talents and interests. People are not asking to be different than what they are; they want to be more fully who they are.

I believe that organizations and individuals share joint responsibility for failing to make this happen, and that failure is the result of either or both operating from fear. I once heard management guru Tom Peters say that if you have not been fired by age thirty, you are not pushing your boundaries. In order to be productive at work, people need to push their boundaries. They need to seek to move beyond their fears, to ask for what they need.

Likewise, organizations need to encourage this exploration and not fire these people, as they might have done in the past when such behaviors would have been labeled "undisciplined, rebellious, not following rules." Organizations must ask themselves if they want robots that fall into line or if they want creative thinkers. Do we want people who are living 25 percent of their potential working for us or do we want people who are 100 percent engaged? E. F. Schumacher, economist and author of *Small Is Beautiful: A Study of Economics as If People Mattered,* wrote many years ago that we have a "moron shortage" in our world.[7] He was referring to the collapse of old hierarchical structures of organizations, where 90 percent of the people were treated as morons. The new emerging structures of organizations are designed to empower people to have more control of their work, and this will help them meet their intrinsic needs.

New organizational structures initially cause more fear, but ultimately, executives, managers, and employees will become more self-confident as they learn the new rules and master new skills. To reduce fears, we need to motivate people through support, recognition, and achievement, while at the same time reducing the organizational behaviors that undermine them.

■ ■ ■

Richard Barrett is the founder and chairman of the Barrett Values Centre. He is an internationally recognized author, consultant, and keynote speaker on values-based leadership. He works with CEOs and senior executives in North and South America, Europe, Australia, and Asia to develop vision-guided, values-driven organizational cultures that strengthen financial performance, build cultural capital, and support sustainable development. He is the creator of the internationally recognized Cultural Transformation Tools (CTT), which have been used to support more than one thousand organizations in forty-two countries in their transformational journeys. Mr. Barrett is the author of *Spiritual Unfoldment: A Guide to Liberating Your Soul*, *Liberating the Corporate Soul: Building a Visionary Organization*, and *Building a Values-Driven Organization: A Whole System Approach to Cultural Transformation*. He is a contributing author to *Psychometrics in Coaching*, chapter 15: "Coaching for Cultural Transformation." Mr. Barrett is a fellow of the World Business Academy, and former values coordinator at the World Bank. For more information, visit the Barrett Values Centre website at www.valuescentre.com.

Liberating the Corporate Soul

Building a High-Performance, Values-Driven Organization

RICHARD BARRETT

Values stand at the very core of human decision making. When we work in an organization whose culture aligns with our personal values, we feel liberated. We are able to bring our full selves to work. We not only bring our energy, our creativity, and our enthusiasm, we also bring our commitment to the well-being of our associates and the success of the organization. Unleashing this energy is tantamount to liberating the corporate soul.

THE CENTRAL ROLE OF VALUES

There are five critical issues preoccupying the boardrooms of both large and small companies around the world:
- How do we increase profits and shareholder value?
- How do we attract and keep talented people?

- How do we build brand loyalty?
- How do we ensure that ethics permeate the corporate culture?
- How do we build a resilient, sustainable company?

There are also five critical issues facing the leaders of our public services:

- How do we increase cost effectiveness?
- How do we deliver high-quality, affordable services?
- How do we attract and keep talented people?
- How do we ensure that ethics permeate the institutional culture?
- How do we build a resilient, sustainable society?

The key to these core issues, in both private- and public-sector organizations, is found in building a high-performance culture. In the private sector, the culture of the organization is the principal source of its competitive advantage and brand differentiation. In the public sector, the culture of the institution is the principal source of its effectiveness and quality of services.

My experience in mapping the values of more than one thousand private- and public-sector institutions, in forty-two countries, over the past ten years allows me to state categorically that *values-driven organizations are the most successful organizations on the planet.* The reasons for this are simple to decipher.

In the private sector:

- The values and behaviors of the leaders drive culture
- Culture drives employee fulfillment
- Employee fulfillment drives customer satisfaction
- Customer satisfaction drives shareholder value

In the public sector:

- The values and behaviors of the leaders drive culture
- Culture drives employee fulfillment
- Employee fulfillment drives mission assurance
- Mission assurance drives customer satisfaction

Note that, in both private and public sectors, the key to success—whether it is in terms of employee or customer satisfaction—begins with the values of the organization. When we speak about "values," we are talking about the deeply held principles, ideals, or beliefs that people hold or adhere to when making decisions. Individuals express their values through their personal behaviors; organizations express their values through their cultural behaviors. Values can be positive or they can be potentially limiting. For example, the positive value of trust is fundamental for creating a cohesive group culture. But, the potentially limiting value of being liked can cause people to compromise their integrity in order to satisfy their need for connection. Similarly, the potentially limiting value of bureaucracy can cause rigidity and limit the agility of an organization.

Our research at the Barrett Values Centre,[1] and that of others, shows a strong link between financial performance and the alignment of an organization's cultural values with employees' personal values. In other words, who you are and what you stand for is becoming just as important as the quality of products and services you provide.

In *Corporate Culture and Performance*, leadership expert John P. Kotter and business logistics professor James L. Heskett show that companies with strong adaptive cultures based on shared values outperform other companies by a significant margin.[2] They found that over an eleven-year period, companies that emphasized all stakeholders grew four times faster than companies that did not. They also discovered that these companies had job creation rates seven times higher, stock prices that grew twelve times faster, and profit performance that was 750 times higher than companies that did not have shared values and adaptive cultures.

In *Built to Last: Successful Habits of Visionary Companies*, Jim Collins and Jerry Porras, authors and researchers in business and leadership, show that companies that consistently focused on building strong values-driven cultures over a period of several decades outperformed companies that did not by a factor of six, and outperformed the general stock market by a factor of fifteen.[3]

CULTURE AND LEADERSHIP

The values that make up the culture of an organization are either a reflection of the underlying beliefs of the current leaders—particularly the chief executive—or a reflection of the heritage of past leaders. Most organizations operate with "default" cultures. Because no one is measuring or paying attention to the culture, the underlying values and beliefs of the leaders become "the way things are done around here."

When there is a lack of alignment between the values of the culture of the organization and the personal values of employees, the result is low performance, which can further result in low levels of staff engagement and poor quality of products and services. All of these factors can have a significant impact on the financial performance of the organization or its ability to deliver services of sustainable high quality.

However, when the values of the organization are in alignment with the aspirational values of employees, the result is high performance. There is a high level of staff engagement and a pursuit of excellence regarding the quality of products and services.

There are two other major benefits to values alignment. First, when values are aligned, the culture of an organization is able to attract and retain talented individuals. This gives organizations a significant commercial advantage, especially when talent is in short supply. Second, values alignment builds a strong brand. Brand values and company values are two sides of the same coin. *The strongest external brands are always those with the strongest internal cultures.*

Ultimately, therefore, whether we are talking about high performance, brand differentiation, or retaining talented individuals, the success of an organization is directly related to the degree of alignment that exists between the underlying values of the leaders and the aspirational values of employees. Long-term, sustainable success is highly dependent on the culture that the leaders create. Significantly, the culture that leaders create is highly dependent on the behaviors of the leaders and their relationships to other leaders in the organization, and on their relationships with their employees. Leaders whose energies are wrapped up in status seeking, empire building, and internal competition create toxic environments with little or no organizational cohesion. Leaders who share the same vision and values, who work for the common good and focus on internal community building, create internal cohesion and values alignment.

To put it another way, organizational transformation begins with the personal transformation of the leaders. Organizations do not transform; people do! The key factor to transforming a low-performance culture into a high-performance culture is leadership. This is why organizations with strong, high-performing cultures tend to replace their leaders by promoting from within, whereas low-performing cultures tend to replace their leaders with external candidates. By promoting from within, thriving cultures are able to retain their successful leadership styles with the least perturbation. Struggling cultures, on the other hand, absolutely need to change their leadership styles. That is why they typically hire from outside the company, with the hope that the new leader will bring a new way of being that translates into a more dynamic culture.

Bringing in an external leader is not the only way to transform an organizational culture. More and more companies are engaging in cultural transformation programs that involve a whole system approach, which I describe in *Building a Values-Driven Organization: A Whole System Approach to Cultural Transformation.*[4] In order to grasp the process and benefits of a whole system approach to cultural transformation, it is important to understand the differences between change, transformation, and evolution,[5] and how to measure the current and desired cultures of an organization, thereby identifying the current and desired leadership styles. From a cultural alignment perspective, it is necessary to have a clear understanding of where an organization is and where it wants to go before embarking on a program of transformation.

CHANGE, TRANSFORMATION, AND EVOLUTION

Toward the end of the last century, many organizations bought into a change concept known as reengineering. In a survey of almost one hundred reengineering projects, two-thirds were judged as producing mediocre or marginal results. The principal reason for failure was the lack of attention given to the human dimension—particularly, people's fear and anxiety of downsizing. Morale slumped in 72 percent of the companies downsized. It was later recognized that what was missing from the reengineering approach was the people or cultural dimension of change. Thomas H. Davenport, President's Distinguished Professor of Information Technology and Management at Babson College in Wellesley, Massachusetts, in an article for *Fast Company* magazine entitled "Why Engineering Failed," notes that "companies that embraced reengineering as a silver bullet are now looking at ways to rebuild the organization's torn social fabric."[6]

This is a clue to the important distinction between change and transformation. Change is a new way of *doing*. Transformation is a new way of *being*. Evolution occurs only when individuals or organizations embrace a continual state of transformation and change.

Change: A different way of doing. Doing what we do now, but doing it in a more efficient, productive, or quality-enhancing way.

Transformation: A different way of being. Involves changes at the deepest levels of beliefs, values, and assumptions. Results in fundamental shifts in personal and corporate behavior and organizational systems and structures. Transformation occurs when we are able to learn from our mistakes, are open to a new future, and can let go of the past.

Evolution: A state of continual transformation and change. Continually improving the way things are done, and at the same time making adjustments in values, behaviors, and beliefs based on learning gained from internal and external feedback. Evolution most easily occurs in systems that celebrate trust, openness, and transparency, and have a profound commitment to learning and self-development.

An Evolutionary Model for Measuring Change and Transformation

Until recently, cultural evolution has been mostly unconscious because there has been no model or tools for measuring culture. The Seven Levels of Organizational Consciousness model, also known as the Barrett model, and the Cultural Transformation Tools (CTT) created by the Barrett Values Centre, provide such a framework. It is now possible to make evolution of consciousness *conscious* by mapping the values of the organizational culture. This model is different from other culture and leadership models because it is evolutionary in nature, whereas most models that attempt to identify cultures or leadership styles are based on concepts that differentiate cultures and leadership styles into mutually exclusive categories that have no evolutionary dimension.

In the Seven Levels of Organizational Consciousness model, each stage of the evolutionary process focuses on a specific existential need. As organizations learn how to satisfy each of these needs, they grow and develop, and as they do, performance and profits improve.

Organizations that have learned to master all the existential needs operate from full-spectrum consciousness, which can best be explained as optimal or comprehensive awareness. Our Barrett Values Centre research shows that, just as full-spectrum individuals are the most effective people on the planet, full-spectrum companies and institutions are the highest-performing organizations on the planet.

The fundamental change that occurs during cultural transformation is a shift from "What's in it for me?" to "What's best for the common good?" This involves moving from an exclusive focus on the pursuit of profit to the pursuit of a broader group of objectives that are instrumental in meeting shareholder, worker, customer, supplier, community, and societal needs.

At the heart of the Seven Levels of Organizational Consciousness model is the concept that all values can be assigned to one of seven stages in the development of individual or collective awareness and consequently measured. (The measurement instruments that are used to map these values are known as the Cultural Transformation Tools, or CTT.) Figure 6 offers a brief overview of these seven levels of existential needs within organizations.

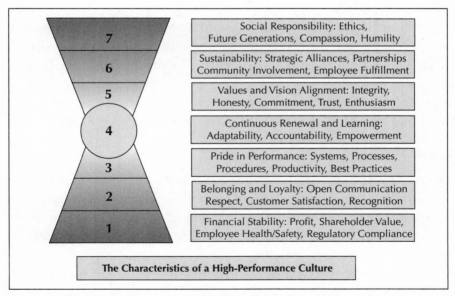

Figure 6: The Seven Levels of Organizational Consciousness model

Level 1: Financial Stability

The first need for any organization is financial survival. Without profits or access to a continuing stream of funds, it will quickly perish. Every organization needs to make financial stability and organizational growth a primary concern. A precondition for success at this level is a healthy focus on the bottom line. Companies need financial surpluses so they can invest in their employees, create new products, or build strong relationships with their customers and the local community. Organizations address the needs of their employees by focusing on job security, employee safety, remuneration, and benefits.

If leaders have fears and anxieties about satisfying their survival needs, this will be reflected in the organizational culture as an excessive focus on short-term results and shareholder value. In such situations, making the quarterly numbers—satisfying the needs of Wall Street or the owners—can preoccupy the minds of the leaders to the exclusion of all other factors. When asked to conform to regulations, they do so at a minimum and have an attitude of begrudging compliance. The anxieties and fears leaders hold about making the numbers can lead to excessive control and caution (being risk-averse), micromanagement, and employee exploitation. Organizations that operate at this level of consciousness tend to expand and grow through takeovers.

When leaders hold fears and anxieties about satisfying their level-1 needs, autocratic conduct, greed, ruthlessness, and territorial behaviors abound. Leaders who operate primarily from this level of consciousness see both people and the earth as resources to be exploited for their personal gain. It is easy for them to rationalize unethical or even illegal conduct, as was the case with Enron.

Level 2: Belonging and Loyalty

The second need for organizations is to establish a sense of belonging and loyalty among employees, and a sense of caring and connection between the organization and its customers. Preconditions for creating a sense of belonging are open communication, mutual respect, and employee recognition. Preconditions for a caring atmosphere are friendliness, responsiveness, and listening. When these qualities are in place, loyalty and satisfaction among employees and customers will be high. Tradition and rituals, such as celebrating birthdays, arrivals, and departures, help cement these bonds.

If the leaders of the organization have fears or anxieties about satisfying their relationship needs, this will be reflected in the culture as fragmentation, dissension, and disloyalty. When leaders meet behind closed doors, or fail to communicate openly, employees suspect the worst. Cliques form, cynicism develops, and gossip becomes rife. These types of behavior are particularly prevalent in family-run businesses. Other behaviors that emerge when leaders hold fears and anxieties about satisfying their level-2 needs include paternalism, favoritism, blame, insensitivity, rumor, conflict avoidance, envy, retaliation, manipulation, and interpersonal conflicts. Sexual harassment, racism, and intolerance may also show up in such organizations. Such conditions leave the organization open to lawsuits that could significantly affect reputation and brand image.

Level 3: Pride in Performance

The third need is to cultivate employee pride in performance. This is achieved by establishing policies, procedures, systems, and processes that create order and promote best practices, quality, and excellence. At this level of consciousness, organizations focus on becoming the best they can be. They set standards and measure their performance through a "dashboard" of performance indicators. Reengineering, Six Sigma, and Total Quality Management are typical responses to issues of performance in organizations that operate from this level of consciousness. These approaches emphasize professional growth and skills training.

If the leaders of the organization have fears or anxieties about satisfying their self-esteem needs, this will be reflected in the organizational culture as steep hierarchies, excessive bureaucracy, and status and prestige symbols, a "silo" and fiefdom mentality. Steep hierarchies often serve no other purpose than to cater to managers' needs for recognition, status, and self-esteem. There is a strong focus on personal achievement rather than collective achievement. Such leaders get their self-esteem from being the best *in* the world, rather than being the best *for* the world. These conditions are often seen in financial institutions, which tend to attract overachievers who are internally competitive, work long hours, and often neglect their families.

Other behaviors that show up in organizations where the leaders have unmet level-3 needs include empire building, elitism, complacency, arrogance, confusion, rigidity, internal politics, power plays, turf issues, unresponsiveness, lack of delegation, and information hoarding. Organizations need to be mindful of the part such behaviors play in creating a climate of fear, where employees do not ask questions and have no incentives to raise ethical issues.

Level 4: Continuous Renewal and Learning

The focus of the fourth level of organizational consciousness is on employee empowerment, operational agility, adaptability, innovation, continuous learning, and the personal growth and development of employees. The critical issue for the organization at this level is how to stimulate innovation so that new products and services can be developed to respond to market opportunities. This requires delegation, teamwork, flexibility, knowledge and information sharing, and the courage and willingness to take risks. A precondition for success at this level of consciousness is encouraging all employees to think and act like entrepreneurs, giving them responsible freedom (accountability) and the opportunity to make a success of their lives.

At this level, there is a shift from a culture of privilege to a culture of meritocracy. Talented individuals are identified and fast-tracked for promotion and development. Fiefdoms and the "silo" mentality are eliminated as employees freely share information and knowledge. Diversity is seen as a positive asset in developing and exploring new business ideas. Managers become process facilitators, delegating decision making to the lowest possible levels of organization. For many managers, this is a new role, requiring them to develop their emotional intelligence skills. A key factor in successfully mastering this level of consciousness is to provide opportunities for managers and employees to gain self-knowledge and understanding through personal growth and development programs.

Level 5: Values and Vision Alignment

The focus at the fifth level of consciousness is on developing a capacity for collective action by engendering employee engagement, commitment, and enthusiasm. For this to happen, leaders must develop a set of shared values, a singular purpose, and an inspiring vision for the organization that focuses on the needs of employees, the needs of customers, the needs of the community, and the needs of society.

The critical issue at this level is to increase cultural resilience by aligning the personal motivations of employees with the purpose and vision of the company, so that every person feels a sense of purpose in coming to work each day. Aligning employees' sense of personal mission with the organization's vision will create a climate of commitment, creativity, and enthusiasm. Personal productivity and creativity increase as individuals align with their passion. The purpose and vision clarifies the intentions of the organization, and the shared values provide guidance on decision making.

When the values are translated into behaviors, they provide a set of parameters that define the boundaries of responsible freedom for all leaders, managers, and employees. The values and behaviors must be reflected in all the policies, procedures, systems, processes, and structures of the organization, with appropriate consequences for those who are not willing or able to comply. A precondition for success is for every leader to "walk the talk," thereby engendering a climate of trust. Prerequisites for trust are integrity, transparency, fairness, openness, and competence.

In level-5 organizations, failures become lessons, and work becomes fun. The key to success at this level of consciousness is the establishment of a strong positive, unique cultural identity that differentiates the organization from its competitors. The culture of the organization becomes an integral part of the brand. This is particularly important in service organizations where employees have close contact with customers and the general public. In such situations the culture and brand become synonymous. At this and subsequent levels of consciousness, organizations preserve their unique culture by promoting from within.

Level 6: Sustainability

The focus of the sixth level of consciousness is on making a difference internally to employees and externally to customers, the local community, and society at large. It is about actualizing the purpose of the organization and implementing the vision. Employees need to know how they are making a difference to the success of the organization. They need a clear line of sight between what they do each day and the purpose or vision of the organization. They need to feed their souls. Without this direct line of sight, they are merely showing up.

They do the work they are given and then go home. They have no sense of connection to the organization other than to satisfy their basic needs: a paycheck, a sense of belonging, and at best, a place where they derive some sense of personal self-esteem.

At the same time, the organization needs to leverage every opportunity it has to fulfill its purpose and vision with respect to employees, customers, the local community, and society. It does this by focusing on employee fulfillment through mentoring, coaching, and giving employees an opportunity to fulfill their destinies; by connecting and collaborating with customers on the design of new products and services; by deepening the organization's relationships with suppliers who share their commitment to the local community and society; and by forming mutually beneficial partnerships and strategic alliances with other like-minded organizations to further the organization's business, community, and societal goals.

Employees and customers need to feel that the company cares about them and their futures. The local community and society need to feel that the organization is sustaining or enhancing their environment and actively creating a positive future for the community. Companies operating at this level of consciousness go the extra mile to make sure they are being responsible citizens. They support and encourage employees' activities in the local community by providing time off for employees to do volunteer work and/or making a financial contribution to the charities in which employees are involved.

A precondition for success at this level of consciousness is developing leaders with a strong sense of empathy. Leaders become mentors, thereby creating pools of talent for succession planning. Leadership development is given significant emphasis at this level of consciousness. With all these activities, the organization continues to build its long-term resilience.

Level 7: Social Responsibility

The focus at the seventh level of organizational consciousness is a deepening and expansion of the previous level: deepening the internal connectedness of the organization and expanding the external connectedness of the organization in order to more fully live the organization's purpose and implement its vision.

Internally, the leaders focus on building a climate of humility and compassion, where the development and growth of employees become their primary concern. Externally, the focus is on local, national, or global activism in building a sustainable future for humanity and the planet. Organizations begin to cooperate with governments and international agencies to change the structural parameters that prevent progress, to fund research and projects that tackle the needs of our global society, and to address environmental and ecological issues that threaten life on the planet.

The critical issue at this level of consciousness is to deepen the organization's commitment to social responsibility, social justice, and human rights, as well as to reduce environmental pollution, preserve ecological diversity, and reduce global carbon emissions. This is the level of selfless service, displayed through a profound commitment to the common good and to the well-being of future generations. To be successful at level 7, organizations must embrace the highest ethical standards in all their interactions with employees, suppliers, customers, shareholders, the local community, and society at large. They must consider the impact of all their decisions on the sustainability and long-term viability of society and the planet.

■

Ultimately, the cultural evolution of an organization is a reflection of the personal evolution of the leaders. Organizations do not transform; people do. The culture is always a reflection of leadership consciousness. Unless the leadership team makes a commitment to change personal behavior, the culture will not change. The first step in such a change is awareness—understanding the link between culture and performance.

■ ■ ■

James F. McMichael, PhD, has served as CEO, state agency executive, presidential advisor, business owner, and community leader. A proven leader, teacher, and speaker, he is a senior organization development consultant and has extensive business, academic, consulting, and training experience. His primary professional interests include team building, strategic planning and thinking, organization design, and creative problem solving. Dr. McMichael is an affiliate of the Center for Professional Development as well as a trainer in the Certified Public Manager Program, both at Florida State University. He was president of a financial management company and was a successful insurance executive. His public posts include being an early pioneer in the field of aging and retirement policy, developing the nation's first retirement plan for dairy farmers, and serving as the executive director of the Wisconsin State Commission on Aging. He has taught at Michigan State University, University of Wisconsin, Thomas College (Georgia), and Florida State University (FSU). His doctoral degree is in political science from FSU, and he is author of *The Spiritual Style of Management: Who Is Running This Show Anyway?* and *Capitalism, a Spiritual Perspective.*

Beyond the Bottom Line

Spiritual Principles for Successful Performance

JAMES F. MCMICHAEL, PHD

The problem of American business today is not that businesses make a profit. That is an essential, not a problem. A business needs to make a profit to exist. The problem is wrapped up in the seemingly desirable phrase, "maximizing profits." Customers get gouged if the firm can get away with it; employees are exploited as an expendable, temporary means of production; and stockholders suffer from extreme volatility as the market demands outlandish profits and punishes those who do not always produce. Even top management can suffer from the nonstop demand to create more profits, so they prepare their golden parachutes very well. This drive to squeeze every last drop of profit from sales has become the standard of how business is judged today. This chapter proposes six fundamental rules that organizations need to follow to survive in this culture, to meet today's challenges, and to stay spiritually sound.

THE BOTTOM LINE

The bottom line is ... the bottom line is *not* the bottom line as a reason for a company to exist! Somewhere we have gone off track with what Adam Smith saw as a means—which we came to call capitalism—for the wealth of nations to be fully developed. Actually, this eighteenth-century moral philosopher and author of *The Wealth of Nations* could have been the inspiration for a scene from a television episode of *Eli Stone,* "Waiting for That Day," where the law firm's senior partner is seen admonishing fellow partners. He tells them, "Capitalism without mercy is evil."

Capitalism is sometimes defined as amoral, nonpolitical, and focused only on profit. But I think the *Eli Stone* folks had it right, at least as far as Smith intended. In 1738, at the age of fifteen, Smith began study of his favorite subject, moral philosophy, at Glasgow University. In his twenties, he first expounded the economic philosophy, "The obvious and simple system of natural liberty."[1] Appointed Chair of Logic in 1751, then Chair of Moral Philosophy at Glasgow University in 1752, he lectured on natural theology as well as economics. In 1759, his first book, which firmly established his reputation, was *The Theory of Moral Sentiments.* Here he wrote, "How selfish so ever man may be supposed, there are evidently some principles in his nature which interest him in the fortune of others and render their happiness necessary to him though he derives nothing from it except the pleasure of seeing it."[2] As Riane Eisler, an eminent social scientist, attorney, and author, says in her book *The Real Wealth of Nations: Creating a Caring Economics,* Smith "made it clear ... that humans can and do act out of 'sentiment' for others."[3]

Smith's optimistic view of others underscored his basic premise: "By directing that industry in such a manner as its produce may be of greatest value, he intends only his own gain, and he is in this, as in many other cases, led by an invisible hand to promote an end which was no part of his intention."[4] While Smith claimed "that an individual would invest a resource, for example, land or labor, so as to earn the highest possible return on it,"[5] rational self-interest requires that you provide value so as to benefit yourself. It is by providing value that society benefits, as well as yourself.

As economic experts James D. Gwartney, Richard L. Stroup, Russell S. Sobel, and David Macpherson put it in *Economics: Public and Private Choice,* "Smith argued that a free exchange market economy would harness self-interest as a creative force. Since one gets ahead in a market economy by helping others in exchange for income, people seeking their own gain will provide valuable goods and services to others."[6]

This is the key: Providing value. That is what we have forgotten. Profit for its own sake will not work, if I read Smith right. Ultimately, we must focus on the value we provide in order to generate that return.

At some level, we have always known that there was more to this buying, manufacturing, and selling of a good or service than profit alone. But for some reason, we keep forgetting. And we seem to be forgetting more than ever these days. So let me say once again: the bottom line is not the bottom line. To put it another way, *profit is a necessary, but not sufficient, reason for an organization to exist.*

MAXIMIZING PROFITS

In common parlance today, the bottom line means profits, which is the end result that most have come to believe is the reason for a business to exist. Making a profit is not the problem. That is essential for a business to survive. The problem is wrapped up in the seemingly desirable phrase, "maximizing profits."

When it becomes apparent that everything a company does is to generate higher levels of profits, it might be a case of maximizing profits. This is something I consider to have dire consequences for the long-term future of our country, and certainly not a spiritual approach to business. I believe each of us has a mission, what some call dharma. Companies are no exception, and when the drive for profit interferes with the mission, there is a major misalignment of the forces that lead to a harmonious society.

We need to look at what has become the way of doing business today. What are some signs of maximizing profits? I doubt many firms will come out and say that profits are the only test of a successful company. But there are examples of major financial writers who basically say just that. If a company is currently generating profits and you see any combination of the following—downsizing, contracting jobs to foreign low-cost suppliers or local contract labor firms, trying to get around needed environmental restrictions, not truly responding to customer complaints (if you can find a way to make a complaint), reducing or eliminating research and development, reducing or eliminating essential fringe benefits for employees such as health-care insurance and retirement plans, requiring key employees to continually work excessive hours, looking to be acquisition targets generating large profits for a limited number of shareholders—you just might have a profit maximizer.

It is interesting to note that Delta Air Lines demonstrated a number of these characteristics while they were in bankruptcy, but they did so out of necessity. The test will be how they operate when, or if, they return to profitability. Wal-Mart also demonstrates a number of these characteristics—and they are profitable. While Delta's profit-maximizing strategies may be somewhat understandable because they are operating in a time of economic distress, Wal-Mart's foundational profit-maximizing strategy can be considered a rather disconcerting business trend.

This drive to squeeze every last drop of profit from sales has become the standard of how a business is judged today. And it completely changes the fundamentals of the business.

EFFICIENCY

Traditionally, those firms that met the needs of their customer most efficiently survived, and those that did not, perished. Recognizing and meeting customer needs and efficiency of operations were the key elements, and everybody benefited from that efficiency. Customers obtained desired services and products at competitive prices, employees were paid reasonable salaries and had good working conditions, and stockholders received a fair return on their investment.

But throw in maximizing profits and nearly everybody loses. Customers get gouged if the firm can get away with it. (Check out oil company profits today.) Employees are exploited as an expendable, temporary means of production. Stockholders suffer from extreme volatility, as the market demands outlandish profits and punishes those who do not always produce. Even top management can suffer from the nonstop demand to create more profits, so they prepare their golden parachutes very well.

Some will say measures such as "contracting out" are efficient. I do not agree. They may be temporary solutions to deal with thorny problems, but most do not save money in the long run and end up reducing quality. One illustration of this idea is the Apple ad where the Microsoft character is told that any PC problems are not his fault. After all, the parts come from everywhere and everybody, while Mac's come from their own people.

I think we need to be careful of the word *efficiency*. While we might all agree that, in an efficient economic system, "production proceeds at the lowest possible per-unit cost," the picture gets a little more focused if we say that an economic system is efficient "if it can provide more goods and services without using more resources," or, if it does not make someone "worse off" in order to make others "better off."[7]

By the same token, if we have a worldview that sees everyone as connected, as one body, so to speak, if we improve one part but hurt another, we do not have efficiency. We have a win-lose situation. What efficiency really calls for is producing the optimum amount, where everyone and everything is at its best—finding win-win solutions.

We are not talking about doggy companies here. We are talking about well-managed companies with proper priorities, such as Southwest Airlines. As they describe on their website, "Southwest Airlines is, first and foremost, a customer service organization. We simply use aircrafts to deliver this product."[8]

In the movie *Meet Joe Black,* the character of Bill Parish (played by Anthony Hopkins) tells his board of his meeting with a proposed deep-pockets purchaser in a merger highly favored by his business school–trained CEO. His thrust is that he has created his firm to be a standard of truthfulness in the media business, a standard he holds dear, but the acquiring firm has only one concern, the bottom line. Facing his own mortality, he knows that maximizing profits is not to be his heritage, and he turns down the merger. Unfortunately, in the real world, those who had the vision to create the firm are often no longer around when decisions such as this one must be made. Bottom line–focused managers might exclusively pursue profits, and the vision is gone.

Speaking of the real world, it will be interesting to see what happens to the *Wall Street Journal* in future years. Now that Rupert

Murdoch's News Corp has taken it over, will the Bancroft family's vision and purpose for the paper be maintained? What are the odds they will?

This is not about bashing management. I have been there. It is a tough job. I truly believe today's senior management is doing what they think is best. The problem lies in what we have come to consider "best." While there are some good signs of new spiritually based companies, my view of over seven thousand companies listed on various exchanges leads me to believe these emerging firms are a very small minority. The financial community is still fixated on the bottom line, and any other goals, such as going "green," are considered only inasmuch as they impact the bottom line.

INVESTOR PRESSURE

What is causing this profit-at-any-cost mentality? Nothing happens by accident. Today's executives are under a lot of pressure. To find a solution, we have to understand the situation.

It all begins with the stock exchanges. The stock exchange began in the sixteenth century, as a means for Dutch merchants to exchange interests in spice-trading companies. It got off to a rocky start, as it did not take long for the merchants to engage in extreme puffery (unsubstantiated claims of superiority or exaggerated praise) in describing their wares.

Things were not much better when the New World got into the act. In the 1700s, soon after trading in interests of various transportation issues began, one scoundrel used inside information to make a bundle off of the dupes who lacked his knowledge. After the 1929 stock market crash that marked the beginning of the Depression, Congress passed the Securities and Exchange Act to regulate the markets. Then, in 2002, after the Enron scandal and a whole series of other "cooked books" disasters, Congress tightened reporting requirements. But it is important not to be misled by big brother's intervention; the byword is still "buyer beware."

Today we deal with profit expectation inflation. Buyers *are* wary. They see extra risks, so they demand extra return. In the 1970s, a return on equity of 15 percent was considered very good. Early in this century, this would have been considered chump change. Let me quote from an excellent investment source, *Investor's Business Daily* (IBD): "Return on equity, or ROE, is calculated by dividing a company's earnings during the past four quarters by shareholders' equity. ROE indicates how well a company is being managed to allow a profit on its shareholder's money. It is also a reliable indicator of a company's future earnings. The best-performing companies tend to have ROEs of 20 to 30% and sometimes even higher. When recommending a stock, we recommend that its ROE be at least 17%."[9]

Talk about pressure! The narrow margin doesn't leave much room for do-gooder stuff.

High-tech companies requiring little capital for startup can generate very high ROEs because their equity is not very large. But the demand for higher and higher earnings still does not let up, and the demand for growth of profits becomes even greater. So you were able to get that 20 percent ROE last year but what have you done for me lately? According to IBD, "Annual earnings per share should show consistent growth over the past three to five years. Look for average annual EPS growth of at least 20% to 25%."[10]

And the pressure continues because these expectations never stop. Not only do investors look for these high growth rates, they look for them *every quarter.* One bad quarter, or even a hint of a bad quarter, and the bottom falls out of your stock, and lots of people lose lots of money, making for unhappy investors. So executives keep that golden parachute around just in case.

I am not blaming IBD; that would be killing the messenger. IBD's numbers are all data based. We need to look at why this pressure to perform exists.

In his book *Investor Capitalism,* Michael Useem, a highly regarded professor of management at the Wharton School, tells of modern efforts of large stockholders, such as pension funds and trusts, to exert more influence over corporate decisions. One of the objectives of this group is to tie executive pay to shareholder wealth; that is, if the executive is to make more, then shareholders need to make more.[11] This sounds fair if you are a shareholder, and it was probably brought about by corporate executives making huge salaries with losing companies.

A major thrust of this movement has come from fixed-benefit pension plans that seriously underfunded their liability. They now need more from their investments to make up for cutting their contributions short. Of course, many have dropped the fixed-benefit pension plan for a much cheaper 401k.

In summary, Useem says that a new order has taken place in the relationship between large investors and public stock corporations. In his list of eight new principles, the first is, "Press for performance. If company managers continue to underperform ... press for strategic change, company restructuring, or, as a final resort, the replacement of management."[12] Not much pressure there.

STOCK OPTIONS

In lieu of even more ridiculous salaries, discouraged by the $1 million deductible salary cap the IRS allows, corporations have come up with many new perks. The executive gets an option to buy the corporation's stock at a set price, usually what it is currently selling for. Instead of buying the stock, however, they work like crazy to drive up the price of the stock so that at some future date they can exercise the option, then turn around and sell the stock, making a nice profit. And how do they drive up the price of the stock? Not by just coasting along. They have to get the profits to keep the price up—not just any old profit, but bigger and bigger and bigger. You get the picture.

SHORT-TERM TRADING HORIZONS

I grew up in a buy-and-hold stock environment. You did your research, found a good company in a good industry, bought it, and monitored its progress to make sure it fit your expectations. If the stock price jumped around a little, you did not pay it much mind as long as the fundamentals stayed solid.

But with the growth of Internet trading and sophisticated stock models, many investors today are in and out of a stock in less than a day. And we are not talking small amounts of money here. These folks not only have a lot of money themselves, but they also invest for many others. A little move one way or the other can trigger massive movements of the stock. So here you are, a corporate executive. Your compensation is tied to stock price, your stock option is your ace in the hole for future delivery, and you have a board who also likes to see your price run up. So what happens to long-term planning, to taking a hit in the short term to position yourself better in the future? What happens to research and development investments?

GLOBAL COMPETITION

It used to be that American companies had to be concerned with what other American companies were doing in their market. No more. American companies are all over the world, and foreign companies are all over America. When I stopped in Georgetown, Kentucky, last year on the way home, the local motel had Japanese newspapers—in Japanese. We were told that a large Toyota plant was located there, and we saw several Japanese businesspeople working away in a conference room planning some future event. Former governor of Wisconsin Lee Sherman Dreyfus once told a story of being in a hotel overlooking Honolulu and reflecting on the ownership of most of what he saw. His line was, "The Japanese don't have to defeat us in war; they just buy us wholesale."

I get so sick of seeing "Made in China." Or, "Produce from Brazil." The dollar cannot compete with the euro or even the yen. Even Adam Smith was in favor of retaliatory tariffs. But fair trade prevails. It would be nice to not have to compete on equal terms with businesses located where labor is so much cheaper, governments freely subsidize, and protective tariffs are in place for their goods. Just put yourself in the place of American CEOs. They know they have to compete for capital. With money pouring into foreign stocks, they feel compelled to maximize profits to attract and keep the capital they need to operate.

BUSINESS SCHOOL TRAINING

I do not want to beat this to death, but most business school curricula place little emphasis on non–bottom line education. Just check out what most of our business leaders of tomorrow are taught. I know there must be some exceptions, but the greater good, the quest for purpose other than profits in the modern world, is not something I have seen emphasized. Sure, we have strategic planning courses that cover mission or other less profit-driven topics, but it is nowhere near the emphasis given to "analytical tools." Let me quote from Florida State University's business school website: "In MBA classrooms at the Florida State University College of Business, we're equipping the CEO's of tomorrow with the analytical tools needed to excel in the marketplace.... As an FSU MBA student, you'll hone skills through competitive project work with other high-achieving students. You'll grow in competence in our business school atmosphere that fosters creativity and rewards problem-solving. Here's the bottom line: Our MBA students graduate prepared to succeed."[13]

Just how do you succeed?

You'd better produce.

Produce what?

Continuous, increasing, high levels of profits.

I think you get the picture. To manage today, balancing all your constituencies is tough. We can still find companies that do a great job, but they are under siege. Most of them do not obsess about the price of their stock, not because they do not care, but because they know their job is to run a company to carry out its mission and provide valuable goods and services to its customers, to take care of its employees, to be good community citizens, to invest in the future, and to make a profit. Most of us know these companies and respect them.

The truth is, we do not trust or have high regard for or respect many corporate executives and the profit-maximizing companies they head. In a report published in the *Wall Street Journal* on September 23, 1999, reporter and editor Ronald Alsop told of a nationwide survey of 10,380 people to determine the standing of business. Businesses that consistently and favorably affected a respondent received a high rating from that person. Businesses that paid high CEO salaries, downsized, or hurt the environment were poorly regarded by respondents. Profits had little to do with people's perception of a company. "Capitalism may demand that companies chase riches, but the survey found that the average American pays little attention to profitability or stock performance when sizing up corporate character," Alsop reported.[14] Johnson & Johnson, for example, was the highest-rated company in the survey's results, yet at the same time, it had an off year in financial results and stock price. Feelings about a company can affect profits in the long run. A quarter of the survey respondents said that in the past year they had boycotted a company's products or urged others to do so when they did not agree with its policies and actions.

In addition to the content of Alsop's story, what I found interesting was the assumption that "capitalism may demand that companies chase riches." Here again, in what could be argued to be the nation's most respected financial publication, is the idea of profits (described as "chasing riches") as the core reason for a company's existence.

BEYOND THE BOTTOM LINE

In November 2004, an article in *Fast Company* examined the actual performance of the companies studied in Jim Collins and Jerry Porras's outstanding book *Built to Last: Successful Habits of Visionary Companies.*[15] In their article, "Was Built to Last Built to Last?" Jennifer Reingold, senior writer at *Fortune,* and Ryan Underwood, political editor/online news editor at *The Tennessean,* reported that all eighteen companies covered in the 1994 book were still in business to varying degrees of success. The authors reiterated that these visionary companies did certain things very differently, things that in large part were more about the internal than the external and had little to do with technology or number crunching. Among these attributes was "adhering to an ideology that went beyond the simple pursuit of profits."[16]

Again, one criteria—if not the main criteria—for their view of the companies' "success" was each company's stock performance. How about customer satisfaction? Or meeting the company's mission?

What we need to do is what many business leaders have been imploring us to do all along: realize that profit is a *result,* not the objective of a business. It is and should be a test we can apply to a product line or service to determine if that line is viable for us. In a free market system, what we are really determining is whether or not there is sufficient demand for the product at a competitive price to justify corporate investment. Our business is to provide that service or product and, in so doing, create a profit, not at an exorbitant expense to the consumer or at the sacrifice of the employee or the stockholder. *The art of spiritual management is to balance all interests so that the result is fair and equitable to all parties concerned,* including senior management.

In her delightful book *Wear Clean Underwear: Business Wisdom from Mom*, *USA Today* columnist Rhonda Abrams stresses over and over again doing the right thing in terms of values. Going beyond the bottom line, she points out that

> while a company could certainly be successful, particularly in monetary terms, by focusing on operations, marketing, and developing a strategic position, those were merely the basic necessities. If your goal is to build a great company, an exceptional company, that will survive over time, your company needs purpose and passion. A great business, it turns out, isn't a *thing* at all; it's a living entity, and it needs a heart, a soul. It needs values, standards, and responsibility.[17]

What can we do? How do we move from the bottom line being everything, to our mission being foremost and profit being a reasonable test of our ability to be in that business?[18]

There Is a Solution

We need to do something, and do it soon. A nation of minimum wage service workers cannot survive. And we cannot keep borrowing to buy. Just ask the U.S. comptroller general about our collective massive debt and what it means for our future. America's businesses need to take action, and outsourcing all our jobs to foreign countries is not the answer.

Then what is?

I propose that there are six fundamental rules that organizations need to follow to survive in this culture, to meet today's challenges, and to stay spiritually sound.

Rule 1: Do not worry about the price of your stock.

I can well remember hearing an executive from Procter and Gamble, one of the eighteen companies highlighted in *Built to Last: Successful Habits of Visionary Companies*, relate how the company operated. In effect, he said that they did not worry about the stock market; they worried about how well they were meeting their customers' needs and making sure no one else was doing a better job. Each of their product managers has profit objectives, to be sure, but what is more important is quality and customer satisfaction. That is where the profits come from. They will, and have, gotten out of product lines that do not meet their tests of value to the customer and profitability—not the profitability the market demands, but the profitability that meets their internal standards.

You determine acceptable levels of profitability, not the stock market.

People will ask, "If we do not make our stock attractive, where will we get capital to operate with?"

My response is, "The old fashioned way—earn it."

Diluting your ownership to raise capital can spur growth that may not serve you well in the long run. We have seen a lot of flash in the pans get a ton of money in initial public offerings, only to grow themselves to death. A local example is Krispy Kreme. They received a large amount of money, started new shops, and initiated new distribution systems. Their stock took off, executives bought several million-dollar homes and boom—things fell apart. They are still in business, but barely.

One of my favorite stories is about Wal-Mart founder Sam Walton after the crash of 1987. Reportedly, a group of financial writers came out to the farm to get his reaction to having lost several billion dollars the day before. His reply was, "See that corn crib over there? You can tell me it's only worth half of what it was worth yesterday, but I still have the corn."[19] Sam Walton did not spend his time worrying about stock prices. He spent time with his employees, encouraging and empowering them to take care of the customer. He knew his business.

Remember when Wal-Mart promoted that their products were made in America and still sold for less, and that they made a good profit and treated employees well? *Made in America* was even the name of Sam's book (which I recommend his kids and the others running the company read). No more. Wal-Mart is just like the rest of the profit maximizers. Target, with their employee involvement and community support, puts them to shame.

Wal-Mart shares usually sell at a higher price/earnings ratio than Target, meaning the market places more value in their earnings. But I am sure Target does not care that Wal-Mart has a higher rating. Target knows they are doing things right. Their three-year earnings-per-share (EPS) growth rate from 2005 to 2008, for example, was 18 percent, versus Wal-Mart's 9 percent. That is double the growth in earnings and doing things right!

I'll say it again: do not depend on the market to determine value for you. You determine it yourself. Those active in the market have their objectives. You have yours.

Rule 2: Rebuild the bonds with your employees.

We have a whole generation of workers who do not trust their employers, who do not intend to stay with them any longer than it takes to get a better job, and who are not interested in going the extra mile. "What have you done for me lately?" they ask. They have seen parents and friends downsized, jobs shipped overseas, pension benefits terminated, and companies using contractors and all kinds of other schemes to get out of paying fringe benefits. "Skeptical" is the kindest description of their attitudes toward employers.

You need to get them on your team, working with you to deal with all the challenges you are facing, those listed above and more. But how to do that?

Honesty is still the best policy. Let people know where things are. If you have bad news, tell them. Some will say, "If this gets out, our stock will go in the dumper." Let it. Remember rule 1. If employees decide to abandon ship, let them. The committed will stay, and you need to get rid of the rest.

Find out what they need and try your best to give it to them. I remember years ago in one of my classes, a young manager said his seasoned boss gave him the best advice he had ever gotten. The advice was simple: listen, listen, listen. That is not to say that you always have to do what your employees want, but you have to listen sincerely, and, if what they want is not possible, let them know why. I remember Tony Pearson, former general manager of Scientific Methods and one of my mentors, telling me, "Jim, everyone deserves their day in court." And you never know where the next great idea might come from.

It is also important to remember that all work and no play make for a dull job. *Have fun at work.* Create opportunities for celebrations, after-hour sports, whatever makes coming to work a joy and not drudgery.

And if you are cringing about the cost or maybe a little less "productive" time, think again of rule 1. You can still preserve your values and perform excellently in the ways that matter. You can review your pricing, look at other cost reductions (such as multiple layers of management), or eliminate marginal product lines. In other words, work on becoming more efficient and effective. If the latter means staff reductions, follow rule 2 and do your best to hold on to the "keepers" somewhere within the organization.

Rule 3: Do not try to do everything. Do less and do it well.

Merger mania drives me crazy. I think Tom Peters, author of *In Search of Excellence,* had it right when he said that merging two lousy companies does not make one great company; it makes one big lousy company.[20]

In my book *The Spiritual Style of Management,* I recommend no more than three hundred employees in any one unit.[21] Like the fast-growing and very creative Ideo corporation, I would rather have a bunch of autonomous successful units than one big mediocre machine. So it might cost you a few dollars in overhead. I do not like overhead, but sometimes the cost is worth it to build unity and identification.

Stay focused on your mission. Do not go fishing for "profitable" companies to add to your collection, thinking the more, the better. It does not work. If something is on sale, there is usually a reason. As a young executive, I helped buy a couple of companies at a real deal. It took us years to get the effects of those deals off the books, and I doubt we ever did make any money on them. Remember why you exist and always do it well. Serve the customer, get feedback, and do it better.

I know how tempting it is. You have this market, now you can add this new service or product to the mix and increase profits. Sounds good. A lot of folks have tried it. But what you lose is focus. What you get is mediocrity. Miami Subs, for example, had a great business selling submarine sandwiches and burgers. Then they added fish and chips, hot dogs, and other menu items. Following that expansion, they went out of business here in Tallahassee.

Rule 4: Do not try to compete where you should not compete.

We have to face it: the world is not fair. Some folks just have an edge we cannot beat. If Americans want to buy tons of stuff that keeps dictators and exploiters in power, what can you do? One thing you can do is not join them. You need to take the high road, not get down in the dirt with those whose standards are just not the ones you believe in and defend. Profit does not demand that you sell out to tyrants and thugs.

Think of it: our wasteful economy puts us in the position of buying oil from some folks we would not want to have over for dinner. Slave wages cause us to contract out jobs to foreign firms that we would not allow to open for business down the street. Capitalism does not demand that we chase profits regardless of the consequences. Capitalism has a conscience. Forget about maximizing profits and concentrate on value to the customer instead. Use your purchasing power to enable good people to do good work in a good environment.

I believe the world market will recognize the good we stand for and still buy American, even if it costs a little more. Good companies, doing good business with good people, will go a long way toward rebuilding the American reputation, and we will all profit.

Rule 5: Remember Adam Smith.

Smith's basic premise was that self-interest demands that we provide goods and services of value in order to benefit ourselves, which means that society will benefit from enlightened self-interest. The wealth of nations lies not in gold and silver, but in the productive capacity of its people and its enterprise. Free that power from restraint, and the "invisible hand" Adam Smith referred to will direct it to the overall common good.

If we are truly capitalists, then we must look to see how we benefit others in our attempts to benefit ourselves. Unwarranted exploitation was what Smith opposed. Exploiting employees, customers, or shareholders to maximize profit would be as repugnant to him as it is to me. I know the power of rationalization; I have used it plenty myself. But strip away all the nice-sounding phrases we like to use, and it leaves exploitation for the sake of that extra dollar of profit.

Rule 6: Let spiritual principles guide your work.

Bottom line, I believe we must be guided by principles, spiritual principles. For me, they are essential in attempting to do the right thing, to deal with all the pressures of the world and not give in to those pressures.

My good friend, Grantham Couch, PhD, former CEO, business-school professor, and fellow spiritual seeker, and I developed a list of principles that guide our lives as a result of our own experience. We do not consider them definitive, and not all may apply to everyone, but we try to use them to guide our lives and thinking in all that we do. I share them with you in hopes they will help you consider the principles you might identify for yourself:

- *Higher Power.* There is a power infinitely greater than anything we can imagine that directs this universe and everything in it, including us. We are not that power.
- *Uniqueness.* All matter in this universe is unique, and has its own particular composition and role to play to complete the universe.
- *Connectedness.* While unique, we are nonetheless interconnected, each element together creating the whole of the universe. Nothing is separate in and of itself.
- *Call to work.* We are not here to simply exist. We contribute our efforts to fulfill the universe and ourselves.
- *Organizational strategies.* Our goal is to create a place where individuals contribute their unique talents together, fulfilling their true selves and the organization's mission.
- *Long-term focus.* While anchored in the present moment, we are aware of the long-term consequences of our actions and continually seek to better the universe as we understand it.
- *Cocreation.* We are cocreators of this universe. God, our Higher Power, provides direction. We provide the action and are responsible for what we create.
- *Community.* As unique elements, we create community for ourselves and our brothers and sisters. We practice the golden rule, let go of control, and operate on trust, knowing good will happen.
- *Consistency.* We are guided by a constancy of purpose that transcends temporary setbacks and difficulties. While staying open to Divine direction, we are firm in our spiritual practice.
- *Respect.* Knowing all is from one Source, we see no hierarchy or superior/inferior relationships. We view all from a deep respect for who they are and what they have to contribute.

- *Listening.* All that we need to know will be given to us if we but listen—with our minds and our hearts. We attempt to absorb all input from that small voice within and that of our coworkers.
- *Different objectives.* We strive to know, love, and serve God, as we understand God. All we do is based on those objectives. Different objectives make all the difference, from the material world to a spiritual perspective. We are not of this world, but we are in the world, and we can know richness and fulfillment not found in seeking for material success. Yet such success often comes. "Seek ye first the Kingdom of Heaven, then all things shall be given unto you."[22]

A BETTER FUTURE

I hope you see the dilemma our companies face. I believe the current trend of choosing to maximize profits to the sacrifice of customer satisfaction, employee morale, and stockholder loyalty will lead to an ultimate end not only of our economy but also of our form of capitalism.

As a political scientist with an interest in public choice theory, I have read many books on political economy. One such major book with a dire prediction of our future is economist Joseph A. Schumpeter's *Capitalism, Socialism and Democracy.* Written in 1950, the book has this to say about the question, can capitalism survive?: "Is it not quite true after all, that there is little parallelism between producing for profit and producing for the consumer and that private enterprise is little more than a device to curtail production in order to extort profits which then are correctly described as tolls and ransoms?"[23]

This negative view of the "little parallelism" between profit and serving the customer is what we are seeing today, what I have called maximizing profit. He goes on to say that the loss of the original creators of the enterprise and the assumption of power by bureaucratic managers seeking their own interests will lead to the end of the enterprise and to capitalism in general.

I truly believe, as did Adam Smith, that we are not doomed to our own failure. I believe that the "principles in [our] nature" that cause us to seek to aid others, the "invisible hand" that leads us and directs our own self-interest to provide value to others, will prevail.

But it will only happen if we stop exclusively stressing the profit-based, bottom-line mentality.

We all, individually and collectively, exist for a reason. For me, that is to know, love, and serve God, as I understand God. I trust God's spirit to direct me to the right path, the way, and the truth. May the spirit be with you.

■ ■ ■

Marjo Lips-Wiersma, PhD, is an internationally recognized expert on workplace spirituality. She is a senior lecturer in management at the University of Canterbury, New Zealand, and coordinates the first New Zealand University course on spirituality in the workplace. She is past chair of the Management, Spirituality, and Religion group of the Academy of Management. Her research is published in international journals such as the *Journal of Organizational Change Management,* the *Journal of Management Development,* the *Journal of Managerial Psychology,* the *Journal of Public Administration and Development,* and the *Journal of Humanistic Psychology.* She specializes in the existential questions facing people and organizations—questions that underpin values, responsibility, and performance. She is also interested in purpose beyond profit and particularly the influence of leadership, discernment, justice, and vision on organizational purpose. She has run workshops in New Zealand, the United States, Great Britain, and the Netherlands.

Kathy Lund Dean, PhD, is an associate professor of management at Idaho State University. She earned her PhD in organizational behavior and ethics from Saint Louis University. Active in both the Organizational Behavior Teaching Society and the Academy of Management for over a decade, she is a founder of the academy's Management, Spirituality, and Religion group. Currently, Dr. Dean is researching nontraditional research methodologies (especially aesthetics), business ethics and decision making, and potential downsides of workplace spirituality. Common consulting work includes strategic planning and executive coaching. Her research appears in a wide variety of management journals, and she has served as associate editor for the *Journal of Management Education* for six years. Prior to entering higher education, Dr. Dean enjoyed a career in retail banking and was partner in a small commercial business. With her family she enjoys hiking and swimming, and in the winter she strategizes on how to spend more time skiing.

Charles J. Fornaciari, PhD, is a professor of management and the Uncommon Friends Chair in Ethics at Florida Gulf Coast University in Fort Myers, Florida. He has published over a dozen journal articles in areas such as the role of spirituality and religion in management, ethics, strategic change, technology in education, and effective learning technique in journals such as the *Journal of Organizational Change Management,* the *Journal of Managerial Issues,* the *Journal of Business Research,* the *Journal of Management Education,* the *Journal of Management, Spirituality and Religion,* the *Journal of Business Ethics Education,* and the *International Journal of Organizational Analysis.* Dr. Fornaciari is a founding member of the Academy of Management's Management, Spirituality, and Religion group. He is also a recipient of the Organizational Behavior Teaching Society's prestigious New Educator Award. He serves as an associate editor for the *Journal of Management Education* and was on the editorial review board of the *Decision Sciences Journal of Innovative Education.*

Identifying and Managing the Shadow of Workplace Spirituality

Practical Guidelines

Marjo Lips-Wiersma, PhD, Kathy Lund Dean, PhD,
and Charles J. Fornaciari, PhD

This chapter argues that managers seeking to honor the workplace spirituality (WPS) of their employees need to consider its often ignored "Shadow," thus increasing the chances that WPS can add value to the organization. First, the authors introduce the concept of the Shadow. Then, they present a 2 x 2 matrix of common organization expressions of the Shadow: instrumentality and control. Next, they explore the quadrants through examples of workplace practice, potential Shadow issues, and the resulting managerial challenges. The chapter concludes with overall suggestions that enable employees and managers to address the Shadow in their organizations.

THE SHADOW

When introducing the topic of workplace spirituality (WPS) to a general or business audience, the audience's response is usually either, "How wonderful; finally, we start looking at how individuals can be whole in organizations and how organizations can do good!" or, "How dangerous; so what you are saying is that organizations are now wanting to engineer our sacred life?"

The premise of this chapter is that workplace spirituality, while in itself neither wholly wonderful nor wholly dangerous, is likely to make a more positive contribution if those who are working from a spiritual perspective understand its potential for misuse. WPS theory and practice usually assume that aligning spirituality and work is wonderful, and that there will be positive outcomes for everyone involved.[1]

We believe, however, that for workplace spirituality to have a true positive outcome, managers also need to explicitly engage the ever-present potential "Shadow," or dark side of human nature. The Shadow is particularly important to ethical WPS theory and practice because, as psychologist Carl Jung argues, without recognition of the

Shadow, a person, and society in general, cannot be whole. Engaging the Shadow is a practical issue in that the potential for employees to be hurt in the name of organizational goals is a significant concern. It is also valuable to explore potential problems of employee spirituality that might emerge as Shadow.

Most faith traditions strongly advocate the need to understand and make meaning of Shadows: the paradoxes, tests, constraints, gravity, and suffering that are part of the human condition. While we invite the reader to study what her or his own spiritual or religious tradition might have to offer with regard to the subject of Shadow, we will start with the writings of the Benedictine monk Anselm Grün. Grün explains that for humanity to progress spiritually, it is important to have an understanding of both "spirituality from above" and "spirituality from below."[2] For Grün, "spirituality from above" emerges from the human desire to ever improve, rise to greater heights, and achieve nearness to God. This type of spirituality provides us with ideals, hope, purpose, and inspiration—in other words, the individual and collective strength to rise above ourselves.

However, with "spirituality from above" alone, we may lose the connection between ideals and reality, feel hopeless or inadequate, or disengage from both the ideal and the real as a result of cynicism and burnout. So, while it is a distinct strength of workplace spirituality theory to engage with spiritual ideals, this may also be its weakness if it ignores individual, collective, and social/economic Shadows, or "spirituality from below."

Grün explains that the Latin word *humilitas* has at its roots the word *humus,* or "the earth." It refers to befriending our individual and collective earthly gravity, the world of our instincts, and the nature of Shadows. Humility, from this perspective, is the courage to see the truth about our individual and collective condition and to make potential Shadow sides visible so we can make conscious decisions in relation to them. It is from this holistic vantage point that we continue our examination.

Carl Jung's concept of Shadow captures that which is unconscious, repressed, undeveloped, and denied. Jung argued that if we deny the existence of Shadow, or at best, fear it, we individually and collectively cease to develop and struggle to become whole. To deny the Shadow, according to Jung, is to deny the possibility of insights about ourselves and our organizations. If the Shadow is unexamined, individuals and societies can become dominated by darkness and lose the opportunity for integration.[3]

INSTRUMENTALITY AND CONTROL

Given the significance of Shadow, any exploration of workplace spirituality requires the exploration of two dimensions of organizational experience that may be especially susceptible to the Shadow: instrumentality and control. By *instrumentality*, we mean the extent to which employees are treated as means toward an organizational profit objective. By *control,* we mean the degree of direction exercised by the organization over its members in the conduct of their work. We take neither the view that organizations, by their very nature, imprison human beings, nor the perspective that human beings, by their very nature, are always likely to make conscious choices irrespective of the system in which they operate. Yet on either continuum, potential problems of employee spirituality can arise.

We have found it helpful to consider the presence and effects of the Shadow in organizations using a 2 x 2 matrix (see figure 7) where instrumentality and control can independently vary from low to high.[4] Each quadrant of the matrix—seduction, evangelization, manipulation, and subjugation—addresses an area where the individual and organization meet and Shadow issues can surface.

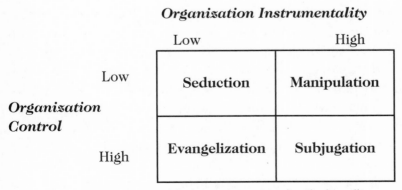

Figure 7: A model of workplace spirituality Shadow effects

Seduction

The top left quadrant of the matrix, *seduction,* describes the practices of organizations with low instrumentality orientations and low levels of control. In these firms, employees are allowed to choose the form and nature of how they pursue individual spiritual growth, but the organization does not specify any formal requirements for outcomes. The Shadow arises when certain employees' WPS practices are allowed to speak for the organization as a whole, or when WPS practices amount to discrimination.

Evangelization

The bottom left quadrant of the matrix, *evangelization,* describes the practices of organizations with low instrumentality orientations and high levels of control. In these firms, spirituality is not viewed as a tool for improving performance, but the form and nature in which WPS is incorporated into the organization is highly specified by management. This may include, for example, organized prayer meetings, inclusion of religious quotes on official company communications, explaining workplace events using religious/spiritual interpretations, and positive notations and evaluations of employee participation in these behaviors. Shadow issues mainly arise from the totality of control that management exerts over its employees' spirituality.

Manipulation

The top right quadrant of the matrix, *manipulation,* describes the practices of organizations with high instrumentality orientations and low levels of control. In these organizations, WPS is viewed simply as another tool to use for improving performance, but the form and nature of how it is incorporated into the organization is determined by individual employees. Organizations in this quadrant will be open to how members choose to pursue WPS, since its form (e.g., prayer groups, religious text discussion groups, or some form of ethics with a religious twist) is less important than its existence. The Shadow concern occurs when an individual wants to feel good and belong in the workplace, but is either deliberately or accidentally ignorant about how his or her spiritual life is being carefully cultivated as a productivity tool.

Subjugation

The bottom right quadrant of the matrix, *subjugation,* describes the practices of organizations with high instrumentality orientations and high levels of control. In these organizations, spirituality is both a clear tool for improving performance, and the form and nature in which WPS is incorporated into the organization is highly specified by management. Shadow issues arise because employees are expected (through some direct or indirect spiritual practice) to bring more of themselves to work in a manner that places the organization above all else.

THE SHADOWS AND THEIR MANAGEMENT CHALLENGES IN PRACTICE

In order to explore in greater depth the Shadow issues and managerial challenges for each quadrant of the matrix, it is helpful to take a look at representative examples of seduction, evangelization, manipulation, and subjugation as they appear in actual practice.

Seduction in Practice

One area where the Shadow of seduction is visible in the United States is the health-care arena, where administrators are struggling to create policies that respect patients' rights to receive treatment or medication while respecting providers' rights to refuse such due to religious beliefs. In the United States, for example, pharmacists may refuse to dispense birth control pills to patients,[5] leading to customers avoiding the pharmacy altogether. Physicians may also refuse, for religious reasons, to perform abortions, sterilizations, or to prescribe contraception.[6] In one instance, California's Supreme Court agreed to hear a case brought by a lesbian whose doctors refused to artificially inseminate her because of her sexual orientation. In another example, a physician refused to prescribe Viagra to a gay man (the case was eventually settled out of court). At issue is a provider's right to pick and choose deniability of services for certain types of patients, a right rife with implications of power and hegemony.

Another occasion when the seduction Shadow surfaces is when the organization lets members choose their own paths, and part of their expression is proselytizing. Given that the work culture is unlikely to be "an oasis of harmony and homogeneity,"[7] some individuals, perceiving the organization's tacit approval, may bring their faith into the firm, begin programs of recruitment, or exclusion, based on spiritual or religious considerations. Because of the indifference of seduction firms, many "in" and "out" groups may all be struggling for control (compared to evangelization organizations, which usually have clear single "in" and "out" groups).

Where the Shadow is indifference, organizations may not care what form WPS takes, and employees may not care how WPS occurs in the whole organization, since they are only engaged in the workplace for their own ends. For these employees and firms, potential Shadow effects include the risk of disconnection and cynicism resulting from a "what's in it for me?" orientation, thus challenging the very nature of the notion of WPS. The Shadow ultimately emerges when individuals disengage from the organization by protecting their own identity, career, or well-being from those exploiting the firm's laissez-faire WPS orientation.

When it comes to seduction, the managerial challenge arises from the conflict between unfettered individual choice and potential organizational fragmentation. In short, the seduction of indifference casts its own Shadow. It is important for managers to decide where the organization is not indifferent and design appropriate policies and procedures. In the United States, for example, courts have generally held that policies preventing religious expression are acceptable as long as they are consistently applied and the organization can demonstrate that providing accommodation would present it with an undue hardship.[8]

Evangelization in Practice

The evangelization Shadow arises when organizations become predominantly filled with employees who adhere to its espoused spirituality or religiosity. Riverview Community Bank in Otsego, Minnesota, is a representative example of this kind of evangelization. Riverview was founded by Chuck Ripka (vice president) and Duane Kropuenske (president) to explicitly express evangelical Christian principles, and it views itself as a ministry that happens to offer financial services.[9] Ripka, for example, talks extensively about God speaking to him, and loan officers pray with their customers to get the best-selling price for their homes. While deliberately Christian, the bank's religious infusion exists not as a tool by which to differentiate itself in the marketplace, but as a home for Christians during the work week to practice their faith. The bank also attracts many Christian customers who put their trust in the bank because of its expressly Christian tenets.

With regard to hiring people of diverse religious backgrounds, Russell Shorto, author and *New York Times* writer, documented Ripka's response in a *New York Times* cover story: "It doesn't matter where they are in their walk," Ripka said. "In the job interview, I sit down and explain to them that we're doing God's work at our bank. We don't say, 'You have to do this' [meaning, become as devout as some in the bank are], but we say it's something that will probably happen." When Ripka was asked whether a Jew or Muslim would feel welcome working at the bank, he replied, "We don't really have that in our community at this point."[10]

Another evangelization Shadow that surfaces in organizations might be where employees and customers trust and follow the leader because she or he has a special relationship with God, and thus, following God's will means following the organization's leader. This can become a very strong tool for control: How can an organization create a participative decision-making environment if its leader claims to have a direct link to God? Which employee in these types of organizations would argue with God?

This Shadow's presence in evangelization suggests that most organization members will buy into management's views of WPS over time and likewise give it strong expression. It is fair to assume that those who question or oppose these views will be unwilling to express their disagreements or will eventually separate themselves from the organization. It is also a probability, from a diversity viewpoint, that such an organization does not attract the best talent because only certain people are drawn to applying for a job.

The managerial Shadow challenge becomes how to make clear to employees the difference between leadership "following God" versus leadership "being God." Even for organizations firmly committed to an explicit faith, almost any solution will involve procedures that allow for differences to be formally included in their systems. For example, most faith traditions have well-developed discernment processes to aid in reflection and decision making.

Managers seeking to reduce this Shadow's impact ultimately face the trade-off inherent in the benefits of a strongly unified culture and its concurrent reduction of diversity. This suggests that management will need to pay particular attention to how it designs and runs employee recruitment and evaluation practices to avoid this Shadow's most harmful effects.

Manipulation in Practice

The manipulation Shadow appears when spiritual practice is subsumed to the instrumental goals of the organization. Take the case where a public for-profit company allows the integration of the sacred with its long-term prospects. In such a case, the "feel-good sense of belonging" mixed with the "we are good employees for the company" sentiment can, in fact, silence dissent and may subtly (as is usually the case with manipulation) discourage members of some faith groups, or such groups as a whole, from asking difficult questions of the company.

In many instances, the manipulation Shadow emerges when organizations seek instrumental ends such as "keeping morale up" or quieting questions—both from within and from outside—that revolve around minor organizational issues. The Shadow can basically be an implicit quid pro quo trade-off between the organization and its members for harmony's sake. At its darkest, however, the Shadow occurs when such faith-based practice is intentionally sanctioned as a public relations strategy, possibly to offset attention paid to organizational practices that are immoral or dangerous. To allow WPS to be co-opted as a publicity trade-off is an extreme form of manipulation.

"Affinity groups" are a common practice with potential for manipulation. These are informal, employee-organized, but organizationally encouraged, interest groups that usually receive company resources to function. The idea behind affinity groups is equal organizational encouragement of disparate employee interests ranging from joggers to Zoroastrians to almost any other conceivable commonality. Organizations hope to avoid unpleasant and expensive possible litigation and to be perceived as inclusive by explicitly choosing not to actively manage which groups can and cannot form.[11]

An example of an affinity group would be the Coca-Cola Company's Christian Fellowship. Control is low in that any employee group within Coca-Cola can set up an affinity group around any interest and be allowed to meet during work time. However, Coke's Christian

Fellowship's statement indicates, among its principles, "We use the Holy Bible, which is the foundation of this fellowship, to reach integrity, accountability, building relationships, respect, and diversity, which are all essential to the company's long-term success."[12]

Manipulation's Shadow presents clear challenges to employee integrity and management feedback. If, for example, the group decided to confront excessive sugar content in some of the soft drinks, would such a group still be supported by management, or would it only be condoned when it was quietly supportive? It becomes important for an organization to consistently make explicit, both to its employees and the outside world, that the views of its affinity groups do not officially represent the organization. This also suggests that organizations avoid the temptation, for their own ends, to publicize the activities of their groups, either internally or externally. They will also have to maintain a true hands-off approach by clearly supporting both complementary and dissenting groups. This can be achieved by proactively designing clear policies and resource-allocation procedures for group formation and operation.

Subjugation in Practice

The subjugation Shadow arises in a "totalizing regime of managerial control where employees are simply programmed automatons who diligently perform the logic of the dominant regime as is engineered by senior management and consultants."[13] In this climate, the human need to belong overrides any form of critical thought, and the organization advocates material success as the sole gateway to attaining nonmaterial desires (such as being a good community member). The subjugation Shadow also shows itself when organizations deliberately appear to shift ethical and functional responsibilities to the individual, using a variety of self-development programs that ultimately provide management with more control. In his book *Management Gurus and Management Fashions,* Brad Jackson, Fletcher Building Education Trust Professor of Leadership at the University of Auckland, chronicles the increasingly dominated self at the hands of well-rehearsed and emotionally slick "self-help" programs that can introduce self-doubt in the employee while sustaining the managers and leaders as the spiritually whole and accomplished ideal.[14]

An often-cited example of subjugation in practice is Amway, an American multilevel marketing distributor. Steve Butterfield, a former employee, provides an extensive description of its practices in his book *Amway: The Cult of Free Enterprise.* Butterfield describes how, step-by-step, one gets drawn into the "Amway lifestyle," including its rallies, products, and positive-thought cult doctrine, until, as he describes it, one's critical intelligence is drowned in a cycle of "fake love and plastic dreams."[15] In an article titled, "The Good, the Bad, and the Ambivalent: Managing Identification among Amway Distributors," Michael Pratt, an assistant professor of organizational behavior in the department of business administration at the University of Illinois, explains how Amway uses techniques such as sense breaking and sense making to harmonize the identities of individual members with its goals.[16] At Amway, encouraging a continual upward spiral of money-making goals was analogue to messages of caring and concern. Amway also appeared to ensure that more of their distributors' non–work lives became intertwined with their identity as distributors by socializing distributors to accept only other Amway employees as "true friends."

Subjugation tools often mirror religious or spiritual practices through their provision of meaning and belonging; thus, their benefits can be tempting for managers. However, their downsides of hegemony and control suggest that organizations must avoid presenting themselves this way, either intentionally or unintentionally. The subjugation Shadow challenges managers to prevent employees from making the organization the raison d'être of their lives and, consequently, replacing their own faith and value systems with the firm's.

One immediate solution is to make policies that encourage employees to literally step outside the organization. Programs that encourage individually chosen renewal paths and self-development are critical. Some common examples include ensuring that employees actually use all of their allotted vacations or do not feel culturally guilty for placing their personal lives above the organization's needs. Other options can include organization-provided development funds that allow employees great latitude in how they will be used.

Implications for Management Practice

In this chapter, we have made the case that managers need to be alert to potential Shadows of WPS. Managers need to ask themselves whether they are comfortable with a form of spirituality that embraces ideals as well as paradoxes, tests, constraints, and gravity, which are also part of the human condition. In other words, does their spirituality encourage humility to see the truth about the human condition and to make potential Shadow sides visible so they can make conscious decisions in relation to them?

At the organizational level, there are some broad questions that any manager working with WPS can ask in order to understand and, where possible, address these Shadows. We offer the following list of questions, but these are by no means exhaustive:

- Who is benefiting and who could be harmed by this form of spiritual practice?
- What might be some of the unintended consequences of this form of spiritual practice?
- Who has been included or excluded from consultation about this form of spiritual practice?
- Who is potentially included or excluded in practicing this form of spiritual practice?
- What is the effect of this form of spiritual practice on all stakeholders?
- Under what conditions will this form of spiritual practice encourage idealism or encourage cynicism?
- Does this form of spiritual practice honor a diversity of spiritual and religious beliefs?

The continuing steady output of popular books and articles on the topic of workplace spirituality clearly indicates the desire for organizations to understand and engage WPS issues. Given the scant attention paid to the Shadow in both popular and academic WPS literature, however, it is imperative that we attempt to understand the implications of these issues. The organizational Shadow is ever present, and a first step for managers in learning how to deal with it is recognizing where and how Shadow may emerge, and developing the tools to address Shadow in their organizations.

■ ■ ■

Jacqueline Miller, executive producer and cocreator of the World Voice Concert, was an American producer for TV-Globo in Rio de Janeiro for the World Cup soccer games. She has coauthored a best-selling book, *Heart at Work*, using the art of storytelling to promote personal and social empowerment. She has produced award-winning television shows, and introduced change-management concepts and creative direct-action programs throughout North and South America, Asia, and Europe. Jacqueline is president and cofounder of Partnerships for Change (PFC), a San Francisco–based nonprofit organization dedicated to positive transformation at the community level. PFC promotes social and economic transformation through direct humanitarian action and sustainable development. As president of PFC, Jacqueline attracts resources to take action where assistance is needed by accessing a vast network of business and political leaders, along with developing media coverage to accelerate global change. Recently, she has been helping orphanages, schools, and monasteries in Southeast Asia and India.

Heart at Work

Signs of Hope

JACQUELINE MILLER

This chapter reviews a laudable initiative undertaken by the United Nations (UN) to establish a global compact for business organizations, with the aim to enhance social responsibility. Five thousand companies have thus far committed to this global compact entailing human rights, labor, environment, and anticorruption. The United Nations Global Compact initiative launched a breakthrough report in 2004 called "Who Cares Wins." Recommendations in this report included more research, investment in and implementation of environmental, social, and governance (ESG) factors in business performance; particular consideration of emerging markets; and inclusion of more high-level research and thinking on these issues in academic institutions and business schools. With this globally oriented initiative, business finally takes responsibility in areas that transcend the bottom line, but also include human care, political awareness, and activism.

Global Compact Principles

The heart of today's workplace is broken, but there are signs of hope and stories of triumph. A number of leaders at the United Nations, for example, are contributing selflessly to the greater good. The United Nations Global Compact initiative has championed corporate social responsibility:

> The Global Compact is an international initiative bringing companies together with UN agencies, labor and civil society to support ten principles in the areas of human rights, working conditions, the environment, and anti-corruption. Through the power of collective action, the Global Compact seeks to advance responsible corporate citizenship so that business can be part of the solution to the challenges of globalisation. In this way, the private sector—in partnership with other social actors—can help realize the Secretary-General's vision: a more stable and inclusive global economy.[1]

With the launch of the "Who Cares Wins" report and "The Principles of Responsible Investment," the Global Compact has brilliantly mobilized the financial sectors. The Global Compact is now the largest voluntary corporate citizenship initiative endorsed by companies from all regions of the world, and it has accelerated corporate social responsibility acceptance and implementation at a rapid pace. As of August 2008, more than five thousand companies worldwide have committed to the Global Compact principles:

Human Rights

- *Principle 1:* Businesses should support and respect the protection of internationally proclaimed human rights within their sphere of influence; and
- *Principle 2:* make sure that they are not complicit in human rights abuses.

Labor

- *Principle 3:* Businesses should uphold the freedom of association and the effective recognition of the right to collective bargaining;
- *Principle 4:* the elimination of all forms of forced and compulsory labor;
- *Principle 5:* the effective abolition of child labor; and
- *Principle 6:* eliminate discrimination in respect of employment and occupation.

ENVIRONMENT

- *Principle 7:* Businesses should support a precautionary approach to environmental challenges;
- *Principle 8:* undertake initiatives to promote greater environmental responsibility; and
- *Principle 9:* encourage the development and diffusion of environmentally friendly technologies.

ANTI-CORRUPTION

- *Principle 10:* Businesses should work against corruption in all its forms, including extortion and bribery.[2]

WHO CARES WINS

When the Global Compact initiative launched the breakthrough "Who Cares Wins" report, they offered a healing balm to troubled corporate interests. In 2004, the critical thinkers who developed this report presented it to the World Economic Forum in Davos, Switzerland. In the opening executive summary, they described the purpose and result of the project:

Twenty financial institutions from 9 countries with total assets under management of over 6 trillion USD have participated in developing this report. The initiative is supported by the chief executive officers of the endorsing institutions. The U.N. Global Compact oversaw the collaborative effort that led to this report and the Swiss Government provided the necessary funding.

The institutions endorsing this report are convinced that in a more globalised, interconnected and competitive world the way that environmental, social and corporate governance issues are managed is part of companies' overall management quality needed to compete successfully. Companies that perform better with regard to these issues can increase shareholder value by, for example, properly managing risks, anticipating regulatory action or accessing new markets, while at the same time contributing to the sustainable development of the societies in which they operate. Moreover, these issues can have a strong impact on reputation and brands, an increasingly important part of company value.

The report aims at increasing awareness of all involved financial market actors, at triggering broader discussions, and supporting creativity and thoughtfulness in approach, rather than being prescriptive. It also aims to enhance clarity concerning the respective roles of different market actors, including companies, regulators, stock exchanges, investors, asset managers, brokers, analysts, accountants, financial advisers and consultants. It therefore includes recommendations for different actors, striving to support improved mutual understanding, collaboration and constructive dialogue on these issues.

The endorsing institutions committed to start a process to further deepen, specify and implement the recommendations outlined in this report by means of a series of individual and collaborative efforts at different levels....

The endorsing institutions are convinced that a better consideration of environmental, social and governance factors will ultimately contribute to stronger and more resilient investment markets, as well as contribute to the sustainable development of societies.[3]

The "Who Cares Wins" report continued with the following recommendations:

Analysts are asked to better incorporate environmental, social and governance (ESG) factors in their research where appropriate and to further develop the necessary investment know-how, models and tools in a creative and thoughtful way. Based on the existing know-how in especially exposed industries, the scope should be expanded to include other sectors and asset classes. Because of their importance for sustainable development, emerging markets received particular consideration and environmental, social and governance criteria should be adapted to the specific situation in these markets. Academic institutions, business schools and other research organizations are invited to support the efforts of financial analysts by contributing high-level research and thinking.

Financial institutions committed to integrating environmental, social and governance factors in a more systematic way in research and investment processes. This must be supported by a strong commitment at the Board and senior management level. The formulation of long-term goals, the introduction of organisational learning and change processes, appropriate training and incentive systems for analysts are crucial in achieving the goal of a better integration of these issues.

Companies are asked to take a leadership role by implementing environmental, social and corporate governance principles and polices and to provide information and reports on related performance in a more consistent and standardised format. They should identify and communicate key challenges and value drivers and prioritise environmental, social and governance issues accordingly. We believe that this information is best conveyed to financial markets through normal investor relation communication channels and encourage, and when relevant, an explicit mention in the annual report of companies. Concerning the outcomes of financial research in this field, companies should accept positive as well as critical results.

Investors are urged to explicitly request and reward research that includes environmental, social and governance aspects and to reward well-managed companies. Asset managers are asked to integrate research on such aspects in investment decisions and to encourage brokers and companies to provide better research and information. Both investors and asset managers should develop and communicate proxy voting strategies on ESG issues as this will support analysts and fund managers in producing relevant research and services.

Pension fund trustees and their **selection consultants** are encouraged to consider environmental, social and governance issues in the formulation of investment mandates and the selection of investment managers, taking into account their fiduciary obligations to participants and beneficiaries. **Governments** and **multilateral agencies** are asked to proactively consider the investment of their pension funds according to the principles of sustainable development, taking into account their fiduciary obligations to participants and beneficiaries.

Consultants and **financial advisers** should help create a greater and more stable demand for research in this area by combining research on environmental, social and governance aspects with industry level research and sharing their experience with financial market actors and companies in order to improve their reporting on these issues.

Regulators are invited to shape legal frameworks in a predictable and transparent way, as this will support integration in financial analysis. Regulatory frameworks should require a minimum degree of disclosure and accountability on environmental, social and governance issues from companies, as this will support financial analysis. The formulation of specific standards should, on the other hand, rely on market-driven voluntary initiatives. We encouraged **financial analysts** to participate more actively in ongoing voluntary initiatives, such as the Global Reporting Initiative, and help shape a reporting framework that responds to their needs.

Stock exchanges are invited to include environmental, social and governance criteria in listing particulars for companies as this will ensure a minimum degree of disclosure across all listed companies. As a first step, stock exchanges could communicate to listed companies the growing importance of environmental, social and governance issues. Similarly, **other self-regulatory organizations** (e.g. NASD, FSA), professional credential-granting organizations (e.g. AIMR, EFFAS), **accounting standard-setting bodies** (e.g. FASB, IASB), public accounting entities, and **rating agencies and index providers** should all establish consistent standards and frameworks in relation to environmental, social and governance factors.

Nongovernmental Organisations (NGOs) can also contribute to better transparency by providing objective information on companies to the public and the financial community.[4]

Principles for Responsible Investment

Another sign of hope is the growing view among investment professionals that environmental, social, and corporate governance (ESG) issues can affect the performance of investment portfolios. Investors fulfilling their fiduciary (or equivalent) duty therefore need to give appropriate consideration to these issues, but to date have lacked a framework for doing so. The Principles for Responsible Investment (PRI), also launched by the United Nations, now provide this framework.

> In early 2005 the then UN Secretary-General, Kofi Annan, invited a group of the world's largest institutional investors to join a process to develop the Principles for Responsible Investment (PRI). Individuals representing 20 institutional investors from 12 countries agreed to participate in the Investor Group. They were supported by a 70-person multi-stakeholder group of experts from the investment industry, intergovernmental and governmental organizations, civil society and academia. The process was coordinated by the United Nations Environment Programme Finance Initiative (UNEP FI) and the UN Global Compact.[5]

The investor group accepted ownership of the principles and had the freedom to develop them as they saw fit. The process, conducted between April 2005 and January 2006, involved a total of five days of face to face deliberations by the investors and four days by the experts, with hundreds of hours of follow-up activity.

The Principles for Responsible Investment that emerged as a result of these meetings reflect the core values of this group of large investors, whose investment horizon is generally long and whose portfolios are often highly diversified. The principles are voluntary and aspirational. They are not prescriptive, but instead provide a menu of possible actions for incorporating ESG issues into mainstream investment decision-making and ownership practices. The principles are open to all institutional investors, investment managers, and professional service partners to support.

When a company signs on to follow the principles, it represents a very real commitment, demonstrating support from the top-level leadership of the whole investment business. And as investors commit to and apply the principles, the hope is not only for better long-term financial returns, but also for a closer alignment between the objectives of institutional investors and those of society at large.

The principles are straightforward, yet if carried out, can have a significant impact in helping investors integrate consideration of ESG issues into their investment decision-making and ownership practices. The principles, which have quickly become the global benchmark for responsible investing, outline six major areas of commitment:

1. We will incorporate ESG issues into investment analysis and decision-making processes.
2. We will be active owners and incorporate ESG issues into our ownership policies and practices.
3. We will seek appropriate disclosure on ESG issues by the entities in which we invest.
4. We will promote acceptance and implementation of the Principles within the investment industry.
5. We will work together to enhance our effectiveness in implementing the Principles.
6. We will each report on our activities and progress towards implementing the Principles.[6]

Following the launch of the principles, phase two of the process began promoting the adoption of the principles by additional investors, providing comprehensive resources to assist investors in implementing the principles and actions, and facilitating collaboration among signatories.

THE KEY IS THE HEART

No one can doubt the impact of the UN Global Compact. The key to arriving at this level of thinking is the heart, because only the heart— or as academics may say, emotional literacy or the emotional quotient—can drive our sense of responsibility to care for others.

The late Anita Roddick, chairman, CEO, and founder of the Body Shop, believed that ethical businesses could be run with heart and still be profitable. She worked on behalf of multiple causes, ranging from environmental issues to debt relief for developing countries. Her philosophy of doing business is summed up in her "favorite four-letter words":

> In my company love, give, care, feel, hope, fair, soul and true—all are to be found in work and are my all-time favorite four-letter words. I have always believed that you can bring your heart to work. Most of us spend most of our time at work. It is the place where we have our greatest daily contact with others, where we expend creative energy and where we form relationships. To fail to understand the role that work plays in the development of people would be wrong. For me, the workplace is much less a factory for the production of goods and much more an incubator for the human spirit. The workplace is where the compulsive search for connection, common purpose and a sense of friendship and neighborhood can find a special place. It is where a continuous sense of spiritual education can take place, and where self-esteem gives us the ability to express ourselves and to contribute selflessly to a greater good.[7]

So often executives sit in their ivory tower making decisions that affect people on the other side of the globe with little attention to the supply chain. They must go to the source of their suppliers and outsourced services to "suffer with" them and see the effects of their decisions. Only then will real heart at work emerge.

Few motivating forces are more potent than giving your staff an opportunity to exercise and express their idealism to influence change—locally, nationally, and globally. As Roddick once said, "Whether caring for locally disadvantaged people, cleaning up the local environment or working with sick animals, staff can feel connected and uplifted. It is another of those not so secret ingredients that help our staff raise their sense of self."[8]

I experienced the power of this personal involvement firsthand in 1990. I had been shocked by the news coverage of the legacies of Nicolae Ceausescu's twenty-six years of dictatorship, so I went to Romania myself to see how Partnerships for Change could help. I was horrified by what I saw. Within just six weeks, we set up the Romanian Relief Drive. Staff clamored to be among the volunteers to help refurbish the orphanages, hold babies with AIDS, and give them something many had never had before—love and care.

Now called the Eastern Europe Relief Drive, the program is still run, on next to nothing, by a handful of young staff members. Their commitment to helping the children in Romania and Albania is humbling to us all. Their desire to help out has been shared by over four hundred and fifty members of our staff from around the world who have gone as volunteers—and come back as changed people. Their values suddenly take a leap into a previously unknown source of power, and they start dreaming of noble purposes.

The most spiritual path in the world is the path of love, and the essence of love is compassionate understanding. In order to love, we need to recognize the physical, material, and psychological suffering of others, to put ourselves "inside the skin" of the other. Shallow observation as an outsider is not enough. We need to be in contact with another's suffering "to suffer with," which is, literally, the definition of *compassion*.

One effective way to open the heart and develop compassion is through "radical sabbaticals," an initiative that Partnerships for Change leads to developing countries. This initiative creates a chance for executives to touch and feel the poorest of the poor.

Another way to bring heart into work is to get staff involved in political activism. For too long, business has been teaching that politics and commerce are two different arenas. Political awareness and activism need to be incorporated into business; in a global world, there are no value-free or politically disentangled actions.

Campaigning is not only about changing the world, it is about changing how individuals work together. Giving people a sense of their own power is as much a part of the goal as resolving the issues. It provides a new forum for staff education, and they can get into issues and areas where they might not normally ever venture. Campaigns are fabulous ways to integrate the behavior of staff at work with the values they hold dear as individual citizens in the larger world. Business leaders need to realize that this is the way forward in the workplace: the personal becomes the political, which becomes the global.

The underlying theme of spirituality at work is "heart at work," and it relates to the amount of care, trust, and love in your workplace. "Heart at work" is already happening in many businesses, as Isaac Tigrett, founder of the Hard Rock Cafe, describes:

> Being one of the Hard Rock Cafe family was therapy for people. Even if they came from a violent home life, here they were loved, and they loved back in return. People always do. I could hire those no one else would take, and in six or seven months they'd be new people. I called it my "High School" and I told 'em I wanted everyone to graduate. I realized early on that we were creating habits, that's all, just habits. That's what success or failure in life comes from: habits. So I determined to create good ones. We graduated some great souls.[9]

One day, it struck Isaac: "If we're so famous, if people love the Hard Rock so much, why not take that and reflect it back at them with a message?" So he started printing epigrams on paychecks, T-shirts, sweatshirts, and such. They were little aphorisms, such as, "Start the day with love"; "Do good, be good, see good"; and the like. The result? "I sold millions of sweatshirts to lots of different kinds of people—some of them pretty rough," Isaac says with an impish gleam, "and on every one of them was that sign: Love all, serve all. That must've done some good!"[10]

Here we have Isaac Tigrett talking love and soul—huge ideas. Isaac later went on to establish the House of Blues in Los Angeles, with Dan Aykroyd, where he defined his mission as wanting "to create a profitable, principled, global entertainment company" that would encourage "racial and spiritual harmony."[11]

BRINGING LOVE AND SPIRITUALITY INTO WORK

Love and spirituality are very much connected with motivation and change. People in modern organizations sometimes struggle to think how to "motivate" their people—as if motivation is some sort of force you apply to a person. In fact, everything that truly motivates people—whether to perform better, to be more dependable and committed, to take initiative, to be courageous, to do the right thing, to adapt to change—is included within love and spirituality. Love helps people believe in themselves and feel valued, and liberates them to have this same effect on others. This builds confidence and trust. Spirituality enables people to connect with each other and with the things that truly matter in the world and their lives. This gives people meaning and purpose and relevance, which is at the heart of true motivation.

In terms of corporate initiatives, love and spirituality are about as natural as you can get. These needs and tendencies are basic human nature, and they are in all of us. So when you decide to bring a bit more love and spirituality into your work, you will be pushing on an open door. It is possible to create a very workable, practical methodology to bring love and spirituality into your work, your team, your department, or a whole organization, right now if you want to. There are good people out there to help you bring a more spiritual ethos into your organization, and the great thing is that these people are loving and caring, too—they practice what they preach.

At the root of any successful change, you will find not only love, but trust, since they go hand in hand. Love and trust, in turn, create the freedom to make the right decisions, to connect with others, to challenge, and to innovate. We tend to think that organizations run on rationale and details, but organizations really run on power. But not just any kind of power. Pure power comes from sustainable passion. And passion that is sustainable comes from purpose. Take a careful look at the most successful companies around the world. They all have a strong sense of purpose and are organizational champions of change driving that purpose. As companies that have a "heart at work," they value and encourage love and spirituality. The compassion and trust among their people leverages diversity and harmony. And that, in anyone's book, makes good business sense.

■ ■ ■

Judi Neal, PhD, is president of Neal & Associates, a consulting firm that focuses on personal and organizational transformation. She holds a PhD in organizational behavior from Yale University and has consulted organizations for twenty-four years, taught management at the University of New Haven and other universities for over seventeen years, and served on the boards of directors of several professional, community, and academic organizations. In 1992, she made spirituality in the workplace a central focus of her research and presentations, and has since gained an international reputation for stressing the importance of spirituality in the workplace. Dr. Neal has been instrumental in professional organizations, including the Academy of Management, where she helped to found the Management, Spirituality, and Religion group. She has spoken at numerous national and international conferences on spirituality in the workplace, and has published numerous articles and several books on spirituality in the workplace. In addition to her professional work, Judi is a part-time musician.

Creating Edgewalker Organizations[1]

The Workplace of the Future

JUDI NEAL, PHD

New kinds of leaders are emerging in today's global world. They are Edgewalkers—people who walk between worlds. They are highly intuitive, deeply spiritual, and well grounded in the practicalities of running an organization. This chapter describes the emergence of Edgewalkers and describes the difficulties and challenges they face in traditional organizations. Besides a handful of Edgewalkers, every organization has people who serve as Flamekeepers, Hearthtenders, Placeholders, and Doomsayers. Most organizations have very few Edgewalkers and far too many Placeholders and Doomsayers. The chapter explores ways of creating an organizational culture that brings out the Edgewalker qualities in people so that the organization can be more values driven, innovative, and leading edge.

> "We look forward to the time when the power to love
> will replace the love of power. Then will our world
> know the blessings of peace."   —*William E. Gladstone*

IMAGINING AN EDGEWALKER ORGANIZATION

When I talk about Edgewalker Organizations, I am writing about something that doesn't exist—at least not in the present. I do believe that they exist in the future, and that there is tremendous possibility for all organizations to be much more creative, much more in harmony with the environment, and much more joyous places to work.

I define Edgewalkers as people who walk between worlds and build bridges between different paradigms, cultures, and realities. Edgewalkers are the people in an organization who sense coming trends, and who create new rules to the business game. They tend to be marginalized, and there are many pressures to make them conform and to be predictable in their behavior, yet they are the greatest resource an organization can have—if the leaders understand and value their unique gifts and skills. Most organizations are uncomfortable, if not downright hostile, to people who are Edgewalkers. But the organizations that learn to embrace those who see things differently, who do not conform perfectly to all the corporate rules, are the ones that will have a competitive edge.

The following profile describes what an Edgewalker Organization might look and feel like.[2] Imagine that your company has just contracted with another company to help your business unit with new product design....

The drive up to the corporate headquarters of Genesis Systems is breathtaking. You ride along tree-lined roads that follow the twists and turns of the brook that feeds Lake Astron. Beautiful sculptures and gardens are nestled here and there among the trees, and tame deer lift their heads from their feeding as you pass by. The winding road takes you partway up the mountain, and then you see a simple but beautiful building in front of you. It is mostly glass, stone, and wood, and there are solar panels on the top of the building. The shape of the building from the front seems to conform to the round contours of the mountain. You also notice a wind turbine higher up the mountain and a charming water wheel next to the waterfall. In the distance you can see other large buildings dotting the hills, and you notice how tastefully they seem to fit into the environment.

You park your car in the lower parking lot, and a solar-powered cart picks you up and drives you to the main entrance. On the lawn in front of the building, several people are playing with some kind of large circular toy that flies between them, although you can't make out exactly what it is. You just notice that it seems to float almost effortlessly for a while when someone throws it. A young man leaps gracefully in the air and grabs this flying disk and spins it off to someone else. A large golden retriever is joyfully barking and running between the players.[3]

There are seven steps leading up to the entrance, and just below the Genesis Systems sign above the door, you read these words carved in marble: "The Universe pays us for being who we are and doing what we love doing." "How odd," you think to yourself, as you ponder what this might mean. As you walk up the last step, the two wooden doors gently open and you hear soft music drifting out from inside the foyer. There are plants everywhere, and you almost feel as if you are in a greenhouse.

Your host, Gary Williams, walks in to meet you, and warmly shakes your hand. Gary is the account executive for your project. You have come here to begin your working relationship with Genesis Systems because your organization has contracted to use the company's product design services to help develop a new consumer product line for your food business. He guides you further into the building and invites you to sit with him in a café setting in the middle courtyard. You notice that the inside of the building is circular and is completely open in the center, with about four levels of balconies surrounding this courtyard. You can see offices on each level, and you realize, from the way the building is designed, that every single one of them must have a view of the outside.[4]

Water from the brook outside has been diverted to a small stream that runs through the building, providing the soothing sound of trickling water in the background in the café area. There are beverage menus on the table, and Gary asks if you would like anything from the coffee bar or juice bar. You ask for a cup of coffee, and Gary brings that back for you and gets himself a fruit smoothie.

As you begin to drink your beverages, Gary outlines the day for you. "First, you will meet with Rob Rabbin, the vice president of corporate consciousness,"[5] Gary says. "All clients meet with Rob so he can explain the company's core values and also talk about some of our unusual ways of working. Rob is a mystic, and we rely on his intuition and his access to higher levels of consciousness to help us make sound business decisions that are good for our clients, good for the company, and good for life on the planet."

Gary goes on to explain their spiritual approach to work: "We like to begin with some shared moments of silence so that our work together comes from our highest source. Rob will introduce you to our concept of 'Spiritual Support Team,' to see if that is something your organization would like to take advantage of. We do not charge for this service, but we believe it makes a powerful difference. Basically, we ask that two people from our company and two people from your organization make an agreement to set aside a half hour every month to share meditation or prayer. It doesn't matter where each person is, they just commit to taking that time, say at 8 a.m. on the first Friday of every month, to connect with Source or the Transcendent. There is no agenda; the only purpose is to connect.[6]

"Next you will meet the chief creative officer, Sonia Borysenkov, who will explain the way the company's engineers work with artists, high school and college students, and indigenous shamans. An integrative, multifunctional team will be assigned to your project. Sonia will introduce you to the team members and we will begin doing some creative, mind-opening exercises that will get us into the kind of consciousness that will help us best serve you and your company."

Gary continues, "Finally, you will end the day with our learning liaison, Bill Kumar, who will ask you for feedback on your day, assess how we might better serve you in the future, and also ask you what you learned that was of value to you. Bill helps us to see every interaction as a positive opportunity for learning and growth. This helps to support the kind of corporate culture that attracts the best and the brightest talent from all over the world."

Gary then asks if you have any questions, and you feel like you have a million of them, but don't know where to start. He laughs and says, "Well you can begin with whatever comes up first, so why don't we get started? I'll take you on a brief tour as we head over to meet with Rob."

Your mind is buzzing. You want to ask questions about the design of the building. Your engineering mind has taken in a lot of details, and you suspect that Genesis Systems is energy self-sufficient.

Why is the building round? How come people were outside playing in the middle of the workday? Are dogs allowed in this workplace? What did that phrase mean above the door? Where did they get the ideas to have a vice president of corporate consciousness and spiritual support teams?

Gary takes you past the meditation center, where you see another circular room with plants, waterfalls, inspiring pictures, candles, cushions, chairs, and symbols from all of the world's great spiritual traditions.[7] Several people are inside sitting quietly, and one person is kneeling on his prayer rug. Next, you go by the corporate library, which includes all the latest technology. Gary explains that their library is actually better and more up-to-date than that of the nearby university.

As you walk by some offices, Gary suggests that you look in and notice the original artwork on the walls. "Genesis has a full-time art director that we hired away from a nationally recognized art museum," he tells you. "She is in charge of our art collection. We feel that our employees will be more inspired if they have access to original art, so they can select a van Gogh or Cézanne or Georgia O'Keeffe painting from a catalog and borrow it from our collection for three months. At the end of three months, they can select a new piece of art."[8]

Just before you get to Rob's office, Gary takes you to the learning and wisdom center. He shows you the various types and sizes of training rooms, and takes you outdoors briefly. He points to the woods and a pathway off to the left. "That's all state-protected land with old-growth forests, and land that has been sacred to the First Peoples. We sponsor regular vision quests for anyone in the company who is interested in taking time to explore the next stages of their life and/or work. We feel that it is very important to be close to nature and living things, and that this closeness energizes and inspires us and helps us to keep a holistic perspective on any of the product development work that we help to create."

You say to him, "I've always wanted to go on a vision quest."

He responds, "Let me take you back into the learning and wisdom center and give you one of our catalogs. We make all our programs available to our clients and vendors at no charge. We are committed to helping all the people we interact with reach their highest potential. That's really our main reason for being in business.[9] *Product design services just happen to be the way we fulfill our mission."*

As you are walking back in, Gary points out a separate circular building nearby, connected by a covered walkway. He said, "That's our family care center. It is a multigenerational care center where we have full-time child- and eldercare staff. Many of our employees are in the so-called Sandwich Generation, where they must care for their children and also for their elderly parents. We have found that the children and the elderly love being together. We have Internet cameras and communication systems so that employees feel connected to their family members throughout the day. Many of them eat lunch with family members at the family care center cafeteria. Our working hours are 8 a.m. to 5 p.m. We have a real commitment to the principle of 'Family First,' and we turn the lights out at 6 p.m. and insist that people go home and get renewal with their family."[10]

Gary takes you up to level three in the building, and as you are walking around the balcony to get to Rob's office, he points out all the small areas for group gatherings, with couches, tables, plants, electronic white boards, and coffee nooks. He tells you that they had an architect design the building so that it was ecological, energy self-sufficient, aesthetically pleasing, and supportive of chance meetings of individuals and groups. "Our research tells us that all these things contribute to creativity, innovation, and job satisfaction," he informs you.

You have now reached Rob's office, and it is unlike any office you have ever seen before. There is a candle burning and very relaxing music playing in the background. On his walls are masks from Africa, hand-carved flutes from South America, and bowls of natural items, such as driftwood, stones, and feathers. Rob himself is a tall, elegant man dressed in loose clothing and sandals—decidedly uncorporate! He reaches out to shake your hand, and you wonder if it is your imagination as you feel a warm energy surround you.[11]

You think to yourself, "This is going to be unlike any other business experience I have ever had!"

CREATING THE EDGEWALKER ORGANIZATION

Organizations are communities of people, and the culture and the effectiveness of the organization is based on the shared values and collective consciousness of the members of the organization. An Edgewalker culture is one that values innovation, creativity, risk taking, unleashing the human spirit, and living in alignment with values of sustainability, justice, compassion, and joy.

The leader in any organization is the primary creator of the culture, and this is especially true in Edgewalker Organizations. Edgewalkers within the organization cannot go out to the creative edge of things any farther than the CEO is willing to go. An Edgewalker Organization must have a leader who is an Edgewalker. This person creates the mindset or overall consciousness of the rest of the organization.

In order to create an Edgewalker culture, it is important to get the right mix of people. In any organization there are five different orientations that people can take, and these affect the extent to which the organization can truly be on the leading edge. These five orientations are:

- Edgewalkers
- Flamekeepers
- Hearthtenders
- Placeholders
- Doomsayers

These orientations are based on two factors: relationship to time and relationship to change. The *relationship to time* factor is a continuum between focus on the past and focus on the future. All time orientations are useful in organizational life. It is important to have people who remember the founding values of the organization and who have a sense of the organizational memory. It is also important that people be focused on the present so that those tasks that need to be done right now are attended to. A focus on the future allows for strategic thinking, innovation, and visioning.

The *relationship to change* factor is a continuum between being closed to change and being open to change. Those who are closed to change help provide stability to the organization and can prevent change for the sake of change. They can also be a real block to innovation and to responding quickly to changes in technology, customer relations, and new product or service development. Those who are open to change are often the ones who initiate change, who have a dissatisfaction with the status quo, and who get bored or uncomfortable with stability. They are the ones who can bring in new ideas, but they are also the ones who can create change just for the sake of change, which can be costly.There is no right or wrong about where someone is on either continuum. What is important, however, is that the organization understands where the culture of the organization needs to be for the organization to be both competitive and sustainable. Figure 8 provides a graphic representation of the five organizational orientations (Edgewalkers, Flamekeepers, Hearthtenders, Placeholders, and Doomsayers) and their relationship to the two factors of time and change. This model can help teams and organizations assess their current orientations, and articulate their desired orientations.

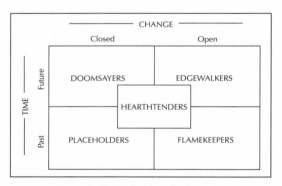

Figure 8: Organizational orientation

In order to understand the implications for organizational culture and performance, we need to examine what each orientation looks like and how it contributes to the whole mix.

Edgewalkers

Edgewalkers are people who walk between worlds and have the ability to build bridges between different worldviews. They have a strong spiritual life and are also very grounded and effective in the everyday material world. They have five qualities of being: self-awareness, passion, integrity, vision, and playfulness. As they grow and develop, they increase their skills in these five stages of development: knowing the future, risk taking, manifesting, focusing, and appreciating.

Edgewalkers are much more oriented toward the future than the past, to the degree that they can sometimes run roughshod over tradition and can close their ears to what has worked in the past. They are also high on the change continuum, with a basic philosophy of "If it ain't broke, fix it anyway."

They are restless and always seeking newness and change. For this reason, they can sometimes be difficult to manage, especially for a traditional manager. The Edgewalker may be more focused on his or her creative ideas than on what is most needed in the organization.

Flamekeepers

Flamekeepers are those people who keep the original vision and values of the organization alive. They are like the Olympic torch bearer, keeping the flame lit at all costs. Or like the keeper of the flame in a temple, who keeps the sacred candles lit morning, noon, and night.

James Collins and Jerry Porras, in their breakthrough study *Built to Last: Successful Habits of Visionary Companies,* concluded that one of the successful habits of visionary companies is what they call "Preserve the Core/Stimulate Progress."[12] They give the example of how CEO Don Petersen and his top management team in the 1980s turned Ford Motor Company around when it was bleeding profits. Petersen is quoted as saying, "There was a great deal of talk about the sequence of the three P's—people, products, and profits. It was decided that people should absolutely come first [products second and profits third]."[13]

This top management team was serving in the role of Flamekeeper by breathing life back into the values of the founder, Henry Ford, who said in 1916, "I don't believe we should make such an awful profit on our cars. A reasonable profit is right, but not too much. I hold that it is better to sell a large number of cars at a reasonably small profit.... I hold this because it enables a larger number of people to buy and enjoy the use of a car and because it gives a larger number of men employment at good wages. Those are the two aims I have in life."[14]

I only know of two organizations that have institutionalized the concept of Flamekeepers. The first is a nonprofit group called the Kripalu Consultant Collaborative (KCC).[15] This is a group of consultants, trainers, coaches, and others that meet two to three times a year. They share an interest in spirituality in the workplace, and they meet to support each other's spiritual and professional growth. The group has designated the founders of the group, Ron and Randy Nelson, and a few others who have been in the group a long time, as Flamekeepers. Their job is to keep the original vision of the organization alive and to continually explore how the organization can more fully live that vision.

The second organization is the strategic programs division of Xerox in Rochester, New York, which created the first truly green, "zero to landfill" copying machine, the Document Center 265DC. The organization went through a massive six-year cultural change to support the development of a whole new series of products. In order to support their larger vision of a culture that focused on people first, they created what was originally called the council of elders and later renamed the council of wisdom keepers. A nominating committee selected sixteen people, two from each of the eight functional groups. In the beginning, the people chosen needed to be fifty-five years or older, and have at least twenty years of service with the organization. Later, Xerox decided that it would be better to have more diversity on the team, since most of the people fifty-five years or older were white males.

The role of these wisdom keepers was to take the temperature of the cultural change program, to serve as ombudsmen, to cut red tape when necessary, and to catch anything significant that might be falling through the cracks.

Flamekeepers are focused on what is best about the past and on preserving the core values of the organization. At the same time, they are open to change and are willing to look at how the organization can build on what has been developed in the past. They may not be your biggest innovators, but once they see how a new product, service, or strategy fits with the core values and is in alignment with the vision of the founders, they will be the biggest supporters of change.

Hearthtenders

Hearthtenders are the people who get the day-to-day work of the organization done. They are the ones who keep the home fires burning when the Edgewalkers are out scouting new territory. They keep things running smoothly and are committed to a sense of family in the organization, and to creating a "home away from home" atmosphere in the organization. Hearthtenders are the ones who remember employees' birthdays and who enjoy the organizational milestone

celebrations. They are the ones who think of creative ways to celebrate accomplishments and to bring people together. They enjoy
working on continuous improvement, and if given half the chance,
will have creative ideas about how to improve the workflow in their
area, or how to better serve customers.

In time orientation, they tend to be focused on the present, and
they are moderately open to change. They are generally satisfied with
their jobs and with the organization, and are happy to keep things the
way they are unless someone has an idea on how to make their work
more streamlined and less stressful. Hearthtenders are shown in the
middle of the model in figure 8, which is an appropriate position because
they provide stability and keep systems running smoothly. Depending on
the climate and culture of the organization, Hearthtenders could move
into any of the other quadrants.

Hearthtenders serve a very important function in the organization, and if you are trying to create an organization that is more values
driven and more innovative, you will want to actively find ways to help
them be either more future oriented, thus moving into the Edgewalker
orientation, or more past oriented, thus moving into the Flamekeeper
orientation. Often Hearthtenders are Edgewalkers or Flamekeepers in
disguise and can be encouraged to be more change oriented if they are
listened to, supported, encouraged, and rewarded.

Placeholders

In contrast to Edgewalkers, who tend to be rare, just about every organization has Placeholders. In *Anatomy of Fire: Sparking a New Spirit
of Enterprise,* leadership expert Tom Brown defines Placeholders as
the people who are holding back organizational progress and innovation.[16] These are the people who see boundaries instead of possibilities, who are focused on the past instead of the future, who use up
resources instead of looking at renewal, and who value doing over
dreaming. They are the ones who want to employ as few people as
possible, in contrast to the leaders who engage all of humankind and
look for ways to grow the enterprise. Placeholders are a drag on organizational energy and are usually the ones who clog the organization's arteries with bureaucratic processes. They will tell you why
something cannot be done and will resist change because "we've
always done it this way."

Placeholders are primarily motivated by fear and ego. They are risk-averse because they are afraid of losing whatever they have. They feel as if they cannot afford to fail, and so they get frozen in place, fighting mightily to keep things the way they are. They might give lip service to change, but they will follow any words of support with statements such as:

- You have to show me where the money will come from.
- Let's put a committee together, and I want a report in three months. Where else has this been done?
- How can you prove that we'll be successful?
- Corporate (or human resources, or management, or the union, or someone else who can be the bad guy) will never go for it.

Placeholders are the self-proclaimed "stability police." They are extremely uncomfortable with change, and they want to keep things as they are or, even better, as they were in the past, when life was simpler.

In the corporate world, a typical way of dealing with Placeholders is to offer early retirement programs. However, the ironic thing is that you are just as likely to lose your Flamekeepers as your Placeholders. Your Flamekeepers will see the early retirement offer as an opportunity to go start their own business in a way that is more in alignment with their values.

Placeholders do have a tremendous amount of organizational memory, and perhaps even some wisdom. A Placeholder is, in many ways, like a pessimistic, angry, cynical Flamekeeper. They probably at one time deeply believed in the vision and values of the organization, and perhaps had their faith and ideals trampled on one too many times. So they retreated into their protective shells and still long for the past. And they try to block any new initiatives that move them even further from what they perceive as their idealized past.

It takes a tremendous amount of work, a high level of interpersonal skills, and maybe even spiritual intelligence, to deal with Placeholders. If you are trying to create more of an Edgewalker culture in your organization, you are likely to create even more fear in Placeholders unless you find a way to deal directly with their motives for being naysayers. From a spiritual perspective, it is important to remember that there is good in every person, and if you are in a change-agent role, you want to find a way to unleash that goodness in your Placeholders.

Programs that increase self-awareness, that focus on values, and that help people rediscover their inherent sense of service and higher purpose, can be very successful for those at lower levels in the organization. One-on-one coaching, whether it is with a professional coach or with a competent boss, can also help Placeholders be more open to change, particularly if they can be shown that they will have some influence on the new direction.

But if your top leaders are Placeholders, your organization is essentially stuck in the mud. Edgewalkers and Flamekeepers will eventually leave out of frustration, and you will be left with people who keep the machinery running but have forgotten the higher purpose and mission of the organization.

Doomsayers

The *Merriam-Webster Dictionary* defines a *Doomsayer* as "one given to forebodings and predictions of impending calamity."[17] Even more than Placeholders, Doomsayers can be a tremendous drag on organizational energy. These folks are not just "the glass is half empty" folks, they are "the glass is broken, the water is going to stain everything, and I'm probably going to bleed to death" folks. They are very concerned about the future, but they always predict the worst possible calamity and then spend their time preparing for doomsday. Or else, in their fear, they just become paralyzed and helpless.

Typically, Doomsayers are marginalized in organizations because they are such an energy drain. They tend to gravitate toward jobs such as safety, environmental engineering, cost accounting, auditing, and other jobs that, by their nature, are supposed to look for what is wrong. The goal of these kinds of jobs is to prevent serious problems from happening and to quickly handle a crisis if it does. Many people in these professions, those who are *not* Doomsayers, handle the prevention work and the crisis work in a calm and professional manner. Doomsayers, on the other hand, turn everything into a drama. They get themselves into a vicious cycle. When they see a potential problem emerging, they do whatever they can to get the attention of people who can do something about it. Often this includes using strong emotion to express their concern.

Doomsayers also use exaggeration to get their point across. Because so many things seem like a crisis to them, and because they tend to exaggerate and blow things out of proportion, they become like the little boy who cried, "Wolf!" People become immune to their cries of alarm, and when there is a real emergency, no one believes them.

Like Placeholders, Doomsayers are change-averse. But their resistance to change is based on a belief that the future holds danger. Their theory about the world is that it is not a safe place, and you have to protect yourself at all costs from bad things happening. And, as Jack Gibb said in his book on trust, our theories create our reality.[18] So if the least little thing goes wrong, Doomsayers are able to say, "See? I told you." They tend to ignore all the things that go right most of the time, and if you point that out to them, they say, "Well, we've been lucky so far, but just you wait."

Doomsayers are very difficult to change. However, if you are creating an Edgewalker Organization, you will have to find a way to deal with them because their negative and fearful energy can be very contagious. Do anything you can to help them develop a more positive relationship with the future. They are already future oriented, but it is a fear-based orientation. If you can help the Doomsayer understand how he or she creates his or her own reality, you will have gone a long way toward transformation. Once they can begin to accept that there may be other ways to think about the future, the Doomsayers will be on their way toward moving to either the Hearthtender quadrant or even the Edgewalker quadrant.

Appreciative Inquiry (AI) entails a particular way of asking questions and envisioning the future that fosters positive relationships and builds on the basic goodness in a person, a situation, or an organization. The 4 "Ds" of Appreciative Inquiry—discover, dream, design, destiny—are a wonderful process for beginning to open up the consciousness of the Doomsayer. Instead of focusing on fixing what is wrong, AI can help them focus on how to create more of what is already working and what it could mean for the future. Doomsayers often find it very difficult to shift their thinking in this way, but it is possible.

When I offer workshops, I often build in a one- or two-hour vision quest in nature as part of the process. This kind of experience can be very helpful to the Doomsayer. Other programs, such as the Noble Purpose program or the ONE program, which help individuals get in touch with their deeper self and their purpose, also have the potential to help Doomsayers see that they could choose a more positive future for themselves. Once they see this on a personal level, they naturally begin to see it on an organizational level as well.

GETTING THE RIGHT MIX

Every large organization will have a mix of people who see the world through one of the five different orientations: Edgewalker, Flamekeeper, Hearthtender, Placeholder, or Doomsayer. If we were to draw a bell curve of the distribution of the typical organization, it might look something like the curve in figure 9:

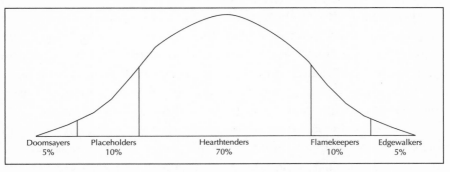

| Doomsayers 5% | Placeholders 10% | Hearthtenders 70% | Flamekeepers 10% | Edgewalkers 5% |

Figure 9: Distribution of orientations in a traditional organization

This particular mix portrays an organization that has equal amounts of Edgewalkers and Doomsayers (5 percent each). They basically cancel each other out and prevent the organization from moving toward a more innovative culture. It also portrays equal amounts of Flamekeepers and Placeholders (10 percent each). Without strong direction from the Edgewalkers, the Flamekeepers and Placeholders keep the organization oriented in the past. The Hearthtenders make up the large majority of the typical organization's orientation (70 percent), and their focus is on the present and keeping the day-to-day work of the organization going.

This traditional mix works fine when the organization is in a relatively stable environment with few competitive challenges. However, it will be a frustrating place for Edgewalkers to work, and if their creativity and values are not respected and nurtured, they will go somewhere else to work for an organization that is more dynamic.

If, on the other hand, your organization is in a rapidly changing, turbulent environment, the kind of environment that Peter Vaill, Senior Scholar and Emeritus Professor of Management in Antioch University's PhD program in Leading and Change, and author of *Learning as a Way of Being,* calls "permanent white water,"[19] then it is essential to have a very different mix. You have a highly competitive environment, technology is changing constantly, your customers change their values and requirements almost overnight, and your old models of predicting the future just do not work anymore. In this kind of environment, you need to have an Edgewalker Organization so that the organization is focused on the future and can quickly adapt to changes in the internal and external environment.

An organization's ability to be successful is directly related to the proportion of Placeholders and Doomsayers to Edgewalkers. Too many Placeholders and Doomsayers can suck the life and inspiration out of a few lone Edgewalkers. And since Edgewalkers are risk takers, they will take all their good ideas and go play in somebody else's sandbox. They will not just sit quietly and turn into deadwood.

Figure 10 shows a very different distribution of people. You will notice that this organization does not have any Doomsayers or Placeholders at all. People who are uncomfortable with change will not be happy in an Edgewalker Organization because this kind of organization not only responds to change, it creates change. It creates new rules to the game and sets the pace for other organizations. Both Doomsayers and Placeholders tend to hold a more fearful and negative view of the world, and their energy would only be a drag on the Edgewalker Organization.

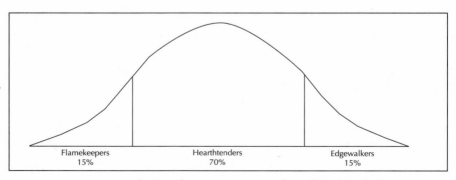

Flamekeepers	Hearthtenders	Edgewalkers
15%	70%	15%

Figure 10: Distribution of orientations in an Edgewalker Organization

There are ways to help Doomsayers and Placeholders move out of their mindsets, and if possible, you want to provide them every opportunity to begin to see the world differently and to join the emerging creative energy of the organization. Several methods of professional development could be helpful, particularly Appreciative Inquiry and personal coaching. If none of these approaches work, the most humane thing to do is to help the person find an environment that feels more comfortable to them. This should be done in the most supportive way possible, using outplacement services, personal development programs, and reasonable severance pay.

In figure 10, there are only three orientations in the distribution curve: Edgewalkers (15 percent), Hearthtenders (70 percent), and Flamekeepers (15 percent). In this model, there are three times as many Edgewalkers as in the traditional organizational model. Although 15 percent is not a large portion of the overall employee base, it is at the level of critical mass and is significant enough to keep the organization moving in creative and inspired new directions. The actual percentages that are the right mix for each organization vary, depending on the kind of business (for example, advertising versus auto manufacturing), the organization's past cultural history, the current stage of development, and the organization's vision of the future.

It is always easier to create a new organization than to change an existing company. When starting from scratch, you can hire the right mix of people to help you fulfill your vision, and you can establish the kinds of values and practices that will keep you on the leading edge. In fact, most innovation and job growth in U.S. companies comes from small, entrepreneurial firms. The large organizations that have been the titans of the corporate world are now the biggest source of the unemployment numbers. These dinosaurs are not known for innovative breakthroughs in their products, services, or management processes. Most positive change comes from the edges of the business world, not the center.

If you do not have the luxury of creating a new start-up, then the question is, how do you help your organization be more of an Edgewalker Organization? One thing you will want to do is to evaluate your current mix of Edgewalkers, Flamekeepers, Hearthtenders, Placeholders, and Doomsayers. A simple way to do this would be to hold focus groups in your organization, explain the definitions of the five orientations, and then ask people to individually create their own distribution curve for the five orientations in your company. Ask people to share their charts and explain why they created that particular distribution. Once everyone has shared, the group can create a collective chart, based on their consensus of what the organization's distribution looks like. Depending on the size of your organization, you may want to do this with several groups, making sure that there is representation of all the levels and functions.[20]

Now, more than ever, our organizations need to attract, develop, and retain Edgewalkers. And we need to support the development of organizations that have a strong commitment to making a positive difference in the world. The Edgewalker Organization is committed to offering leading-edge products and services that enhance people's lives and the planet. They are committed to sustainability, diversity, and nurturing the human spirit. They do this through embracing the people who have strong Edgewalker qualities and through supporting people in developing a stronger relationship to the future and greater openness to change.

■ ■ ■

Notes

Love and Truth: The Golden Rules of Leadership

1. Lance Secretan, *Managerial Moxie* (Rocklin, Calif.: Prima Publishing, 1993).
2. Brad Blanton, *Radical Honesty: How to Transform Your Life by Telling the Truth* (New York: Dell Publishing, 1994).
3. Will Schutz, *The Human Element: Productivity, Self-Esteem and the Bottom Line* (San Francisco: Jossey-Bass, 1994).
4. Mary Cusack, "Here's a Radical Idea—Tell the Truth," *Fast Company,* Alice van Housen, Issue 10, August 1997.

Letting the Heart Fall Open: Spirit, Vulnerability, and Relational Intelligence in the Workplace

1. *Merriam-Webster Dictionary* (New York: Random House, 2001), 676.
2. Roger Lewin and Birute Regine, *Weaving Complexity and Business: Engaging the Soul at Work* (New York: Texere Publishing, 2001).
3. Linda Hartling, "Relational Intelligence: A Key to Success in the New Economy," *WCW Research Report* (Spring/Summer 2001).
4. Jeffrey Pfeffer, *The Human Equation: Building Profits by Putting People First* (Boston: Harvard Business School Press, 1998).
5. Tom Peters and Robert Waterman, *In Search of Excellence: Lessons from America's Best Run Companies* (New York: Harper & Row, 1982).
6. Joyce Fletcher, *Disappearing Acts: Gender, Power, and Relational Practice at Work* (Cambridge, Mass.: MIT Press, 2001).
7. Sumru Erkut and Winds of Change Foundation. *Inside Women's Power: Learning from Leaders* (Wellesley, Mass.: Wellesley Centers for Women, Wellesley College, 2001).
8. As reported in an article in the *New York Times*, Amy Zipkin "Management: The Wisdom of Thoughtfulness" (*New York Times*, May 31, 2000).
9. Howard Gardner, *Frames of Mind: The Theory of Multiple Intelligences* (New York: BasicBooks, 1983).
10. Christopher Koch, interview with Howard Gardner, "The Bright Stuff," *CIO* (March 1996). Retrieved from *http://inst.sfcc.edu/~mwehr/Humanrel/15EmotIntArt.htm*.

WORKING SPIRITUALLY: Aligning Gifts, Purpose, and Passion

1. L. Ferguson, *The Path for Greatness: Spirituality at Work* (Victoria, B.C.: Trafford Publishing, 2001), 10.
2. K. Gibran, "On Work," *The Prophet* (New York: Alfred A. Knopf, 1923), 13.

YOU ARE THE MESSAGE! The Power of Authentic Speaking

1. D. Warren, *James Cagney: The Authorized Biography* (London: Robson Books, 1998).
2. M. Oliver, "The Summer Day," *New and Selected Poems* (Boston: Beacon Press, 1992).
3. These words of Sydney J. Harris are found in numerous quotation sites on the Internet, including www.thinkexist.com, www.brainyquote.com, and www.quote opia.com.

BRAIN SHAPING AT WORK: Wiring Our Brains for Integrity, Leadership, Creativity, and [Insert Your Favorite Trait or Skill Here]

1. E. J. Gibson, *An Odyssey in Learning and Perception* (Cambridge, Mass.: MIT Press, 1991).
2. M. M. Merzenich, R. J. Nelson, M. P. Stryker, M. S. Cynader, A. Schoppmann, J. M. Zook, "Somatosensory Cortical Map Changes Following Digit Amputation in Adult Monkeys," *The Journal of Comparative Neurology* 224 (1984): 591.
3. P. Tallal, S. L. Miller, G. Bedi, G. Byma, X. Wang, S. S. Nagarajan, C. Schreiner, W. M. Jenkins, M. M. Merzenich, "Language Comprehension in Language-Learning Impaired Children Improved with Acoustically Modified Speech," *Science* 271 (1996): 81; M. M. Merzenich, W. M. Jenkins, P. Johnston, C. Schreiner, S. L. Miller, P. Tallal, "Temporal Processing Deficits of Language-Learning Impaired Children Ameliorated by Training," *Science* 271 (1996): 71.
4. M. Herzog and M. Fahle, "The Role of Feedback in Learning a Vernier Discrimination Task," *Vision Research* 37 (1997): 2133.
5. L. P. Shiu and H. Pashler, "Improvement in Line Orientation Discrimination Is Retinally Local but Dependent on Cognitive Set," *Perception and Psychophysics* 52 (1992): 582; M. Ahissar and Hochstein, "Attentional Control of Early Perceptual Learning," *Proceedings of the National Academy of Sciences USA* 90 (1993): 5718; D. B. Polley, E. E. Steinberg, and M. M. Merzenich, "Perceptual Learning Directs Auditory Cortical Map Reorganization through Top-Down Influences, *The Journal of Neuroscience* 26 (2006): 4970.
6. A. R. Seitz, H. R. Dinse, "A Common Framework for Perceptual Learning," *Current Opinion in Neurobiology* 17 (2007): 148.
   Note: In addition to this excellent review, my son's insight about catchy songs may be illustrative here. The other day he told me, "When you learn music, the piece of music loves you and you learn to love it. But with catchy music, you may not love it at first; it just catches. After hearing it over and over in your head, you kind of learn to love it because you know it so well." Catchy music,

and other similar kinds of stimulation, may have stimulus parameters that harness the neurological structures that are linked to reward, short-circuiting the usual requirement for attentional focus on something you want to learn.

7. B. A. Wright, "Why and How We Study Human Learning on Basic Auditory Tasks, *Audiology & Neuro-otology* 6 (2001): 207; B. A. Wright and A. T. Sabin, "Perceptual Learning: How Much Daily Training Is Enough?" *Experimental Brain Research* 180 (2007): 727; A. T. Sabin, "Perceptual Learning Enhancement: The Influence of Non-Target Condition and Condition Order" (qualifying research project, 2008).

8. J. A. Mossbridge, E. O'Connor, M. B. Fitzgerald, and B. A. Wright, "Perceptual Learning Evidence for Separate Processing of Asynchrony and Order Tasks," *Journal of Neuroscience* 26 (2006): 12708; J. A. Mossbridge, B. N. Scissors, and B. A. Wright, "Learning and Generalization on Asynchrony and Order Tasks at Sound Offset: Implications for Underlying Neural Circuitry," *Learning and Memory* 15 (2008): 13.

9. R. C. deCharms, "Reading and Controlling Human Brain Activation Using Real-Time Functional Magnetic Resonance Imaging," *Trends in Cognitive Sciences* 11 (2007): 473.

10. M. Shermer, phone interview with author, June 18, 2008.

11. M. Shermer, *The Mind of the Market: Compassionate Apes, Competitive Humans, and Other Tales from Evolutionary Economics* (New York: Times Books, 2007).

12. F. de Waal, lecture at Northwestern University, April 10, 2008.

13. S. D. Preston and Frans de Waal, "Empathy: Its Ultimate and Proximate Bases," *Behavioral and Brain Sciences* 25 (2002): 1.

14. O. Golan and S. Baron-Cohen, "Systemizing Empathy: Teaching Adults with Asperger Syndrome or High-Functioning Autism to Recognize Complex Emotions Using Interactive Multimedia," *Development and Psychopathology* 18 (2006): 591.

15. R. A. Barker, "How Can We Train Leaders If We Do Not Know What Leadership Is?" *Human Relations* 50 (1997): 343.

16. D. V. Day, "Leadership Development: A Review in Context," *The Leadership Quarterly* 11 (2000): 581.

17. R. Koestner, M. Walker, L. Fichman, "Childhood Parenting Experiences and Adult Creativity," *Journal of Research in Personality* 33 (1999): 92.

18. H. J. Eysenck, *Genius: The Natural History of Creativity* (Cambridge, Mass.: Cambridge University Press, 1995).

19. R. Epstein, S. M. Schmidt, R. Warfel, "Measuring and Training Creativity Competencies: Validation of a New Test," *Creativity Research Journal* 20 (2008): 7.

20. M. DiChristina, "How to Unleash Your Creativity," *Scientific American Mind* 19 (3) (June/July 2008).

21. J. Cameron, *The Artist's Way: A Spiritual Path to Higher Creativity* (New York: Jeremy P. Tarcher, 1992).
22. K. Robinson, *Out of Our Minds: Learning to be Creative* (Hoboken, N.J.: John Wiley & Sons, 2001).
23. S. P. Marshall, *The Power to Transform: Leadership That Brings Learning and Schooling to Life* (San Francisco: Jossey-Bass, 2006).
24. Stephanie Pace Marshall, phone interview with author, May 12, 2008.

INSPIRED LEADERSHIP: Leading with Spirit

1. Institute of HearthMath, "Overview." Retrieved from www.heartmath.org.
2. Institute of HeartMath, *Science of the Heart: Exploring the Role of the Heart in Human Performance—An Overview of Research Conducted by the Institute of HeartMath.* E-book retrieved from www.heartmath.org/research/research-science-of-the-heart.html.

References

Church, Dawson, ed. *Healing the Heart of the World: Harnessing the Power of Intention to Change Your Life and Your Planet.* Santa Rosa, Calif.: Elite Books, 2005.

Hayakawa, Ellen. *The Inspired Organization: Spirituality and Energy at Work.* Victoria, B.C.: Trafford Publishing, 2003.

Institute of HeartMath. *Science of the Heart: Exploring the Role of the Human Heart in Human Performance—An Overview of Research Conducted by the Institute of HeartMath.* Boulder Creek, Calif.: Institute of HeartMath, 2001.

Wise, Anna. *High Performance Mind: Mastering Brainwaves for Insight, Healing and Creativity.* New York: Penguin Group, 1996.

SPIRITUALITY AND ETHICAL LEADERSHIP: Moral Persons and Moral Managers

1. L. T. Hosmer, "Trust: The Connecting Link Between Organizational Theory and Philosophical Ethics," *Academy of Management Review* 20 (1995): 379–403; K. T. Dirks and D. Ferrin, "Trust in Leadership: Meta-analytic Findings and Implications for Research," *Journal of Applied Psychology* 87 (2002): 611–628; P. Kottler and N. Lee, *Corporate Social Responsibility: Doing the Most Good for Your Company and Your Cause* (New York: Wiley & Sons, 2005).
2. S. A. Waddock and S. B. Graves, "The Corporate Social Performance-Financial Performance Link," *Strategic Management Journal* 18 (1997): 303–319.
3. M. E. Brown and L. K. Trevino, "Ethical Leadership: A Review and Future Directions," *Leadership Quarterly* 17 (2006): 595–616; M. E. Brown, L. K. Trevino, and D. A. Harrison, "Ethical Leadership: A Social Learning Perspective for Construct Development and Testing," *Organizational Behavior and Human Decision Processes* 97 (2005): 117–134; L. K. Trevino, L. P. Hartman, and M. Brown, "Moral Person and Moral Manager: How Executives Develop a Reputation for Ethical Leadership," *California Management Review* 42 (2000): 12–142.

4. I. Mitroff and E. A. Denton, "A Study of Spirituality in the Workplace," *Sloan Management Review* (Summer 1999): 83–92.

5. D. Duchon and D. A. Plowman, "Nurturing the Spirit at Work: Impact on Work Unit Performance," *The Leadership Quarterly* (2005): 816.

6. B. J. Zinnbauer and K. I. Pargament, "Religiousness and Spirituality," in *Handbook of the Psychology of Religion and Spirituality,* ed. R. F. Paloutzian and C. L. Park (New York: Guilford, 2005), 21–42.

7. M. Kriger and Y. Seng, "Leadership with Inner Meaning: A Contingency Theory of Leadership Based on the Worldviews of Five Religions," *The Leadership Quarterly* 16 (2005): 771–806.

8. R. N. Kanungo and M. Mendonca, "What Leaders Cannot Do Without: The Spiritual Dimensions of Leadership," in *Spirit at Work: Discovering the Spirituality in Leadership,* ed. J. A. Conger (San Francisco: Jossey-Bass, 1994), 162–198.

9. C. Peterson and M. E. P. Seligman, *Character Strengths and Virtues: A Handbook and Classification* (Oxford: Oxford University Press, 2004); A. Compte-Sponville, *A Small Treatise on the Great Virtues: The Uses of Philosophy in Everyday Life* (New York: Metropolitan Books, 2001).

10. R. Galford and A. S. Drapeau, "The Enemies of Trust," *Harvard Business Review* (February 2003): 88–95.

11. L. Stein, "Flying Low," *U.S. News & World Report,* May 5, 2003.

12. J. A. Morris, C. M. Brotheridge, and J. C. Urbanski, "Bringing Humility to Leadership: Antecedents and Consequences of Leader Humility," *Human Relations* 58 (2005): 1323–1350.

13. J. Collins, *Good to Great* (New York: HarperBusiness, 2001).

14. J. A. Morris, C. M. Brotheridge, and J. C. Urbanski, "Bringing Humility to Leadership."

15. T. Smith, "Justice as a Personal Virtue," *Social Theory & Practice* 25 (1999): 361–384; Peterson and Seligman, *Character Strengths and Virtues;* Compte-Sponville, *A Small Treatise on the Great Virtues.*

16. A. Colby and W. Damon, *Some Do Care: Contemporary Lives of Moral Commitment* (New York: Free Press, 1992).

17. A. Colby and W. Damon, "The Development of Extraordinary Moral Commitment," in *Morality in Everyday Life: Developmental Perspectives,* ed. M. Killen and D. Hart (Cambridge: Cambridge University Press, 1995), 311.

18. J. S. Young, C. S. Cashwell, and V. J. Woolington, "The Relationship of Spirituality to Cognitive and Moral Development and Purpose in Life: An Exploratory Investigation," *Counseling & Values* 43 (1998): 63–69; C. J. Chang-Ho, "Religious Orientations in Moral Development," *Journal of Psychology and Christianity* 23 (2004): 22–30; A. M. Maclean, L. J. Walker, and M. K. Matsuba, "Transcendence and the Moral Self: Identity Integration, Religion, and Moral Life," *Journal for the Scientific Study of Religion* 43 (2004): 429–437.

19. L. A. Kohlberg, *The Psychology of Moral Development: The Nature and Validity of Moral Stages,* vol. 2 (San Francisco: Harper & Row, 1984); J. R. Rest, D.

Narvaez, M. J. Bebeau, and S. J. Thomas, *Postconventional Moral Thinking: A Neo-Kohlbergian Approach* (Mahwah, N.J.: Lawrence Erlbaum, 1999).

20. L. W. Fry, "Toward a Theory of Spiritual Leadership," *The Leadership Quarterly* 14 (2003): 693–727.

21. N. Eisenberg, "Emotion, Regulation, and Moral Development," *Annual Review of Psychology* 51 (2000): 665–697.

22. C. A. Rayburn, "Vocation as Calling," in *Connections Between Spirit and Work in Career Development,* ed. D. P. Bloch and L. J. Richmond (Palo Alto, Calif.: Davies-Black, 1997), 162–183; J. L. Magee and A. L. Delbercq, "Vocation as a Critical Factor in a Spirituality for Executive Leadership in Business," in *Business, Religion, & Spirituality: A New Synthesis,* ed. O. F. Williams (Notre Dame, Ind.: University of Notre Dame Press, 2003), 94–110.

23. P. H. Mirvis, "'Soul Work' in Organizations," *Organization Science* 8 (1997): 193–206.

24. L. Hardy, *The Fabric of This World: Inquiries into Calling, Career Choice, and the Design of Human Work* (Grand Rapids, Mich.: Eerdmans, 1990).

25. L. Reave, "Spiritual Values and Practices Related to Leadership Effectiveness," *Leadership Quarterly* 16 (2005): 655–687.

26. R. J. Foster, *Celebration of Discipline: The Path to Spiritual Growth,* rev. ed. (New York: Harper & Row, 1998).

27. K. Kurth, "Spiritually Renewing Ourselves at Work: Finding Meaning through Serving," in *Handbook of Workplace Spirituality and Organizational Performance,* ed. R. A. Giacalone and C. L. Jurkiewicz (Armonk, N.Y.: M. E. Sharpe, 2003), 447–460.

28. Fry, "Toward a Theory of Spiritual Leadership."

29. Ibid.

30. C. L. Jurkiewicz and R. A. Giacalone, "A Values Framework for Measuring the Impact of Workplace Spirituality on Organizational Performance," *Journal of Business Ethics* 49 (2004): 129–142; R. A. Giacalone and C. L. Jurkiewicz, "Right from Wrong: The Influence of Spirituality on Perceptions of Unethical Business Activities," *Journal of Business Ethics* 46 (2003): 85–97.

31. J. C. Garcia-Zamor, "Workplace Spirituality and Organizational Performance," *Public Administration Review* 63 (2003): 355–363.

I-THOU AT THE WORKPLACE: An Interpersonal Spirituality from the Teachings of Martin Buber

References

Buber, Martin. *I and Thou*. Translated by Walter Kaufman. New York: Free Press, 1971.

Friedman, Maurice. *Encounter on the Narrow Ridge: A Life of Martin Buber*. St. Paul: Paragon House, 1993.

———. *Martin Buber: The Life of Dialogue*. 4th ed. New York: Routledge, 2002.

Ross, Dennis S. *God in Our Relationships: Spirituality between People from the Teachings of Martin Buber*. Woodstock, Vt.: Jewish Lights Publishing, 2003.

WHAT MAKES AN ORGANIZATION SPIRITUAL? Applied Spirituality in Organizational Structure, Design, Processes, and Practices

1. M. Benefiel, *The Soul of a Leader: Finding Your Path to Fulfillment and Success* (New York: Crossroad Publishing, 2008), 138–141.
2. Ibid., 142–158.
3. International Center for Spirit at Work, "About the International Spirit at Work Award," *www.spiritatwork.org/index.php/isaw_aboutaward*.
4. M. Benefiel, *Soul at Work: Spiritual Leadership in Organizations* (New York: Church Publishing, 2005), 17–26.
5. Benefiel, *Soul of a Leader*, 31–48.
6. J. Biberman and Len Tischler, eds., *Spirituality in Business: Theory, Practice, and Future Directions* (New York: Palgrave MacMillan, 2008).
7. J. Marques, "Spiritual Performance from an Organizational Perspective: The Starbucks Way," *Corporate Governance* 8, no. 3 (2008): 248–257.

ADDRESSING WELLNESS PROBLEMS IN THE WORKPLACE THROUGH SPIRITUALITY: Six Risks and Six Spiritual Solutions

1. A. Maslow, *Motivation and Personality* (New York: Addison-Wesley Publishing, 1954; rev. 1987 by Robert Frager and James Fadiman).
2. G. Norwood, "Maslow's Hierarchy of Needs," www.deepermind.com/ maslow.htm; Don Clark, "Leadership and Human Behavior," www.nwlink.com/~donclark/leader/leadhb.html.
3. J. Marques, S. Dhiman, and R. King, *Spirituality in the Workplace: What It Is, Why It Matters, and How to Make It Work for You* (Fawnskin, Calif.: Personhood Press, 2007).
4. W. A. Guillory, *The Living Organization: Spirituality in the Workplace* (Salt Lake City: Innovations International, 2000): x.
5. L. Reid and F. Evers, *Working with Spirit: Engaging Spirituality to Meet the Challenges of the Workplace* (Toronto: Path Books, 2004).
6. C. L. Cordes and T. W. Dougherty, "A Review and an Integration of Research on Job Burnout," *Academy of Management Review* 18, no. 1 (1993): 621–656.
7. D. Rosenberg McKay, "Job Burnout," About.com, http://careerplanning.about.com/od/workrelated/a/burnout_sht.htm.
8. Ibid.
9. "Chrysler to Cut Ontario Jobs," www.thestar.com, February 14, 2007.
10. M. Kivimäki, J. Vahtera, J. Pentti, and J. E. Ferrie, "Factors Underlying the Effect of Organizational Downsizing on Health of Employees: Longitudinal Cohort Study," *British Medical Journal* 320 (April 2000): 971–975.

11. C. D. Dooley, J. Prause, and K. A. Ham-Rowbottom, "Underemployment and Depression: Longitudinal Relationships," *Journal of Health and Social Behavior* 41 (December 2000): 421–436.
12. Kathleen D. Ryan and Daniel K. Oestreich, *Driving Fear Out of the Workplace: How to Overcome the Invisible Barriers to Quality, Productivity, and Innovation* (San Francisco: Jossey-Bass, 1991).
13. Ibid., 9.
14. Lao-tzu, *Tao Te Ching: A New English Version with Foreword and Notes by Stephen Mitchell* (New York: Harper, 1992), ch. 9.

OVERCOMING FEAR AND BUILDING TRUST: Creating Healthy Organizations

1. F. Herzberg, *Work and the Nature of Man* (New York: T. Y. Cromwell, 1966) and *One More Time: How Do You Motivate Employees?* (Boston: Harvard Business Press, 2008); Abraham Maslow, *Motivation and Personality* (New York: Harper & Row, 1970 and 1987 re-edited); Peter Drucker, *The Effective Executive* (New York: HarperCollins Publishers, 1993); Peter Block, *The Answer to How Is Yes* (San Francisco: Berrett-Koehler, 2002); Daniel Yankelovich, *New Rules: Searching for Self-Fulfillment in a World Turned Upside Down* (New York: Bantam, 1982); and Patrick Lencioni, *The Five Dysfunctions of a Team: A Field Guide for Leaders, Managers, and Facilitators* (San Francisco: Jossey-Bass, 2005).
2. F. Herzberg, *Work and the Nature of Man*, 71–79.
3. Ibid.
4. W. Schmidt and J. P. Finnigan, *TQ Manager: A Practical Guide for Managing in a Total Quality Organization* (San Francisco: Jossey-Bass, 1993).
5. S. Covey, *The 7 Habits of Highly Effective People* (New York: Simon and Schuster, 1989).
6. A. Maslow, *Motivation and Personality* (New York, HarperCollins, 1987).
7. E. F. Schumacher, *Good Work* (New York: Harper & Row, 1977).

LIBERATING THE CORPORATE SOUL: Building a High-Performance, Values-Driven Organization

1. R. Barrett, *Building a Values-Driven Organization: A Whole System Approach to Cultural Transformation* (Boston: Butterworth-Heinemann, 2006).
2. J. P. Kotter and J. L. Heskett, *Corporate Culture and Performance* (New York: Free Press, 1992).
3. J. C. Collins and J. I. Porras, *Built to Last: Successful Habits of Visionary Companies* (New York: HarperCollins, 1994).
4. R. Barrett, *Building a Values-Driven Organization*.
5. R. Barrett, *Liberating the Corporate Soul: Building a Visionary Organization* (Boston: Butterworth-Heinemann, 1998), 12–13.
6. T. H. Davenport, "The Fad That People Forgot," *Fast Company* (October 1995): 69–74.

BEYOND THE BOTTOM LINE: Spiritual Principles for Successful Performance

1. From *Revolution to Reconstruction: Biographies: Adam Smith*. Website: odur.let.rug.nl/~usa/B/asmith/adams 1.htm.

2. A. Smith, *The Theory of Moral Sentiments,* 1759. The Library of Economics and Liberty; the Concise Encyclopedia of Economics. www. econlib.org?library.

3. R. Eisler, *The Real Wealth of Nations: Creating a Caring Economics* (San Francisco: Berrett-Koehler, 2007), 140.

4. A. Smith, *An Inquiry into the Nature and Causes of the Wealth of Nations,* book 4, ch. 2. The Library of Economics and Liberty; the Concise Encyclopedia of Economics. www. econlib.org?library.

5. A. Smith, *Wealth of Nations,* 1776. The Library of Economics and Liberty; the Concise Encyclopedia of Economics. www. econlib.org?library.

6. J. D. Gwartney, R. L. Stroup, R. S. Sobel, and D. Macpherson, *Economics: Private and Public Choice,* 9th ed. (New York: Harcourt, 2008), 16.

7. Wikipedia, "Economic efficiency," http://en.wikipedia.org/wiki/Economic_efficiency.

8. You can read more about Southwest's mission at www.southwest.com/aboutswa/ourmission.

9. Investor's Business Daily, http://www.investors.com.

10. Investors Business Daily, "What Is CAN SLIM?" www.investors.com/learn/c01b.asp.

11. M. Useem, *Investor Capitalism: How Money Managers Are Changing the Face of Corporate America* (New York: Basic Books, 1996).

12. Ibid., 274.

13. Florida State University College of Business, "MBA Programs at a Glance," http://cob.fsu.edu/grad/mba.cfm.

14. R. Alsop, "The Best Corporate Reputations in America: Just as in Politics, Trust, Reliability Pay Off Over Time," *Wall Street Journal,* September 23, 1999.

15. J. C. Collins and J. I. Porras, *Built to Last: Successful Habits of Visionary Companies* (New York: HarperCollins, 1994).

16. J. Reingold and R. Underwood, "Was Built to Last Built to Last?" *Fast Company* (November 2004): 105.

17. R. Abrams, *Wear Clean Underwear: Business Wisdom from Mom; Timeless Advice from the Ultimate CEO* (New York: Dell, 2000).

18. Quotes supporting concern for purpose other than the bottom line from many outstanding writers and thinkers about business purpose and policy, including P. Drucker, C. Handy, B. Largent, L. C. Thurow, R. Eisler, and others, can be found at our website, www.spiritfilledpress.com.

19. From a report with Sam Walton.

20. T. Peters, "What's Culture Got to Do with It?" www.tompeters.com/entries.php?note=009550.php.

21. J. McMichael, *The Spiritual Style of Management* (Havana, Fla.: Spirit Filled Press, 1997).

22. Scripture verse adapted from Matthew 6:33.

23. J. A. Schumpeter, *Capitalism, Socialism and Democracy*, 3rd ed. (New York: Harper Perennial, 1962), 80.

IDENTIFYING AND MANAGING THE SHADOW OF WORKPLACE SPIRITUALITY: Practical Guidelines

1. J. Biberman and M. Whitty, eds., *Work and Spirit: A Reader of New Spiritual Paradigms for Organizations* (Scranton, Pa.: University of Scranton, 2000); M. Conlin, "Religion in the Workplace: The Growing Presence of Spirituality in Corporate America," *BusinessWeek* (November 1, 1999), 150–158; M. Gunther, "God and Business: The Surprising Quest for Spiritual Renewal in the American Workplace," *Fortune* (July 16, 2001): 58–80; J. Milliman, J. Ferguson, D. Trickett, and B. Condemi, "Spirit and Community at Southwest Airlines: An Investigation of a Spiritual Values-Based Model," *Journal of Organizational Change Management* 12, no. 3 (1999): 221–233.

2. A. Grün and M. Dufner, *Spiritualiteit van Beneden* (Ten Have, Neth.: Kampen, 1994).

3. C. G. Jung, *The Collected Works of C. G. Jung* (Princeton, N.J.: Princeton University Press, 1967).

4. For the formal background of the quadrant model, please see M. S. Lips-Wiersma, K. Lund Dean, and C. J. Fornaciari's paper presented at the 2008 Academy of Management Meetings, "The Workplace Spirituality Movement: Identifying the Shadow of Management and Managing the Shadow."

5. M. Schoeff, "Bill Seeks to Expand Right to Religious Expression at Work," *Workforce Management* 85, no. 4, (2006): 3; R. Stein, "Pharmacists' Rights at the Front of New Debate," *Washington Post,* March 28, 2005; www.washington-post.com/wp-dyn/articles/A5490-2005Mar5427_5492.html.

6. L. Parker, "Some Doctors Refuse Services for Religious Reasons," *USA Today* (August 3, 2007), 1A, 3A.

7. J. Martin, *Organizational Culture: Mapping the Terrain* (London: Sage, 2002), 95.

8. K. Lund Dean, C. J. Fornaciari, and S. R. Safranski, "The Ethics of Spiritual Inclusion," in *Spirituality in Business: Theory, Practice, and Future Directions,* ed. J. Biberman and L. Tischler (New York: Palgrave Macmillan, 2008), 188–202.

9. R. Shorto, "Faith at Work," *New York Times Magazine* (October 31, 2004), 40–46, 62, 66, 69.

10. Ibid., 42.

11. K. Lund Dean, C. J. Fornaciari, and S. R. Safranski, "The Ethics of Spiritual Inclusion."

12. D. Miller, *God at Work: The History and Promise of the Faith at Work Movement* (New York: Oxford University Press, 2007), 184.

13. P. Fleming and G. Sewell, "Looking for the Good Soldier, Svejk," *Sociology* 36, no. 4 (2002): 857–873.

14. B. Jackson, *Management Gurus and Management Fashions: A Dramatistic Inquiry* (London: Routledge, 2001).

15. S. Butterfield, *Amway: The Cult of Free Enterprise* (Boston: South End Press, 1985).

16. M. G. Pratt, "The Good, the Bad and the Ambivalent: Managing Identification among Amway Distributors," *Administrative Science Quarterly* 45, no. 3 (2000): 456–493.

HEART AT WORK: Signs of Hope

1. Exhibit 1, "Brief description of the U. N. Global Compact," *Who Cares Wins* (Geneva: United Nations Department of Public Information, 2004), viii. Retrieved from www.unglobalcompact.org/docs/news_events/8.1/WhoCaresWins.pdf.

2. Exhibit 2, "U. N. Global Compact Principles," *Who Cares Wins,* ix.

3. "Executive summary," *Who Cares Wins,* i–ii.

4. Ibid., ii–iv.

5. "Principles for Responsible Investment," (UNEP Finance Initiative, [n.d.]).

4. Retrieved from www.unpri.org/files/pri.pdf.

6. Ibid., 6–7.

7. Reprinted with permission from Jacqueline Miller. Exerpted from *Heart at Work* (McGraw Hill, 1996).

8. Ibid.

9. Ibid.

10. Ibid.

11. Isaac Tigrett, as quoted in *Nation's Restaurant News* (October 27, 1997). Retrieved from http://findarticles.com/p/articles/mi_m3190/is_/ai_19944813.

CREATING EDGEWALKER ORGANIZATIONS: The Workplace of the Future

1. Adapted from "The Edgewalker Organization," in Judi Neal, *Edgewalkers: People and Organizations That Take Risks, Build Bridges, and Break New Ground* (Westport, Conn.: Praegerm, 2006), chs. 6–7.

2. This scenario is a composite based on innovative practices from several ideas, as well as images I had from meditating on the future with the idea of bringing this organizational design into the present.

3. Sounds True, in Boulder, Colorado, has a policy of allowing dogs in the workplace as long as they are well behaved toward humans and other canines, and as long as no one in the work area has allergies to dogs.

4. This building design is similar to that of the Johnson & Johnson corporate headquarters in New Brunswick, New Jersey.

5. Robert Rabbin is a wonderful writer on spirituality in the workplace. This mention here is to honor him for his work, and to make reference to his article, "Vice President of Corporate Consciousness," *Spirit at Work Newsletter* (October 1997).

6. J. Robert Ouimet explains how spiritual support groups work in his dissertation summary titled, "The Golden Book," available at www.our-project.org.

7. More and more organizations have meditation rooms or silence rooms. They include Ouimet-Tomasso, ANZ Bank, Pfizer, and Rodale Press, for example.

8. Johnson & Johnson has a program just like this in their New Brunswick, New Jersey, Corporate Headquarters.

9. *Times of India,* an International Spirit at Work Award recipient, states in their award application, "The organisation structure is consumer focused and the customer is seen as God. Everyone in the organisation joins together to provide an offering to this God (customer) with the best possible news and views, of highest quality at fastest speed. The organisation is not solely governed by profits. The aim of the organisation is to make employees and stakeholders happy and achieve their highest potential by using the organisation as a platform for self actualization."

10. This section is modeled on some of the practices of SAS, a major software company in Cary, North Carolina.

11. This description is based on the shaman character Jason Hand in Richard Whiteley's book *The Corporate Shaman: A Business Fable* (New York: Harper-Collins, 2002).

12. J. Collins and J. Porras, *Built to Last: Successful Habits of Visionary Companies* (San Francisco: HarperBusiness, 1997). See chapter 3, "More than Profits," for more information on how to "preserve the core," 46–79.

13. D. Petersen, quoted in Collins and Porras, *Built to Last,* 52.

14. H. Ford, quoted in Collins and Porras, *Built to Last,* 53.

15. More information about the Kripalu Consultant Collaborative can be found at www.spiritintheworkplace.com.

16. T. Brown, *Anatomy of Fire* (Lexington, Ky.: Management General, 2002), ch. 2, p. 3. E-book retrieved from www.anatomyoffire.com.

17. *Merriam-Webster Online Dictionary,* retrieved from www.m-w.com/cgi-bin/dictionary?va=doomsayer.

18. J. Gibb, *Trust: A New View of Personal and Organizational Development* (Los Angeles: Guild of Tutors Press, 1978).

19. P. Vaill, *Learning as a Way of Being: Strategies for Survival in a World of Permanent White Water* (San Francisco: Jossey-Bass, 1997).

20. An Edgewalker Organizational assessment tool has been created by Judi Neal & Associates. For more information on the organizational assessment tools, contact Judi Neal at judi@edgewalkers.org, or visit www.edgewalkers.org.

Index

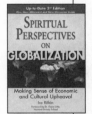
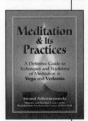

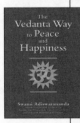

Spiritual Biography / Reference

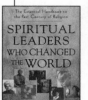

Spiritual Leaders Who Changed the World
The Essential Handbook to the Past Century of Religion
Edited by Ira Rifkin and the Editors at SkyLight Paths; Foreword by Dr. Robert Coles
An invaluable reference to the most important spiritual leaders of the past 100 years.
6 x 9, 304 pp, 15+ b/w photos, Quality PB, 978-1-59473-241-6 **$18.99**

Spiritual Biography—SkyLight Lives

SkyLight Lives reintroduces the lives and works of key spiritual figures of our time—people who by their teaching or example have challenged our assumptions about spirituality and have caused us to look at it in new ways.

The Life of Evelyn Underhill
An Intimate Portrait of the Groundbreaking Author of Mysticism
by Margaret Cropper; Foreword by Dana Greene
Evelyn Underhill was a passionate writer and teacher who wrote elegantly on mysticism, worship, and devotional life.
6 x 9, 288 pp, 5 b/w photos, Quality PB, 978-1-893361-70-6 **$18.95**

Mahatma Gandhi: His Life and Ideas
by Charles F. Andrews; Foreword by Dr. Arun Gandhi
Examines from a contemporary Christian activist's point of view the religious ideas and political dynamics that influenced the birth of the peaceful resistance movement.
6 x 9, 336 pp, 5 b/w photos, Quality PB, 978-1-893361-89-8 **$18.95**

Simone Weil: A Modern Pilgrimage
by Robert Coles
The extraordinary life of the spiritual philosopher who's been called both saint and madwoman.
6 x 9, 208 pp, Quality PB, 978-1-893361-34-8 **$16.95**

Zen Effects: The Life of Alan Watts
by Monica Furlong
Through his widely popular books and lectures, Alan Watts (1915–1973) did more to introduce Eastern philosophy and religion to Western minds than any figure before or since.
6 x 9, 264 pp, Quality PB, 978-1-893361-32-4 **$16.95**

More Spiritual Biography

Bede Griffiths: An Introduction to His Interspiritual Thought
by Wayne Teasdale
The first study of his contemplative experience and thought, exploring the intersection of Hinduism and Christianity.
6 x 9, 288 pp, Quality PB, 978-1-893361-77-5 **$18.95**

The Soul of the Story: Meetings with Remarkable People
by Rabbi David Zeller
Inspiring and entertaining, this compelling collection of spiritual adventures assures us that no spiritual lesson truly learned is ever lost.
6 x 9, 288 pp, HC, 978-1-58023-272-2 **$21.99**
(A book from Jewish Lights, SkyLight Paths' sister imprint)

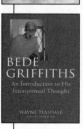

Sacred Texts—SkyLight Illuminations Series

Offers today's spiritual seeker an accessible entry into the great classic texts of the world's spiritual traditions. Each classic is presented in an accessible translation, with facing pages of guided commentary from experts, giving you the keys you need to understand the history, context and meaning of the text. This series enables you, whatever your background, to experience and understand classic spiritual texts directly, and to make them a part of your life.

CHRISTIANITY

The End of Days: Essential Selections from Apocalyptic Texts—Annotated & Explained *Annotation by Robert G. Clouse*
Helps you understand the complex Christian visions of the end of the world.
5½ x 8½, 224 pp, Quality PB, 978-1-59473-170-9 **$16.99**

The Hidden Gospel of Matthew: Annotated & Explained
Translation & Annotation by Ron Miller
Takes you deep into the text cherished around the world to discover the words and events that have the strongest connection to the historical Jesus.
5½ x 8½, 272 pp, Quality PB, 978-1-59473-038-2 **$16.99**

The Lost Sayings of Jesus: Teachings from Ancient Christian, Jewish, Gnostic and Islamic Sources—Annotated & Explained
Translation & Annotation by Andrew Phillip Smith; Foreword by Stephan A. Hoeller
This collection of more than three hundred sayings depicts Jesus as a Wisdom teacher who speaks to people of all faiths as a mystic and spiritual master.
5½ x 8½, 240 pp, Quality PB, 978-1-59473-172-3 **$16.99**

Philokalia: The Eastern Christian Spiritual Texts—Selections Annotated & Explained *Annotation by Allyne Smith; Translation by G. E. H. Palmer, Phillip Sherrard and Bishop Kallistos Ware*
The first approachable introduction to the wisdom of the Philokalia, which is the classic text of Eastern Christian spirituality.
5½ x 8½, 240 pp, Quality PB, 978-1-59473-103-7 **$16.99**

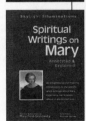

The Sacred Writings of Paul: Selections Annotated & Explained
Translation & Annotation by Ron Miller
Explores the apostle Paul's core message of spiritual equality, freedom and joy.
5½ x 8½, 224 pp, Quality PB, 978-1-59473-213-3 **$16.99**

Sex Texts from the Bible: Selections Annotated & Explained
Translation & Annotation by Teresa J. Hornsby; Foreword by Amy-Jill Levine
Offers surprising insight into our modern sexual lives.
5½ x 8½, 208 pp, Quality PB, 978-1-59473-217-1 **$16.99**

Spiritual Writings on Mary: Annotated & Explained
Annotation by Mary Ford-Grabowsky; Foreword by Andrew Harvey
Examines the role of Mary, the mother of Jesus, as a source of inspiration in history and in life today. 5½ x 8½, 288 pp, Quality PB, 978-1-59473-001-6 **$16.99**

The Way of a Pilgrim: The Jesus Prayer Journey—Annotated & Explained
Translation & Annotation by Gleb Pokrovsky; Foreword by Andrew Harvey
This classic of Russian spirituality is the delightful account of one man who sets out to learn the prayer of the heart, also known as the "Jesus prayer."
5½ x 8½, 160 pp, Illus., Quality PB, 978-1-893361-31-7 **$14.95**

Sacred Texts—cont.

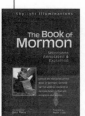

MORMONISM

The Book of Mormon: Selections Annotated & Explained
Annotation by Jana Riess; Foreword by Phyllis Tickle
Explores the sacred epic that is cherished by more than twelve million members of the LDS church as the keystone of their faith.
5½ x 8½ , 272 pp, Quality PB, 978-1-59473-076-4 **$16.99**

NATIVE AMERICAN

Native American Stories of the Sacred: Annotated & Explained
Retold & Annotated by Evan T. Pritchard
Intended for more than entertainment, these teaching tales contain elegantly simple illustrations of time-honored truths.
5½ x 8½, 272 pp, Quality PB, 978-1-59473-112-9 **$16.99**

GNOSTICISM

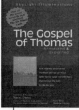

Gnostic Writings on the Soul: Annotated & Explained
Translation & Annotation by Andrew Phillip Smith; Foreword by Stephan A. Hoeller
Reveals the inspiring ways your soul can remember and return to its unique, divine purpose.
5½ x 8½, 144 pp, Quality PB, 978-1-59473-220-1 **$16.99**

The Gospel of Philip: Annotated & Explained
Translation & Annotation by Andrew Phillip Smith; Foreword by Stevan Davies
Reveals otherwise unrecorded sayings of Jesus and fragments of Gnostic mythology.
5½ x 8½, 160 pp, Quality PB, 978-1-59473-111-2 **$16.99**

The Gospel of Thomas: Annotated & Explained
Translation & Annotation by Stevan Davies Sheds new light on the origins of Christianity and portrays Jesus as a wisdom-loving sage.
5½ x 8½, 192 pp, Quality PB, 978-1-893361-45-4 **$16.99**

The Secret Book of John: The Gnostic Gospel—Annotated & Explained
Translation & Annotation by Stevan Davies The most significant and influential text of the ancient Gnostic religion.
5½ x 8½, 208 pp, Quality PB, 978-1-59473-082-5 **$16.99**

JUDAISM

The Divine Feminine in Biblical Wisdom Literature
Selections Annotated & Explained
Translation & Annotation by Rabbi Rami Shapiro; Foreword by Rev. Cynthia Bourgeault, PhD
Uses the Hebrew books of Psalms, Proverbs, Song of Songs, Ecclesiastes and Job, Wisdom literature and the Wisdom of Solomon to clarify who Wisdom is.
5½ x 8½, 240 pp, Quality PB, 978-1-59473-109-9 **$16.99**

Ethics of the Sages: *Pirke Avot*—Annotated & Explained
Translation & Annotation by Rabbi Rami Shapiro Clarifies the ethical teachings of the early Rabbis. 5½ x 8½, 192 pp, Quality PB, 978-1-59473-207-2 **$16.99**

Hasidic Tales: Annotated & Explained
Translation & Annotation by Rabbi Rami Shapiro
Introduces the legendary tales of the impassioned Hasidic rabbis, presenting them as stories rather than as parables. 5½ x 8½, 240 pp, Quality PB, 978-1-893361-86-7 **$16.95**

The Hebrew Prophets: Selections Annotated & Explained
Translation & Annotation by Rabbi Rami Shapiro; Foreword by Zalman M. Schachter-Shalomi
Focuses on the central themes covered by all the Hebrew prophets.
5½ x 8½, 224 pp, Quality PB, 978-1-59473-037-5 **$16.99**

Zohar: Annotated & Explained *Translation & Annotation by Daniel C. Matt*
The best-selling author of *The Essential Kabbalah* brings together in one place the most important teachings of the Zohar, the canonical text of Jewish mystical tradition.
5½ x 8½, 176 pp, Quality PB, 978-1-893361-51-5 **$15.99**

Sacred Texts—cont.

ISLAM

The Qur'an and Sayings of Prophet Muhammad
Selections Annotated & Explained
Annotation by Sohaib N. Sultan; Translation by Yusuf Ali; Revised by Sohaib N. Sultan
Foreword by Jane I. Smith
Explores how the timeless wisdom of the Qur'an can enrich your own spiritual journey.
5½ x 8½, 256 pp, Quality PB, 978-1-59473-222-5 **$16.99**

Rumi and Islam: Selections from His Stories, Poems, and Discourses—
Annotated & Explained
Translation & Annotation by Ibrahim Gamard
Focuses on Rumi's place within the Sufi tradition of Islam, providing insight into the mystical side of the religion.
5½ x 8½, 240 pp, Quality PB, 978-1-59473-002-3 **$15.99**

EASTERN RELIGIONS

The Art of War—Spirituality for Conflict
Annotated & Explained
by Sun Tzu; Annotation by Thomas Huynh; Translation by Thomas Huynh and the Editors at Sonshi.com; Foreword by Marc Benioff; Preface by Thomas Cleary
Highlights principles that encourage a perceptive and spiritual approach to conflict.
5½ x 8½, 256 pp, Quality PB, 978-1-59473-244-7 **$16.99**

Bhagavad Gita: Annotated & Explained
Translation by Shri Purohit Swami; Annotation by Kendra Crossen Burroughs
Explains references and philosophical terms, shares the interpretations of famous spiritual leaders and scholars, and more.
5½ x 8½, 192 pp, Quality PB, 978-1-893361-28-7 **$16.95**

Dhammapada: Annotated & Explained
Translation by Max Müller and revised by Jack Maguire; Annotation by Jack Maguire
Contains all of Buddhism's key teachings.
5½ x 8½, 160 pp, b/w photos, Quality PB, 978-1-893361-42-3 **$14.95**

Selections from the Gospel of Sri Ramakrishna
Annotated & Explained
Translation by Swami Nikhilananda; Annotation by Kendra Crossen Burroughs
Introduces the fascinating world of the Indian mystic and the universal appeal of his message.
5½ x 8½, 240 pp, b/w photos, Quality PB, 978-1-893361-46-1 **$16.95**

Tao Te Ching: Annotated & Explained
Translation & Annotation by Derek Lin; Foreword by Lama Surya Das
Introduces an Eastern classic in an accessible, poetic and completely original way.
5½ x 8½, 192 pp, Quality PB, 978-1-59473-204-1 **$16.99**

STOICISM

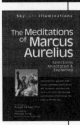

The Meditations of Marcus Aurelius
Selections Annotated & Explained
Annotation by Russell McNeil, PhD; Translation by George Long; Revised by Russell McNeil, PhD
Offers insightful and engaging commentary into the historical background of Stoicism.
5½ x 8½, 288 pp, Quality PB, 978-1-59473-236-2 **$16.99**

Spirituality of the Seasons

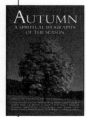

Autumn: A Spiritual Biography of the Season
Edited by Gary Schmidt and Susan M. Felch; Illustrations by Mary Azarian
Rejoice in autumn as a time of preparation and reflection. Includes Wendell Berry, David James Duncan, Robert Frost, A. Bartlett Giamatti, E. B. White, P. D. James, Julian of Norwich, Garret Keizer, Tracy Kidder, Anne Lamott, May Sarton.
6 x 9, 320 pp, 5 b/w illus., Quality PB, 978-1-59473-118-1 **$18.99**

Spring: A Spiritual Biography of the Season
Edited by Gary Schmidt and Susan M. Felch; Illustrations by Mary Azarian
Explore the gentle unfurling of spring and reflect on how nature celebrates rebirth and renewal. Includes Jane Kenyon, Lucy Larcom, Harry Thurston, Nathaniel Hawthorne, Noel Perrin, Annie Dillard, Martha Ballard, Barbara Kingsolver, Dorothy Wordsworth, Donald Hall, David Brill, Lionel Basney, Isak Dinesen, Paul Laurence Dunbar. 6 x 9, 352 pp, 6 b/w illus., Quality PB, 978-1-59473-246-1 **$18.99**

Summer: A Spiritual Biography of the Season
Edited by Gary Schmidt and Susan M. Felch; Illustrations by Barry Moser
"A sumptuous banquet.... These selections lift up an exquisite wholeness found within an everyday sophistication."— ★ *Publishers Weekly* starred review
Includes Anne Lamott, Luci Shaw, Ray Bradbury, Richard Selzer, Thomas Lynch, Walt Whitman, Carl Sandburg, Sherman Alexie, Madeleine L'Engle, Jamaica Kincaid.
6 x 9, 304 pp, 5 b/w illus., Quality PB, 978-1-59473-183-9 **$18.99**
HC, 978-1-59473-083-2 **$21.99**

Winter: A Spiritual Biography of the Season
Edited by Gary Schmidt and Susan M. Felch; Illustrations by Barry Moser
"This outstanding anthology features top-flight nature and spirituality writers on the fierce, inexorable season of winter.... Remarkably lively and warm, despite the icy subject." — ★ *Publishers Weekly* starred review
Includes Will Campbell, Rachel Carson, Annie Dillard, Donald Hall, Ron Hansen, Jane Kenyon, Jamaica Kincaid, Barry Lopez, Kathleen Norris, John Updike, E. B. White.
6 x 9, 288 pp, 6 b/w illus., Deluxe PB w/flaps, 978-1-893361-92-8 **$18.95**
HC, 978-1-893361-53-9 **$21.95**

Spirituality / Animal Companions

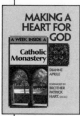

Blessing the Animals: Prayers and Ceremonies to Celebrate God's Creatures, Wild and Tame *Edited by Lynn L. Caruso*
5¼ x 7¼, 256 pp, Quality PB, 978-1-59473-253-9 **$15.99**; HC, 978-1-59473-145-7 **$19.99**

Remembering My Pet: A Kid's Own Spiritual Workbook for When a Pet Dies
by Nechama Liss-Levinson, PhD, and Rev. Molly Phinney Baskette, MDiv; Foreword by Lynn L. Caruso
8 x 10, 48 pp, 2-color text, HC, 978-1-59473-221-3 **$16.99**

What Animals Can Teach Us about Spirituality: Inspiring Lessons from Wild and Tame Creatures *by Diana L. Guerrero* 6 x 9, 176 pp, Quality PB, 978-1-893361-84-3 **$16.95**

Spirituality—A Week Inside

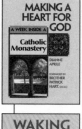

Come and Sit: A Week Inside Meditation Centers
by Marcia Z. Nelson; Foreword by Wayne Teasdale
6 x 9, 224 pp, b/w photos, Quality PB, 978-1-893361-35-5 **$16.95**

Lighting the Lamp of Wisdom: A Week Inside a Yoga Ashram
by John Ittner; Foreword by Dr. David Frawley
6 x 9, 192 pp, 10+ b/w photos, Quality PB, 978-1-893361-52-2 **$15.95**

Making a Heart for God: A Week Inside a Catholic Monastery
by Dianne Aprile; Foreword by Brother Patrick Hart, OCSO
6 x 9, 224 pp, b/w photos, Quality PB, 978-1-893361-49-2 **$16.95**

Waking Up: A Week Inside a Zen Monastery
by Jack Maguire; Foreword by John Daido Loori, Roshi
6 x 9, 224 pp, b/w photos, Quality PB, 978-1-893361-55-3 **$16.95**; HC, 978-1-893361-13-3 **$21.95**

Spirituality

Next to Godliness: Finding the Sacred in Housekeeping
Edited and with Introductions by Alice Peck
Offers new perspectives on how we can reach out for the Divine.
6 x 9, 224 pp, Quality PB, 978-1-59473-214-0 **$19.99**

Bread, Body, Spirit: Finding the Sacred in Food
Edited and with Introductions by Alice Peck
Explores how food feeds our faith. 6 x 9, 224 pp, Quality PB, 978-1-59473-242-3 **$19.99**

Renewal in the Wilderness: A Spiritual Guide to Connecting with God in the Natural World *by John Lionberger*
Reveals the power of experiencing God's presence in many variations of the natural world. 6 x 9, 176 pp, b/w photos, Quality PB, 978-1-59473-219-5 **$16.99**

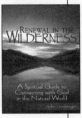

Honoring Motherhood: Prayers, Ceremonies and Blessings
Edited and with Introductions by Lynn L Caruso
Journey through the seasons of motherhood. 5 x 7¼, 272 pp, HC, 978-1-59473-239-3 **$19.99**

Soul Fire: Accessing Your Creativity *by Rev. Thomas Ryan, CSP*
Learn to cultivate your creative spirit. 6 x 9, 160 pp, Quality PB, 978-1-59473-243-0 **$16.99**

Technology & Spirituality: How the Information Revolution Affects Our Spiritual Lives *by Stephen K. Spyker* 6 x 9, 176 pp, HC, 978-1-59473-218-8 **$19.99**

Money and the Way of Wisdom: Insights from the Book of Proverbs
by Timothy J. Sandoval, PhD 6 x 9, 192 pp, Quality PB, 978-1-59473-245-4 **$16.99**

Awakening the Spirit, Inspiring the Soul
30 Stories of Interspiritual Discovery in the Community of Faiths
Edited by Brother Wayne Teasdale and Martha Howard, MD; Foreword by Joan Borysenko, PhD
6 x 9, 224 pp, HC, 978-1-59473-039-9 **$21.99**

Creating a Spiritual Retirement: A Guide to the Unseen Possibilities in Our Lives
by Molly Srode 6 x 9, 208 pp, b/w photos, Quality PB, 978-1-59473-050-4 **$14.99**
HC, 978-1-893361-75-1 **$19.95**

Finding Hope: Cultivating God's Gift of a Hopeful Spirit
by Marcia Ford 8 x 8, 200 pp, Quality PB, 978-1-59473-211-9 **$16.99**

The Geography of Faith: Underground Conversations on Religious, Political and Social Change *by Daniel Berrigan and Robert Coles* 6 x 9, 224 pp, Quality PB, 978-1-893361-40-9 **$16.95**

Jewish Spirituality: A Brief Introduction for Christians *by Lawrence Kushner*
5½ x 8½, 112 pp, Quality PB, 978-1-58023-150-3 **$12.95** *(A book from Jewish Lights, SkyLight Paths' sister imprint)*

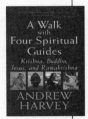

Journeys of Simplicity: Traveling Light with Thomas Merton, Bashō, Edward Abbey, Annie Dillard & Others *by Philip Harnden*
5 x 7¼, 144 pp, Quality PB, 978-1-59473-181-5 **$12.99** 128 pp, HC, 978-1-893361-76-8 **$16.95**

Keeping Spiritual Balance As We Grow Older: More than 65 Creative Ways to Use Purpose, Prayer, and the Power of Spirit to Build a Meaningful Retirement
by Molly and Bernie Srode 8 x 8, 224 pp, Quality PB, 978-1-59473-042-9 **$16.99**

Spirituality 101: The Indispensable Guide to Keeping—or Finding—Your Spiritual Life on Campus *by Harriet L. Schwartz, with contributions from college students at nearly thirty campuses across the United States* 6 x 9, 272 pp, Quality PB, 978-1-59473-000-9 **$16.99**

Spiritually Incorrect: Finding God in All the *Wrong* Places *by Dan Wakefield; Illus. by Marian DelVecchio* 5½ x 8½, 192 pp, b/w illus., Quality PB, 978-1-59473-137-2 **$15.99**

Spiritual Manifestos: Visions for Renewed Religious Life in America from Young Spiritual Leaders of Many Faiths *Edited by Niles Elliot Goldstein; Preface by Martin E. Marty*
6 x 9, 256 pp, HC, 978-1-893361-09-6 **$21.95**

A Walk with Four Spiritual Guides: Krishna, Buddha, Jesus, and Ramakrishna
by Andrew Harvey 5½ x 8½, 192 pp, 10 b/w photos & illus., Quality PB, 978-1-59473-138-9 **$15.99**

What Matters: Spiritual Nourishment for Head and Heart
by Frederick Franck 5 x 7¼, 128 pp, 50+ b/w illus., HC, 978-1-59473-013-9 **$16.99**

Who Is My God?, 2nd Edition: An Innovative Guide to Finding Your Spiritual Identity
Created by the Editors at SkyLight Paths 6 x 9, 160 pp, Quality PB, 978-1-59473-014-6 **$15.99**

Religious Etiquette / Reference

How to Be a Perfect Stranger, 4th Edition: The Essential Religious Etiquette Handbook *Edited by Stuart M. Matlins and Arthur J. Magida*
The indispensable guidebook to help the well-meaning guest when visiting other people's religious ceremonies. A straightforward guide to the rituals and celebrations of the major religions and denominations in the United States and Canada from the perspective of an interested guest of any other faith, based on information obtained from authorities of each religion. Belongs in every living room, library and office. Covers:

African American Methodist Churches • Assemblies of God • Bahá'í • Baptist • Buddhist • Christian Church (Disciples of Christ) • Christian Science (Church of Christ, Scientist) • Churches of Christ • Episcopalian and Anglican • Hindu • Islam • Jehovah's Witnesses • Jewish • Lutheran • Mennonite/Amish • Methodist • Mormon (Church of Jesus Christ of Latter-day Saints) • Native American/First Nations • Orthodox Churches • Pentecostal Church of God • Presbyterian • Quaker (Religious Society of Friends) • Reformed Church in America/Canada • Roman Catholic • Seventh-day Adventist • Sikh • Unitarian Universalist • United Church of Canada • United Church of Christ
6 x 9, 432 pp, Quality PB, 978-1-59473-140-2 **$19.99**

The Perfect Stranger's Guide to Funerals and Grieving Practices: A Guide to Etiquette in Other People's Religious Ceremonies *Edited by Stuart M. Matlins*
6 x 9, 240 pp, Quality PB, 978-1-893361-20-1 **$16.95**

Spirituality & Crafts

The Knitting Way: A Guide to Spiritual Self-Discovery
by Linda Skolnik and Janice MacDaniels
Examines how you can explore and strengthen your spiritual life through knitting.
7 x 9, 240 pp, b/w photographs, Quality PB, 978-1-59473-079-5 **$16.99**

The Scrapbooking Journey: A Hands-On Guide to Spiritual Discovery
by Cory Richardson-Lauve; Foreword by Stacy Julian
Reveals how this craft can become a practice used to deepen and shape your life.
7 x 9, 176 pp, 8-page full-color insert, plus b/w photographs, Quality PB, 978-1-59473-216-4 **$18.99**

The Painting Path: Embodying Spiritual Discovery through Yoga, Brush and Color *by Linda Novick; Foreword by Richard Segalman*
Explores the divine connection you can experience through creativity.
7 x 9, 208 pp, 8-page full-color insert, plus b/w photographs
Quality PB, 978-1-59473-226-3 **$18.99**

The Quilting Path: A Guide to Spiritual Discovery through Fabric, Thread and Kabbalah *by Louise Silk*
Explores how to cultivate personal growth through quilt making.
7 x 9, 192 pp, b/w photographs and illustrations, Quality PB, 978-1-59473-206-5 **$16.99**

Contemplative Crochet: A Hands-On Guide for Interlocking Faith and Craft *by Cindy Crandall-Frazier; Foreword by Linda Skolnik*
Illuminates the spiritual lessons you can learn through crocheting.
7 x 9, 208 pp, b/w photographs, Quality PB, 978-1-59473-238-6 **$16.99**

The Soulwork of Clay: A Hands-On Approach to Spirituality
by Marjory Zoet Bankson; Photographs by Peter Bankson
Takes you through the seven-step process of making clay into a pot, drawing parallels at each stage to the process of spiritual growth.
7 x 9, 192 pp, b/w photographs, Quality PB, 978-1-59473-249-2 **$16.99**

Spiritual Practice

Soul Fire: Accessing Your Creativity by Rev. Thomas Ryan, CSP
Shows you how to cultivate your creative spirit as a way to encourage personal growth.
6 x 9, 160 pp, Quality PB, 978-1-59473-243-0 **$16.99**

Running—The Sacred Art: Preparing to Practice
by Dr. Warren A. Kay; Foreword by Kristin Armstrong
Examines how your daily run can enrich your spiritual life.
5½ x 8½, 160 pp, Quality PB, 978-1-59473-227-0 **$16.99**

Hospitality—The Sacred Art: Discovering the Hidden Spiritual Power
of Invitation and Welcome by Rev. Nanette Sawyer; Foreword by Rev. Dirk Ficca
Explores how this ancient spiritual practice can transform your relationships.
5½ x 8½, 192 pp, Quality PB, 978-1-59473-228-7 **$16.99**

Thanking & Blessing—The Sacred Art: Spiritual Vitality through
Gratefulness by Jay Marshall, PhD; Foreword by Philip Gulley
Offers practical tips for uncovering the blessed wonder in our lives—even in try-
ing circumstances. 5½ x 8½, 176 pp, Quality PB, 978-1-59473-231-7 **$16.99**

Everyday Herbs in Spiritual Life: A Guide to Many Practices
by Michael J. Caduto; Foreword by Rosemary Gladstar Explores the power of herbs.
7 x 9, 208 pp, 21 b/w illustrations, Quality PB, 978-1-59473-174-7 **$16.99**

Divining the Body: Reclaim the Holiness of Your Physical Self by Jan Phillips
8 x 8, 256 pp, Quality PB, 978-1-59473-080-1 **$16.99**

Finding Time for the Timeless: Spirituality in the Workweek
by John McQuiston II Simple stories show you how refocus your daily life.
5½ x 6¾, 208 pp, HC, 978-1-59473-035-1 **$17.99**

The Gospel of Thomas: A Guidebook for Spiritual Practice
by Ron Miller; Translations by Stevan Davies
6 x 9, 160 pp, Quality PB, 978-1-59473-047-4 **$14.99**

Earth, Water, Fire, and Air: Essential Ways of Connecting to Spirit
by Cait Johnson 6 x 9, 224 pp, HC, 978-1-893361-65-2 **$19.95**

Labyrinths from the Outside In: Walking to Spiritual Insight—A Beginner's Guide
by Donna Schaper and Carole Ann Camp
6 x 9, 208 pp, b/w illus. and photos, Quality PB, 978-1-893361-18-8 **$16.95**

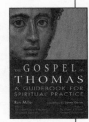

Practicing the Sacred Art of Listening: A Guide to Enrich Your Relationships
and Kindle Your Spiritual Life—The Listening Center Workshop
by Kay Lindahl 8 x 8, 176 pp, Quality PB, 978-1-893361-85-0 **$16.95**

Releasing the Creative Spirit: Unleash the Creativity in Your Life
by Dan Wakefield 7 x 10, 256 pp, Quality PB, 978-1-893361-36-2 **$16.95**

The Sacred Art of Bowing: Preparing to Practice
by Andi Young 5½ x 8½, 128 pp, b/w illus., Quality PB, 978-1-893361-82-9 **$14.95**

The Sacred Art of Chant: Preparing to Practice
by Ana Hernández 5½ x 8½, 192 pp, Quality PB, 978-1-59473-036-8 **$15.99**

The Sacred Art of Fasting: Preparing to Practice
by Thomas Ryan, CSP 5½ x 8½, 192 pp, Quality PB, 978-1-59473-078-8 **$15.99**

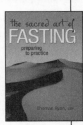

The Sacred Art of Forgiveness: Forgiving Ourselves and Others through God's Grace
by Marcia Ford 8 x 8, 176 pp, Quality PB, 978-1-59473-175-4 **$16.99**

The Sacred Art of Listening: Forty Reflections for Cultivating a Spiritual Practice
by Kay Lindahl; Illustrations by Amy Schnapper
8 x 8, 160 pp, b/w illus., Quality PB, 978-1-893361-44-7 **$16.99**

The Sacred Art of Lovingkindness: Preparing to Practice
by Rabbi Rami Shapiro; Foreword by Marcia Ford 5½ x 8½, 176 pp, Quality PB, 978-1-59473-151-8
$16.99

Sacred Speech: A Practical Guide for Keeping Spirit in Your Speech
by Rev. Donna Schaper 6 x 9, 176 pp, Quality PB, 978-1-59473-068-9 **$15.99**
HC, 978-1-893361-74-4 **$21.95**

About SKYLIGHT PATHS Publishing

SkyLight Paths Publishing is creating a place where people of different spiritual traditions come together for challenge and inspiration, a place where we can help each other understand the mystery that lies at the heart of our existence.

Through spirituality, our religious beliefs are increasingly becoming a part of our lives—rather than *apart* from our lives. While many of us may be more interested than ever in spiritual growth, we may be less firmly planted in traditional religion. Yet, we do want to deepen our relationship to the sacred, to learn from our own as well as from other faith traditions, and to practice in new ways.

SkyLight Paths sees both believers and seekers as a community that increasingly transcends traditional boundaries of religion and denomination—people wanting to learn from each other, *walking together, finding the way.*

For your information and convenience, at the back of this book we have provided a list of other SkyLight Paths books you might find interesting and useful. They cover the following subjects:

Buddhism / Zen	Global Spiritual	Monasticism
Catholicism	Perspectives	Mysticism
Children's Books	Gnosticism	Poetry
Christianity	Hinduism /	Prayer
Comparative	Vedanta	Religious Etiquette
Religion	Inspiration	Retirement
Current Events	Islam / Sufism	Spiritual Biography
Earth-Based	Judaism	Spiritual Direction
Spirituality	Kabbalah	Spirituality
Enneagram	Meditation	Women's Interest
	Midrash Fiction	Worship

3/20